Martha

LET US BLESS THE LORD
THE LORD YEAR TWO

LET US BLESS THE LORD ^{YEAR TWO}

Meditations on the Daily Office

EASTER THROUGH PENTECOST

Volume 4

Barbara Cawthorne Crafton

MOREHOUSE PUBLISHING

HARRISBURG / PENNSYLVANIA

Morehouse Publishing, P.O. Box 1321, Harrisburg, PA 17105

Morehouse Publishing, 445 Fifth Avenue, New York, NY 10016

Morehouse Publishing is an imprint of Church Publishing Incorporated.

Cover art: Mark Cassino/SuperStock

Cover design: Laurie Westhafter

Library of Congress Cataloging-in-Publication Data

Crafton, Barbara Cawthorne.
    Let us bless the Lord. Year two : meditations on the Daily office / Barbara Cawthorne Crafton.
        p.   cm.
    Contents: v. 1. Easter through Pentecost.
    ISBN 0-8192-1983-5 (casebound : v. 1)
        1. Devotional calendars—Episcopal Church.   2. Bible—Meditations.
3. Divine office.   4. Episcopal Church—Prayer-books and devotions—English.
I. Title.
BV4812.C73   2006
242'.3—dc22
                                                              2005007921

Printed in the United States of America

06 07 08 09 10 11   10 9 8 7 6 5 4 3 2 1

CONTENTS

FOREWORD:
NORTHEAST CORRIDOR

This morning, Q heads west and I head east: we will stop at the bank and the post office, walk to the train station together, and then go our separate ways. For the thousandth time, we will give thanks that we live in a place where you don't need a car to get where you're going.

Public transportation is, well, public. You have not carefully selected those with whom you will ride. You don't know them all; you may not know any of them. It is as far from the lone self-sufficiency of driving everywhere all by oneself as one can get, and yet it is completely self-sufficient—no matter how old you are, whether or not you can afford a car payment and insurance and repairs and gasoline, you can ride. The investment banker finds a seat next to the young man whose earphones don't quite shield his companion from his hip-hop serenade, and the younger man gets a chance to read the older man's *Wall Street Journal* and wonder about what life is like for a person who reads such a thing very day; to see, to his surprise, an article on P. Diddy; to reflect, perhaps, on the probability that P. Diddy, increasingly "Mr. Combs" these days, probably reads the *Journal* every day to manage his many millions. He is far richer than the investment banker. Perhaps life is not as simple as the young man thought. Nor, perhaps, as his older seatmate may have imagined all these years.

The snowy landscape along the tracks whizzes by. The train is a fine place for Morning Prayer: *Glorify the Lord, O chill and cold, drops of dew and flakes of snow. Frost and cold, ice and sleet, glorify the Lord, praise him and highly exalt him for ever,* sing the Three Young Men of ancient times, and you sing along with them in your mind and ask yourself how much they can have known about snow and sleet. You wonder if perhaps even the weather is not as simple as you think.

People's shoes, some immaculate, some stained with salt and mud and rolled over at the heels with wear. People's hair, carefully combed for the new day or covered with hats or concealed with scarves or catching the light from the morning sun as it pours through the windows. People's coats: identical Burberrys, expensive fur coats, cheap, thin wool coats that have seen one too many seasons and must somehow manage a few more.

You learn a lot on the train. There is much for which a person can pray and never run out of material, all the way in to Penn Station.

Easter

ⅴ SUNDAY, EASTER DAY

Pss 148, 149, 150 * 113, 114, or 118
Exodus 12:1–14 * Isaiah 51:9–11
John 1:1–18 * Luke 24:13–35

"Stay with us, because it is almost evening . . ."
LUKE 24:29

Maybe the two didn't know who Jesus was, but even on an hour's acquaintance they had already decided they liked him. They were attracted to something in him and didn't want to let him go on his way at the end of the day. In retrospect, it seemed to them that their hearts had quickened when they talked with him about the scriptures, putting the terrible sorrow they carried with them into the larger context of the divine love and the divine power.

And so they reached for the comfort of companionship, at first. Just another human being, a wise and encouraging one with some good things to say, to help them move forward. There are still good people out there, they thought to themselves. This man was happily met. There would be other good souls. Life would go on. It was good to be reminded of that. *Let's invite our new friend to dinner.*

And it was at that dinner that they realized there was more to hear than the promise that life would go on. More than just learning to live with a loss. More than just a new friend. At dinner their loss was restored. At dinner, the death of death itself became visible to them.

And, afterwards, it seemed to them that they had known it all along. Known it as soon as he had started speaking. They hadn't, of course. It had taken them a while to *get* it—some listening, some thinking, some quiet talking. And it took the breaking of the bread— their last living memory of the earthly Jesus—before they remembered just where they had seen those hands break bread before.

MONDAY IN EASTER WEEK

Pss 93, 98 * 66
Exodus 12:14–27
1 Corinthians 15:1–11
Mark 16:1–8

Last of all, as to one untimely born,
he appeared also to me.
1 CORINTHIANS 15:8

The English words don't do this verse justice: "untimely born" doesn't just mean born at the wrong time. It means *mistakenly* born, a miscarriage, an abortion. Much more than just *last*.

Paul was always aware of his own history, of how strange it must seem to other Christians that he had been a militant enemy of Christ before he became his apostle. He knew it was monstrous to many that he, of all people, should have been entrusted with the gospel to the Gentiles. It must have looked to them as it looked to us when porn king Larry Flint got born again.

When you have made a shambles of your life, the best defense is usually a good offense. Don't sit on it and hope nobody finds out about it; that's a recipe for living in fear. Don't try to hide it: *you* be the one to bring it up first. Answer for it as best you can, and then accept the consequences of having done it. We can't undo history.

And we can't stand in the way of God's using it for our good, either. The dumbest thing you ever did, the biggest mistake you ever made—they are the building blocks of the good thing God is making of you. Maybe you wish with all your heart that they weren't there, but maybe you wouldn't know what you know, or be who you are, if they weren't.

TUESDAY IN EASTER WEEK

Pss 103 * 111, 114
Exodus 12:28–39
1 Corinthians 15:12–28
Mark 16:9–20

*For he must reign until he has put
all his enemies under his feet.*
1 CORINTHIANS 15:25

Look carefully at medieval paintings of the crucifixion: there is often a skull buried in the dirt at the foot of the cross. Whose is it? It is Adam's skull. Adam, through whom sin and death came into the world, lying in mute witness to the saving act of Christ, through whom they leave.

And look at some ancient icons of the Harrowing of Hell: Jesus, risen and mighty, hauling an ancient Adam and a wrinkled Eve up from the netherworld. There are others behind them, people who lived and died never knowing Christ, simply because they were born too soon. Up they come, blinking in the bright sunlight of resurrection. And mighty Jesus stands there at the gate of hell with his foot on a snake. Who is *that*? It is Satan, beaten down under his feet.

The painters imagine a world untouched by the things that crush us in our world: no sin, no death, no malice, or evil. All gone. Christ has defeated them all in their holy pictures.

But still we die. Still we sin. More all the time, it seems, and in ever more imaginative ways. Surely the victory is not complete, is it? Surely the world would be a very different place if what we see in the old holy pictures were really true?

But it is true. We affirm it: it is now, and it is not yet. It has been and also will be. It will come into being, and all these things are— will be—present at once. There is no time in the domain of God. We have it only here.

So the world is already a very different place from what we experience it to be. It is not the universe that is full of holes. It is our seeing of it.

WEDNESDAY IN EASTER WEEK

Pss 97, 99 * 115
Exodus 12:40–51
1 Corinthians 15:(29) 30–41
Matthew 28:1–16

. . . no foreigner shall eat of it . . .
EXODUS 12:43

Today, of course, Jewish families often invite non-Jews to their Seders, to hear the songs and the stories, to eat the special foods, to hear the youngest child ask the question about why this night is different from all other nights, introducing the story of the Passover. *We escaped. God intervened directly in our plight and we got away.*

We often hear them talk about their chosen-ness in scripture. They still do, sometimes, when the issue of Israeli settlements comes up, or the Holocaust. Chosen-ness means something different now from what it must have meant to the Israelites as they crossed over on dry land and turned to see the destruction of their oppressors. It has been a long time since any Jew thought that being the chosen people meant a free ride around trouble.

But they remembered their great deliverance. It didn't mean nothing bad would ever happen again, but it *was* a miracle. The amazing things that happen in our lives aren't less amazing because they don't last forever, or because other things happen later on. To live in the moment of miracle, knowing full well that there will be other moments, to remember the gift of chosen-ness every time it is given and especially when it is not.

THURSDAY IN EASTER WEEK

Pss 146, 147 * 148, 149
Exodus 13:3–10
1 Corinthians 15:41–50
Matthew 28:16–20

. . . indeed, star differs from star in glory.
1 CORINTHIANS 15:41

They say that our sun isn't really anything to write home about, as suns go: many are larger. Some are as big as 150 of Old Sol.

And the earth isn't much, either. Mars and Jupiter and Saturn are all much bigger.

But if our own familiar celestial bodies feel jealous of their larger relatives, we don't know about it. The sun and the earth seem to us to be supremely and unselfconsciously themselves, busy about their own beauty, emanating and incubating our lives through the eons with a self-contained steadiness we assume is our birthright.

One of these days, that steadiness will falter and fail. Then another beauty will appear in the place where it was, another kind of power. Something different from what we know now.

That we can't imagine it will not delay its coming for even a moment. The end of the universe is not contingent upon our imagination, or anything else about us. Our input is unnecessary.

There can't be a resurrection, we think, because I can't picture it. Jesus can't be the Son of God because I'm not clear on how such a thing could be. But I only dimly understand the concept of a black hole in space, and nobody knows why aspirin works. There are lots of things I don't understand and yet accept. And all religious language is metaphor. We don't fully understand a word of it.

FRIDAY IN EASTER WEEK

Pss 136 * 118
Exodus 13:1–2, 11–16
1 Corinthians 15:51–58
Luke 24:1–12

. . . and we will be changed.
1 CORINTHIANS 15:52

Well, of course. We didn't think we'd stay the same, did we? Well, actually, yes, we *did* imagine heaven to be just like earth, only we'd be thinner and nothing would ever break down or wear out. We imagine it: blue sky, bright sun, happy, all our families and friends in love and friendly, even the ones who didn't like each other here. But they'd still be themselves and we'd still be *us*. You could still tell who we were. Ourselves, only perfect.

The survival of the personality is among our most cherished hopes of the life beyond this one. That life seems to us to be of little worth without it—but only at first. Only before we learn to sink into the stillness of prayer without words, learn the gentle way down to a place below all the things we experience, including ourselves. Somewhere in that stillness you leave behind—forever—your need for yourself. Your anxiety about your own continuation.

The world still delights you: it is one interesting place. But we can hold it lightly, and we will appreciate it more.

SATURDAY IN EASTER WEEK

Pss 145 * 104
Exodus 13:17–14:4
2 Corinthians 4:16–5:10
Mark 12:18–27

Even though our outer nature is wasting away,
our inner nature is being renewed day by day.
2 CORINTHIANS 4:16

Life is changed, not ended, the celebrant said in the Eucharistic prayer during the funeral. We don't leave; we just change form. Our way of being alive is different.

This idea is easier to accept when death has been slow in coming, when we could see the wasting away, could see that "being alive" means both more and less than having a heartbeat and some brain waves. This was the sudden death of a man in his prime, with no warning. Harder? Who can compare one sorrow to another? It is hard in a different way, that's all.

But the strengthening of the inner nature goes on lifelong, if we allow and encourage it. We don't have to wait for our bodies to weaken before we strengthen our spirits. The whole of the spiritual life can be—and has been—seen as preparation for a holy death, but people usually die as they live: your holy life will be true to itself in all its stages, including its ending.

So will a holy person never complain, never become annoyed, never lash out unfairly at someone who's trying to help him? That's unlikely: *holy* doesn't mean *superhuman*. But a life trained to look for the things of God will already know that they appear in some pretty odd places and will be on the alert for them in this novel situation, the leaving of life. His very brain stem carries remembered snatches of prayer, remembered hymns; these holy things will still offer comfort, comfort that people who do not have them in their history cannot know.

SUNDAY, EASTER II

Pss 146, 147 * 111, 112, 113
Exodus 14:5–22
1 John 1:1–7
John 14:1–17

[Jesus said to his disciples,]
"Do not let your hearts be troubled."
JOHN 14:1

Troubled? Sad, for sure. But troubled comes later on, after the first flush of grief is past. The silence on the other end of the relationship makes you wonder if there's anyone there. The banality of your ongoing, unpartnered life makes you angry and bitter, and then you're ashamed of being angry and bitter.

You had not realized until now how much of your faith was tied up in the life of one person. You believe in God, Jesus says, believe also in me. Ah, you think, I believed in a human being, put all my trust is someone no more permanent than I am. No wonder I am so shaken. Human beings can't be each other's gods. Only God is God.

We can't help doing it, of course. It's the way we are. Our hearts are so full, and they give themselves so completely to what they love. And eventually what we love gives way under our weight, and we get clobbered. Again. It happens every time.

Try to remember that your beloved is not God. He will die, or you will: one of you will be left alone. Love each other well, even if it must be foolishly, as it always must be; you will be sorry if fear of losing love keeps you from knowing it, and you will know firsthand that it really *is* the case that it is better to have loved and lost than never to have loved at all. Accept the kindness of those who see your sorrow, and forgive the blindness of those who cannot allow themselves to see it; know that it is hidden fear, not coldheartedness, that blinds them.

And then abide with God, after you have lost everything else. So different from the unseen good fairy you may once have thought he was, before your life taught you anything different. So eternally present, so unafraid of your wildest grief or most violent rage. Steadier than your heartbeat, closer to you than your own thoughts and audible, sometimes, within them. Because your spiritual senses have been changed by your trauma, you are now aware of things differently. Be patient with yourself as you learn what that way is. And then drink deeply and often at the well.

MONDAY IN EASTER II

Pss 1, 2, 3 * 4, 7
Exodus 14:21–31
1 Peter 1:1–12
John 14:(1–7) 8–17

"If you love me, you will keep my commandments."
JOHN 14:15

Faith is not just another word for doing the right thing. But, on the other hand, you will desire to do the right thing if you have faith. Sometimes you will succeed. Other times, it will not be crystal clear to you or anyone else just what the right thing is. But you will always try.

The reason that you will try is that faith is a relationship with Christ, and Christ embodies the good and the true. He makes us desire to be good and true. Makes us uncomfortable when we are not. Gives us joy in goodness, even if it means sacrifice on our part. There have been people who faced death willingly for the sake of another, and did so because of their faith in Christ.

The commandments of Christ, after all, are pretty simple: love God and love your neighbor as much as you love yourself. Utterly simple, and just as utterly beyond us, without reliance upon a power beyond our own pale power. We're pretty self-centered beings. It is true, though, that a lifetime of allowing oneself to be formed by Christ imparts a strength and a wisdom we didn't come into this world with. The longer we stay in the neighborhood of God's love, the more able we become to recognize the good and the more desirous we are of acting on it.

Love God and do what you like, St. Augustine said many centuries ago. Who you follow will color what you do.

TUESDAY IN EASTER II

Pss 5, 6 * 10, 11
Exodus 15:1–21
1 Peter 1:13–25
John 14:18–31

I will not leave you orphaned; I am coming to you.
JOHN 14:18

Orphaned is exactly the word for it: alone, dry, in a desert, deserted in a solitude that feels as if it will last forever.

Of course, that all depends on what we think forever is.

We already know that time looks different from the end than the way it looks from the beginning. Fifty years used to seem like forever when you were a kid. So did the months you had to wait until Christmas. So did a year of school. But something began to happen in middle age: time speeded up. It began to race, out of control, year piling upon year so quickly that you confuse last year's Christmas cards with this year's.

So you look at your recent bereavement and you think about it: you hope that the crazy speeding up of time will continue. That the time won't seem like that long, not as long as it seems now when you contemplate how long you'll be living alone. It'll be years, you know. And you hope those years will feel as short as other years have been feeling lately.

Because you want there to be something at the other end of them, something that includes the two of you and your history and your love, includes everything, something old that has been made new.

The whole point of Jesus' coming is to defeat this sorrow. The speeding of time is God-given: it will not only increase, but it will increase to the point where there is no such thing as time at all: that's what it's like in the kingdom of heaven. Nothing lost. Everything is now. Including the two of you.

WEDNESDAY IN EASTER II

Pss 119:1–24 * 12, 13, 14
Exodus 15:22–16:10
1 Peter 2:1–10
John 15:1–11

Every branch that bears fruit he prunes
to make it bear more fruit.

JOHN 15:2

As soon as it gets warm enough to work the soil—any day now—I'm moving all the roses to the side of the house, where I should have put them in the first place. They're climbers: they can climb up the wall.

I need to do this while it's still cool, because moving is hard on them. When it's cool, their systems slow down and they aren't as shocked by change. I should have done this last fall, so they could have had a winter of suspended animation, but I was just too busy.

One way to help them conserve their strength is to prune them decisively. It's a hard thing to do, cutting off a living branch. But one is seldom sorry in the end. While I'm out there, I'd better cut back the two big butterfly bushes. Way down—from ten feet high to about two. That's not easy, either. And the lavender, from about a foot to only a couple of inches. Ouch.

Everybody in the garden needs to lose what he or she doesn't need in order to preserve what is needed. Maintaining unnecessary things takes energy you need for the essential ones. And sometimes we ourselves are not the ones best equipped to assess what needs to go: it *all* feels essential to us. Pruning is a surgery we can't usually perform on ourselves. Another hand is needed. But it must be a wise hand. One that knows what to take and what to leave. The hand of one who knows the possibilities of our future.

There is really only one hand we can trust with this painful necessity. Some of our wounds prune us: they deprive us of something we only think we need, and we grow because of that very deprivation.

THURSDAY IN EASTER II

Pss 18:1–20 * 18:21–50
Exodus 16:10–21
1 Peter 2:11–25
John 15:12–27

For it is a credit to you if, being aware of God,
you endure pain while suffering unjustly.
1 PETER 2:19

Hmmn. Remember that they thought the world was coming to an end in a matter of months. We can handle anything, they must have told each other, if the time is short. But that was a long time ago. We can't afford to turn away from suffering now, not our own or anyone else's.

Long after people stopped waking up in the morning expecting the world to end that afternoon, though, the powerful continued to love passages like this one. *God wants you on the bottom and me on top.* The church helped the poor hold still under all this for a long, long time: it was powerful, too. God wants things just the way they are here. Be patient and wait for heaven. Behave yourself in the small things of your own small life: that's what morality is. Don't concern yourself with larger issues of good and evil.

Interesting—to endure pain while suffering unjustly is also a tenet of the practice of civil disobedience. You don't seek to evade arrest in an act of civil disobedience: you allow the powers that be to punish you, precisely to make your point about the injustice of an unjust law. Your suffering shames the powerful. Let enough of you speak this quiet, nonviolent "No" and evil will crumble before it. It might take a long time. But ours is not the world of 1 Peter: we've got time to care about a righteousness larger than our own.

FRIDAY IN EASTER II

Pss 16, 17 * 134, 135
Exodus 16:22–36
1 Peter 3:13–4:6
John 16:1–15

Indeed, an hour is coming when those who kill you will think that by doing so they are offering worship to God.
JOHN 16:2

Preach a sermon in a New York City church and the chances are good that there will be someone in the congregation who lost a loved one in the World Trade Center bombing. Or who was involved in it himself. You can tell who they are: they may begin to cry during your sermon. Or they will identify themselves to you after church, and you will spend some time with them as they tell you what floor she was on, how old he was, when they talked for the last time, what he said. By now they are used to talking about this to strangers: it has become a like sad poem committed to memory.

This day, I preached about martyrs. Real martyrs, I said, may give their lives willingly for someone else, but they don't take other people with them. The suicide bombers weren't martyrs: they were murderers. We really shouldn't call them suicide bombers: they're homicides. There is a place in our faith for martyrdom, but that's not it.

This day, there was one woman to whom the sermon meant more than it did to anyone else. Her daughter was on the 93rd Floor. We talked a bit after the service and agreed to have lunch sometime soon.

Her eyes brimmed with tears as we said good-bye. Maybe such a sermon shouldn't be preached? I don't think so. As painful as it is to talk about a permanent sorrow, it's more painful never to mention it at all.

SATURDAY IN EASTER II

Pss 20, 21:1–7 (8–14) * 110:1–5 (6–7), 116, 117
Exodus 17:1–16
1 Peter 4:7–19
John 16:16–33

"Do you now believe? The hour is coming,
indeed it has come, when you will be scattered,
each one to his home, and you will leave me alone."
JOHN 16:31–32

You want faith. A dependable life of prayer. You want to be a person who loves the Lord. And you *are* that person: sometimes you sail through life like a beautiful boat, your white sails full of wind. That's a happy state.

And then you lose it. And you don't know why. You were so *secure*; it was so easy to pray. What happened?

Could be anything. For the disciples, it was shock and fear and bereavement that plundered their faith. That does it for a lot of people. So does trouble in a close relationship. So does guilt over something unconfessed. So does illness—not always, but sometimes.

When this falling away happens to us, it's probably because we forgot to expect change. Nothing we have here lasts: it all goes away. We can't hitch our spirits permanently to any person or thing or movement or even to any idea. Even ideas about God.

We'd best be circumspect about what we really know about God, always. It may not be as much as we think it is. We'd best listen, always, for the unexpected voice of God whenever we find ourselves in a place strange to us: there isn't anywhere we can go to where God cannot accompany us. But we can't expect our *experience* of God to be the same in all these different places. The disorientation of change shakes everything in us, including our faith, and we won't be able to respond to it by insisting to ourselves that it hasn't happened.

SUNDAY, EASTER III

Pss 148, 149, 150 * 114, 115
Exodus 18:1–12
1 John 2:7–17
Mark 16:9–20

*Whoever says, "I am in the light," while hating
a brother or sister, is still in the darkness.*

1 JOHN 2:9

Go to your computer and do an Internet search on "God Hates Fags." You will find the website of the Westboro Baptist Church of Topeka, Kansas, a church composed of one man and his family, including his young children. The mission of this church is the same as the mission of the man's life, which is to denounce homosexuality. On the website, Matthew Shepard, the young man who was murdered in Wyoming for being gay, is depicted burning in the fires of hell and warning other gay people who are still alive to cease and desist. The church attended Matthew's funeral and picketed it. They hurled insults at his grieving parents.

And they believe themselves to be in the light.

But you can't hate like that and follow Christ at the same time. The two cancel each other out. We can disagree about important ethical concerns. We can argue. But we can't hate each other like that. It takes us nowhere but hell.

Interesting that the God Hates Fags website is all about going to hell. Maybe the very condition of focusing on judgment and punishment takes us there—before we even know what's happened. Maybe that's what hell is like: a narrow view of reality that cannot see love plainly visible. Cannot hear music or see color. Sits smack in the middle of God's goodness, but can apprehend only anger.

Not a place most of us would want to be. But then, the heaven of such a faith is everyone else's hell.

MONDAY IN EASTER III

Pss 25 * 9, 15
Exodus 18:13–27
1 Peter 5:1–14
Matthew (1:1–17); 3:1–6

You will surely wear yourself out,
both you and these people with you.
EXODUS 18:18

Wow—Moses had a great father-in-law. His advice—*delegate!*—is so sane, and he offers it with such concern and respect.

And Moses really needed that advice. He was trying to serve a large group of people the same way he would serve a small one, and that can't work. You don't have the same relationship with thousands of people that you have with fifty or sixty.

Clergy miss this important truth sometimes, and so do their congregations. He should have time for an hour with me whenever I want an hour with him, you think, just as my priest did when I was young. But if the church of your youth was small and your current one is huge, that won't happen. It's not because the clergy used to be friendly and now they're standoffish. It's just because there are still only twenty-four hours in a day.

It would be wonderful if we could do everything with the utmost thoroughness and take as long as we wanted doing it. If we could do it all and do it right. If every similar task could be done in exactly the same way every time, with exactly the same results. It would be wonderful if there were no ambiguity in the things we do.

But not two of our moments are ever the same. Each time we do the same thing we do it just a little differently, in a matrix other than the one we used the time before. We look around us at what we really have to work with, pick up what we have brought with us from the past and tuck it under one arm as we step off into the future with it, for better or for worse. We'll find out soon enough which it is.

TUESDAY IN EASTER III

Pss 26, 28 * 36, 39
Exodus 19:1–16
Colossians 1:1–14
Matthew 3:7–12

"Do not presume to say to yourselves,
'We have Abraham as our ancestor.' . . ."
MATTHEW 3:9

Privilege feels permanent, to those who enjoy it. If you are on top, it's hard to imagine yourself anywhere else.

It's certainly possible for an *individual* to be born, live, and die in a position of wealth and power: we only live for eighty years or so. But it is sure that no *nation* will remain on top forever: every society has its day, and then it subsides into history. Rome was the mighty power of its day, and today the remains of its imperial power are an antiquarian's delight and nobody's worst nightmare. Portugal was a major maritime power, a wealthy explorer and colonizer of distant lands; today it is the poorest country in the European Union.

Logic dictates that America will not be an exception to the cycle of rising and falling that every other empire has followed. Our enormous wealth and power feels permanent to us, but it cannot really *be* permanent. No society remains on top forever.

Usually people respond with discomfort or even anger when someone talks this way. It feels disloyal, wanting in patriotism, as if our ongoing hegemony were solely a matter of our *esprit de corps*. It even feels blasphemous, to some: God set us here, a city on a hill, and trusting in God is trusting in our ongoing greatness.

But our coins don't say, "We trust in ourselves." They say "In God we trust." Nations—even ours—come and go. Only God stays.

WEDNESDAY IN EASTER III

Pss 38 * 119:25–48
Exodus 19:16–25
Colossians 1:15–23
Matthew 3:13–17

. . . the Spirit of God descending like a dove . . .
MATTHEW 3:16

You see it in religious art, a white dove hovering over Jesus' head as he stands knee-deep in the water; often, fish are depicted swimming around his ankles, just so we understand what we're seeing.

The dove gets the small parts in scripture. But they're *good* small parts: Noah sends one out after the rain stops to check on the water level, and it returns with an olive branch in its beak. Then he sends it out again in a few days, and it does not return—found a new home and moved in, I guess. The dove does better than the raven he sent out first, who comes right back with nothing, having found nowhere to light. The psalmist longs for the wings of a dove, so that he might fly away to a better place. And one of the many pet names the amorous lover of the Song of Songs uses for his sweetheart is "my dove."

I know some doves personally: we have them at our bird feeder. There they are a little different: they argue constantly with each other over who gets to eat first, as they're so plump that only two of them can occupy the tray at the same time. They raise a clucking ruckus as they jockey for position, pushing and shoving one another away from the sunflower seed. Our doves are not courageous little scouts, like Noah's: theirs are the second calls we hear in the morning, not the first. They wait until one other songbird sends up a chirp and then they begin, an ascending trill followed by a series of three low coos.

The thing about doves is, they're *common*. They're everywhere in the country. If the spirit of God descending upon the Son of God was like a dove instead of like a peacock or an eagle, it speaks to me of the availability and universality of his power. It is not elite; it is everywhere, of modest origins, willing to wait. This anointing with the spirit was different from its dramatic visits to people in the Old Testament: they fell to the ground in something that sounds like a seizure. Jesus just gets out of the water and gets to work: first to the hard work of self-examination and then to the work of his life.

THURSDAY IN EASTER III

Pss 37:1–18 * 37:19–42
Exodus 20:1–21
Colossians 1:24–2:7
Matthew 4:1–11

"You speak to us, and we will listen;
but do not let God speak to us, or we will die."
EXODUS 20:19

When a New Testament scholar talks of Jesus as "the new Moses," it is because of verses like this one. Moses mediates between God and humanity in his delivery of the law to the people. The majesty of law is the way we relate to God in Judaism, recommended to us by Moses' power to deal directly with God on behalf of the people who lack that power. *Do what he tells you: this is the man who can face God and not die from it.*

Jesus mediates through the law, too, in his authoritative articulation of the law of love, the spiritual distillation of "all the law and the prophets." So he *is* like Moses in that respect. But it is his power to abide in the presence of God that makes him a mediator *in his person*: it is *as a being* that he is between us and God, not just as a particularly hardy specimen able to withstand the bright light of the divine. Jesus at once separates and joins God and humanity, simultaneously revealing and bridging the great gulf between creator and created.

We domesticate him: he was a really great preacher, a crackerjack healer of the sick, a profoundly gifted ethical teacher. Did you see the way he raised that guy from the dead? These categories we can understand: he is like us, only a whole lot mightier. Like Superman.

But scripture confounds such an easy Jesus: it shows us a Jesus making mistakes and learning from them, snapping at people in irritation, weeping at the death of a friend, a Jesus begging to be spared of his own death. Our desire for Superman is such that we don't always see these glimpses of Jesus for what they are, but they are there. Their witness forbids us from reducing him to a superhuman Man of Steel. We can't separate Jesus from God. His power is not really in *what he can do*, but in *who he is* for us, something clearly beyond our ability to comprehend. We can make up stories about Superman, and we've probably made up some about Jesus, too. The Son of God, though, we can't make up. None of us could even begin.

FRIDAY IN EASTER III

Pss 105:1–22 * 105:23–45
Exodus 24:1–18
Colossians 2:8–23
Matthew 4:12–17

*The people who sat in darkness have seen
a great light, and for those who sat in the region
and shadow of death light has dawned.*

MATTHEW 4:16

Today, you can visit the infamous apartheid-era prison on Robben Island. You can walk into the cell Nelson Mandela occupied for twenty-seven long years. Today, it is a popular South African tourist destination. But it used to be the end of the road to despair—the "region and shadow of death."

Mandela refused to despair, though, and so did his people. How difficult it must have been to maintain hope! But they did it: living under the thumb of an oppressor whose moral standing in the world diminished with every passing day, they drew strength from Mandela's survival and steadiness—his strength and, he would be quick to point out, that of many others. Because he had spent the long years of his confinement in a state of readiness, he was not blinded by the sudden light of his liberation from it. He was ready for it.

The worst of trials does not last forever. It comes to an end. It will not always be like this: there will come a time when it is all over and you are left with the rest of your life to live. Perhaps you will be injured by it, and will have to learn to do the things you used to do differently. Perhaps you will see the signs of your coming liberation and perhaps you will not. Either way, prepare for your freedom now, before it comes. Then your joy will double: now, as you prepare for it and then again, on the day when it finally appears.

SATURDAY IN EASTER III

Pss 30, 32 * 42, 43
Exodus 25:1–22
Colossians 3:1–17
Matthew 4:18–25

"Follow me, and I will make you fish for people."
MATTHEW 4:19

"Fishers of men" was how it used to read, before such language fell out of use. Okay: "people" is fine. It still sounds funny, though, doesn't it? Almost as if evangelists were predators.

And some of them *are*, of course, which is why so many people don't want to be one. It feels intrusive, even bullying; to many, trying to talk people into becoming Christians seems disrespectful of whatever heritage or beliefs they have brought with them.

What makes an evangelist a predator seems to me to have to do with how he values the one he seeks to convert. Is he truly interested in the person as a person, or only as another pelt to add to his collection of successful conversions? Am I interested only in putting another notch into my prayer book, or can I count the person beloved even if he or she never signs up? Am I willing to be a step along a life's journey whose ending is not known, or must I control the route?

Jesus never demanded conversion to anything before he would help people: heal them, feed them, counsel them, set them free in some way. He had no tests, and never sought to limit the love of God. He preached the kingdom, loved his fellow human beings, and left the response up to them. The response is always up to us anyway. Nobody makes faith decisions for us; they're too important. We have to make them ourselves.

ꓦ SUNDAY EASTER IV

Pss 63:1–8 (9–11), 98 * 103
Exodus 28:1–4, 30–38
1 John 2:18–29
Mark 6:30–44

On its lower hem you shall make pomegranates of blue,
purple, and crimson yarns, all around the lower hem,
with bells of gold between them all around—
a golden bell and a pomegranate alternating
all around the lower hem of the robe.

EXODUS 28:33–34

A aron must have been a sight for sore eyes: all those pomegranates! Every detail of priestly attire as it existed when the book of Exodus was written down, years after Moses and Aaron both were history, seems to have been important enough to project its intricacies backward onto whoever tailored Aaron's clothes.

That's what we do with church things: we imagine that our favorite things have always been there. But they haven't: they were all new once. Some of them had practical uses when they were new: the poncho-like chasuble worn by a modern priest wasn't a liturgical garment at first—it was just what first-century Romans wore as outerwear. Chanting prayers and psalms and scripture readings wasn't originally so much about meditation as it was about audibility: song carried better than the spoken word. Incense wasn't just a metaphor for ascending prayer: it masked the odors of burning meat, blood, and dead animals in the gory liturgies of temple worship in Jerusalem. Jesus didn't really speak in King James English, so it's okay to have the scriptures in our own words.

Of course, they've changed all the hymns and the prayers now, my friend says on returning to church after an absence of many decades. He misses the good old words: they had sat comfortably in his memory since childhood, and the new ones were a little jarring. Life is fast and unsettling, full of doubt and loose ends. We like to surround ourselves with sameness to balance out the flux of it, and yet we know that we sing and pray and preach from our place in history and that all these activities will vary from era to era. Secure and full of trust is what we want to be, walking through a shaky and sometimes treacherous world. But we must also be sinewy and flexible, so as not to break under the suddenness of all our changes in life.

MONDAY IN EASTER IV

Pss 41, 52 * 44
Exodus 32:1–20
Colossians 3:18–4:6 (7–18)
Matthew 5:1–10

Blessed are the poor . . .
MATTHEW 5:3

The beatitudes present a paradox to people who don't know a lot of scripture: the bad news/good news pairs provide one more way for Jesus to do what he always does—invert the world's valuations of things. The last is first, he says so many times in so many places, and the first will be last. All the things the world thinks will make us happy are fading away, and the very place of our unhappiness will be the place from which joy springs. And so it is the poor who are happy, the meek who inherit, the hungry who are satisfied: the kingdom of heaven is different from the kingdom of this world.

What would you write to someone who is living in darkness, a reader asks. I don't know if she means herself, her husband, her child, her friend. Is hers the pain of love and concern or the pain of personal suffering? I don't know.

But here is what I would write: *The meek will inherit. The hungry will be satisfied. The mourners will laugh. It will not always be like this.* If we can imagine a better time, we can pray in its direction. If we can pray it, we can receive guidance for our action in healing the portion of it that is within our reach. Some of it may be beyond us. Sometimes part of "It will not always be like this" happens in heaven.

For what can happen here, pray and work. For what must wait for glory, pray and be assured: we shall see God.

TUESDAY IN EASTER IV

Pss 45 * 47, 48
Exodus 32:21–34
1 Thessalonians 1:1–10
Matthew 5:11–16

. . . I threw it into the fire, and out came this calf!
EXODUS 32:24

My, my. What a surprise. Well, now, that's not *exactly* how it happened: Aaron makes it sound like the calf molded itself in the fire. Not exactly: he and others *formed* it. The plan and the design was theirs, a quick capitulation to the whining of the Israelites for new gods they could see and carry with them as they traveled, like the gods all the neighboring peoples had. Aaron *made* the golden calf: it wasn't an accident.

In today's business headlines, we learn that the biggest tree yet in the forest of corporate CEO scandals has fallen. His defense was that he really didn't keep up with the financials much; he left that to subordinates. But the jury didn't believe him: he was in charge. He knew, or he should have known.

The things we do don't just *happen*. We *do* them. A word of grammatical advice: suspect the passive voice whenever you hear it. You may be hearing the language of evasion. You can't keep the truth quiet forever, anyhow. It always has God on its side. Sooner or later, it rises to the surface of even the muddiest pool, there for anyone to see.

So we might as well tell the whole truth from the beginning. God already knows it, and everyone else is going to figure it out soon enough. It's one thing to do something silly or wrong or both, and another thing to make it even worse it by lying about it afterward.

WEDNESDAY IN EASTER IV

Pss 119:49–72 * 49, (53)
Exodus 33:1–23
1 Thessalonians 2:1–12
Matthew 5:17–20

*But we were gentle among you, like a nurse
tenderly caring for her own children.*
1 THESSALONIANS 2:7

But wait a minute—a nurse didn't care for her *own* children. She cared for the children of other people. Is this a scribe's mistake? Perhaps Paul misspoke? Or is there something in this choice of an image we might learn?

Children raised by people other than their parents is a consistent, minor theme in scripture—Moses, for instance. Young man Joseph, carried off to Egypt to remake himself in Pharaoh's house. The young Samuel, taken to the temple to be raised by Eli, left there by the very mother who longed with such passion to bear him. There was something attractive to these ancient writers in removing a person from the setting that gave him birth, remaking him in another image. *Who is my mother?* Jesus himself asks, rhetorically, *Who are my brothers?*

Paul continues this idea with his notion of adoption: in baptism, we have been adopted as God's children. We are remade, given a second birth. Whatever we were before, we can be re-formed in the image of God. Expect to change as you grow in the faith. Sometimes this change was symbolized by the taking of a new name: Saul became

Paul, Simon became Peter. Even today, some Christians take a new name upon the occasion of their baptism or their confirmation.

We become new people, new brothers and sisters. We have new parents, parents besides the parents to whom we were born. Nurture of this kind is more important to celibate, childless Paul than our first nurture, when we were little. For him, our nurse, the one who actually nourishes us in the faith, becomes our real mother as we head into our new life.

THURSDAY IN EASTER IV

Pss 50 * (59, 60) or 114, 115
Exodus 34:1–17
1 Thessalonians 2:13–20
Matthew 5:21–26

. . . first be reconciled to your brother or sister,
and then come and offer your gift.
MATTHEW 5:24

Although it has degenerated into a coffee-less fellowship hour popping up in the middle of a church service, the Peace in the liturgy is really about reconciliation. You were supposed to exchange a greeting with the person against whom you held a grudge, not race around the church kissing everybody you could lay your hands on and greeting people you hadn't seen in a week with little shrieks of joy.

Why? Why concern ourselves with repairing our rifts now, right before Communion? Because the Eucharist is a feast of love, a meal in the family of God, and enmity between any of us gets in the way of our experience of God's love. It may not be obvious. You may not feel it. But nobody can live in a state of estrangement from another person and be completely at home with God. It gets in the way.

So what then? Insincere Hollywood-style air kisses between people who can't stand each other, on their way up to the altar of

God? Empty shows of false friendliness are no substitute for the hard work of healing and forgiveness that the restoration of fellowship entails. The Kiss of Peace is symbolic, sober, quiet, minimal. Perhaps it celebrates the completion of forgiveness, or perhaps it observes only its first tentative beginnings. Or perhaps each kiss of peace is another halting step somewhere in between the two. Wherever it falls on that continuum, its beginning is cause for rejoicing in heaven.

FRIDAY IN EASTER IV

Pss 40, 54 * 51
Exodus 34:18–35
1 Thessalonians 3:1–13
Matthew 5:27–37

. . . even in plowing time and in harvest time you shall rest.
EXODUS 34:21

Notice that the language of this commandment is not that of permission: it's an order. We have to do it. Like all the other commandments, it is moral duty. We have a moral obligation to rest,

Then why do so many of us we feel so guilty when we do?

It took Q about four years to understand that he was retired. His discomfort was palpable: what was he supposed to be doing now? Almost immediately he went back to the only thing he has ever done, and began to teach part-time. I think he's only taken one semester off since his retirement.

I am retired from parish ministry, something I can't even *write* without a ridiculous pang of guilt. Never mind that I work hard at my writing and accept as many speaking engagements as I can: shouldn't I be running a parish somewhere? Isn't that what a priest is supposed to do? I still feel like a person who is shirking her responsibilities. Ugh. I think I may have been born feeling that way.

We are hard on ourselves, stern taskmasters. Productivity is such a central value in our lives that we can't set it down for even a moment. We would make good hamsters, running and running on our wheels to nowhere.

But we are ordered to rest. That was wise of God, to make it mandatory: he must have known how driven some of us would be. Maybe we can't fully retire: some of us are just not suited for it. But, retired or no, we are all ordered to take it easy on ourselves. Once a week. Without fail. That's an order.

SATURDAY IN EASTER IV

Pss 55 * 138, 139:1–17 (18–23)
Exodus 40:18–38
1 Thessalonians 4:1–12
Matthew 5:38–48

"Love your enemies . . ."
MATTHEW 5:44

Right away, we must suspect something: maybe love is not a feeling. Even Jesus can't command our emotions. So there's one thing we know is not true: our ability to fulfill this command will not be hostage to the vicissitudes of our emotions. You're not going to have to come up with warm, happy feelings for someone who has injured you before Jesus will talk to you about it.

So, then, love is something other than a feeling. Instead it is a choice we make, a choice that happily contains feelings, but which can be made in their absence, in expectation that they will someday rejoin us. In the beginning of learning to love our enemy, we choose to be the one to end our feud—regardless of who began it. We begin to pray for the one we once cursed—a modest beginning, just the mention of his name, no insincere embroidery of false blessings are needed from us. We decide to do this before our feelings have altered in the slightest degree. Before anything at all has changed. Our decision to begin is based solely on our desire to live life differently.

When you pray for your enemy, you will change. Maybe not later this afternoon: it's a process, not a moment. The one for whom you pray will change, too, in ways you may never know or ways that may become startlingly visible to you one day. And the world will change, too. It will be just a little bit better than before.

SUNDAY, EASTER V

Pss 24, 29 * 8, 84
Leviticus 8:1–13, 30–36
Hebrews 12:1–14
Luke 4:16–30

For it will take seven days to ordain you . . .
LEVITICUS 8:33

Seven days? Aaron got off easy. It's can be seven years or even more today, from the moment you begin to wonder if God might be calling you to be a priest until the moment when you are actually ordained one.

People who are in the midst of this discernment are said to be "in the process." Committee after committee must pass judgment on you, attempting to discern the impossible: what kind of priest will this person be? "The process" seems interminable when you are in it, and I, for one, never really believed I would be ordained a priest until the day after I was.

It can make a person paranoid, unless you take steps to regain some sense of your own autonomy. Very early on, you realize that worrying about how it's going to turn out will get you exactly nothing except a miserable life, and will turn you into a person nobody should ordain to anything. You understand that all you can do is your best, that nobody can do more than that. You throw up your hands and tell God, *Okay. Just do whatever it is you're going to do. I'm ready.*

These days, I am one of the people who interviews aspiring priests. Among other things, I look for that openhearted attitude— *Here I am. Just do whatever you're going to do*—and feel confidence in the vocation before me when I see it. The person who can learn to relax about his own life will be able to lead without micromanaging the lives of others. The person who needs to be ordained probably should not be; one who can learn a willingness to be denied something passionately desired will probably be able to survive the disappointments of parish ministry, where we regularly don't get things that we want very much.

God just scooped Aaron up out of the desert and made him a priest. All they had to worry about were his vestments, which seemed to have been really something. His descendants were able to inherit that status, another time saver. Take a good look at your clergy next time you run into one of them, and be kind: they've been through the wringer.

MONDAY IN EASTER V

Pss 56, 57, (58)* 64, 65
Leviticus 16:1–19
1 Thessalonians 4:13–18
Matthew 6:1–6, 16–18

And your Father who sees in secret will reward you.
MATTHEW 6:4

St. Paul's Chapel in lower Manhattan, newly famous for its role in the rescue and recovery effort after the World Trade Center bombing, has always been a treasure of New York, an example of eighteenth-century aesthetics that surprises most people who enter it for the first time: St. Paul's is pink and turquoise inside. Our forebears turn out to have been a little less august than we thought.

It is the oldest continuously used public building in Manhattan—George Washington went to church there—so its walls are covered with memorial plaques honoring the great and near-great of the city's past. A half-hour's wander through them is a trip back in time: the yellow fever epidemic, the dead soldiers of many wars, men lost at sea, women in childbirth.

One man in particular sticks in my mind when I read this passage from Matthew, about not trumpeting one's good works, allowing virtue to be its own reward. His plaque is large and ornate; clearly his family was one of substance. His excellent qualities are engraved in the marble, chronicled for generations after him to see and admire.

This was the verse his family chose to carve at the bottom of the list of his accomplishments, with one important addition: the plaque's version reads, "And your father who sees in secret will reward you *openly*."

I see. The family was important enough to request a change in Holy Writ and get it: the word "openly" does not appear in any version of this verse. It's a verse about *renouncing* worldly praise, not courting it. You may not get a reward that everyone can see for making the hard choices that are in accordance with your ethics, or for practicing your piety. You may go your whole life before your reward comes, and in the end your reward may not be that for which you hope at all. That's the point.

The poor rich man: his "open" reward was a marble plaque in a church. I bet he would have traded it gladly for a longer life.

TUESDAY IN EASTER V

Pss 61, 62 * 68:1–20 (21–23) 24–36
Leviticus 16:20–34
1 Thessalonians 5:1–11
Matthew 6:7–15

*". . . they think that they will be heard
because of their many words."*
MATTHEW 6:7

Jesus goes on to teach his disciples the prayer we know as his. It's used by Christians everywhere, although it doesn't mention Christ at all, but it was also used by the first-century Rabbi Hillel, roughly Jesus' contemporary. It's a Jewish prayer.

And it's simple. So simple and so short that most of us know it by heart.

Prayer doesn't need to be wordy. We don't need to cover everything in it, as if God wouldn't know what to do if we didn't spell it all out exhaustively. The content of prayer isn't what's important; it's the fact of prayer itself. It's that we turn to God. I am convinced that you could go the rest of your life and never say another word in prayer and you'd be fine: just your silent resting in the presence of God is enough. God can take it from there.

Sometimes we are so gabby in our prayer that we couldn't possibly hear anything God chose to say in the midst of it. We distrust silence and wish to fill it with verbiage as soon as possible. But God comes in quiet, in the silence of our spirits after we've said it all. Or if we've said nothing at all. God knows what we need.

Talk to God if you wish. Tell God whatever you want to say. But save some time to sit in the presence of God in silence. Perhaps right after you have said, *For the kingdom, and the power and the glory are yours, now and forever.*

WEDNESDAY IN EASTER V

Pss 72 * 119:73–96
Leviticus 19:1–18
1 Thessalonians 5:12–28
Matthew 6:19–24

You shall be holy, for I the LORD your God am holy.
LEVITICUS 19:2

What follows in this passage is a set of commandments similar to the famous ten of Exodus, but not exactly the same: stealing and lying, the Sabbath and graven images are there, but killing and adultery are not. Labor practices are included, and business practices. The list is recognizable as coming from the same world, but it is not exactly the same.

It is good to see these slight variations, for it reminds us of something important: the giving of the commandments on stone tablets is a powerful metaphor of permanence, but it is a metaphor. What we see in this and other summaries of the law is its actual development: they aren't the same, they are passed from person to person and written down later, and they vary. We see the society of Israel codifying, in the early stages of its communal life, the conduct it will expect of its members.

While the mythic giving of the law may not be what we would recognize as history, in our journalistic sense of that word, the idea of the law as that which forms the community is as lasting as those stone tablets. It was the portable genius of ancient Israel, the inheritance that still enables the Jewish people to survive anywhere.

How would the people define themselves? As a military power? As a vast commercial empire? In terms of might or wealth? The nations that defined themselves in those ways long ago vanished from the face of the earth. No, it would be none of these things: they would be holy as God is holy. The people would mirror righteousness and justice. It would be the grandeur of the law upon which Israel would build its common life.

THURSDAY IN EASTER V

Pss (70), 71 * 74
Leviticus 19:26–37
2 Thessalonians 1:1–12
Matthew 6:25–34

"Consider the lilies of the field. . . ."
MATTHEW 6:28

It is the time of the lilies. They are hard to pass by, they are so allur-
ing: one wants to look into their mysterious throats, to note their
lovely trumpet shapes, take in their brilliant colors. Fat bumblebees
don't even try to resist: they cling drunkenly to pollen-covered sta-
mens and stagger out a little while later, their legs and thoraxes covered with telltale yellow dust.

I bring lilies home from church a few weeks after every Easter,
the pure white Easter lilies, so by now there are dozens of them in
our garden, too. They will not bloom their first summer: they were
forced at the florist for Easter Day, and that's it for the year. But the
following year they appear, five or six gorgeous long trumpets on a
stem. Every year, for years and years, they will come. And they put
out new plants, too, little ones by their sides, who grow up and bring
forth pearly trumpets, too.

They put out their scent in the evening: to get it in the daytime,
you have to put your nose right in the flower, and should expect to
share that space with the bumblebee. But in the dark their perfume
fills the air, intoxicating and fruity, dense. In your summer garden:
the unmistakable smell of Easter.

In the dark of an early spring morning, you open the church for
the first service. It has been a long and exhausting Holy Week, and
you are tired. You will have a family feast and then put your feet up
this afternoon. You are looking forward to horizontality.

But as soon as the door swings open, the scent of the lilies hits
you and you are no longer tired. All your memories spring to life:
childhood Easters, Easter songs, "Welcome Happy Morning!" and

"Come Ye Faithful, Raise the Strain!" and "He is Risen." Other churches on other dark mornings with nobody else there yet, just you and the deep fragrance, and you silent and wondering, happy to be there alone for a moment in the fruitful dark, waiting to turn on the light so as not to break the spell of all the yesterdays that crowd together in your heart. He is the Alpha and the Omega, you think, the first and the last. Oh, yes. And you breathe it in, again and again.

They put out their scent in the evening. In the dark, with nobody watching. And their spirit breath fills you beyond mere happiness.

ᚋ FRIDAY IN EASTER V

Pss 106:1–18 * 106:19–48
Leviticus 23:1–22
2 Thessalonians 2:1–17
Matthew 7:1–12

"Ask, and it will be given you."
MATTHEW 7:7

*U*m, *we need to turn the watering can the other way, with its han-dle facing out, for What's-Her-Name,* I tell Q. *It gives her a better approach.* What's-Her-Name would rather drink from the old metal watering can than from a dish, so I keep it full to the brim. I came upon her doing this once, and watched her until she noticed me and scurried away. Another time I came upon her up on her hind legs, as tall as she could make herself, drinking from the birdbath. She likes to find her own sources of water, in the wild: puddles, water in a saucer under a flower pot, trickles of water meandering down the path from the watering of plants. Finding water herself is independent, an important What's-Her-Name value.

Look, she's doing it again, I tell Q. What's-Her-Name is standing at the watering can, her chin level with the rim, drinking steadily.

Isn't that cute? "Cute" isn't a word that usually springs to mind where What's-Her-Name is concerned. But this is cute. The birdbath thing was cute.

What's-Her-Name is not one for cuddling. She'll accept a neck rub, but is at pains to hide her evident pleasure at it and will never sidle up to you and ask for one. She's compromised the plantings in every window box we've ever had by jumping up into them to stare in the window at us, a startling sight if you're not expecting it. I believe this means she wants to come inside, although she has never said so: I only think so because, when you open the kitchen door, you hear the immediate thump of a cat hitting the cellar door and in under two seconds she has shot into the house.

She hates asking for things. I feel exactly the same way. Having to ask underscores one's dependence. The asker is weak, needy; the *askee* has all the power. I don't want people to know I need anything. This is ridiculous. Everyone has needs. We all need help now and then.

Maybe we refuse to ask because we think the answer will be No. What's-Her-Name was found in a junkyard without her front claws: that can't have been a good thing. Maybe underneath our independence is loneliness and fear, fear that help will not be on the way. We make a preemptive public relations strike in favor of our own independence, confidently asserting it every chance we get, before anybody asks. No, no, I'm fine, we say, don't need a thing.

But it is nice if someone keeps the watering can filled to the brim, and turns it around so it is easy to reach. Whether we admit it or not, someone cares for us and invites us to care for each other in a life more full of love than of lonely pride.

SATURDAY IN EASTER V

Pss 75, 76 * 23, 27
Leviticus 23:23–44
2 Thessalonians 3:1–18
Matthew 7:13–21

"Enter through the narrow gate. . . ."
MATTHEW 7:13

*H*e's on the straight and narrow now, someone will say of a reformed criminal. That's interesting: goodness is narrow, and evil is wide. Lots of options for misbehaving, not many for righteousness.

At first it seems obvious that the widest spectrum of choices possible is the road to happiness. Free to do anything at all, answerable to no one. Summer vacation, all the time. But the pleasure of all that freedom doesn't last: like schoolchildren in August, itching to get at the smooth white sheets of paper, the new pencils. Without really knowing it, we long unexpectedly for some structure in our lives.

Narrowness can be an aid to the spiritual life. Having a dependable structure for prayer conditions you to pray: the same thing every time, in the same place, at the same time. You learn quickly to expect a prayerful state when you assemble all the things that encourage it. This is a very different experience from waking up each morning and asking yourself, *Now, what do I feel like doing?* The answer is liable to be going back to sleep or clicking on the television. You slide into this or that, more or less by default, and soon your day is over with nothing to show for it. A few days like this are a good thing, but many more invite depression. Too many choices lead, paradoxically, to no genuine choice at all.

Of course you can do anything you want. Nobody can make you do anything. But what do you *choose* to do? Where do you *want* to go? Don't wander too far from the road that leads there, or you might not remember where it is.

SUNDAY, EASTER VI

Pss 93, 96 * 34
Leviticus 25:1–17
James 1:2–8, 16–18
Luke 12:13–21

"Be on your guard against all kinds of greed; for one's life
does not consist in the abundance of possessions."
LUKE 12:15

So many catalogues in the mailbox every day, selling travel clothes, bathing suits, bed linens, face creams, cooking supplies, camping equipment, sports equipment, even one selling *reading* equipment—do you really need special equipment to read? And so many ads for easy credit to buy all these things: loans on your house, the same credit card from six or eight different banks in six or eight different states.

There are people in America whose credit card debt is in six figures. They pay only the interest. It is 24 percent per year. They will pay for years, for the rest of their lives, probably, and never even come near the principal. Just the interest.

This has become so entrenched a part of our lives that Americans are startled to learn that people in many countries don't use credit cards. That, in some places, some people don't borrow money to buy or build a home—they save up for it, and live with family until they have enough. Many of us don't realize that easy credit is part of what makes our cost of living so high: it's not just that we have more money to start with, it's that we spend more than we have. And that's only easy at first.

And many of us really don't believe that we can stop. That there's another way to live. That we have more than anyone needs, more cars, shoes, jackets, sets of dishes. That each new toy will amuse us for only a little while—we think each one will finally do the trick. Those who sell depend on our short attention span to make us eager for next must-have. Nothing about this transaction in the least resembles joy.

Nothing lasts. Nothing physical, nothing you can buy. Not even a diamond is forever. Only God can satisfy us forever. We are chronically thirsty until we begin to look for living water, hungry all the time until we taste the true bread.

MONDAY IN EASTER VI

Pss 80 * 77, (79)
Leviticus 25:35–55
Colossians 1:9–14
Matthew 13:1–16

"Listen! A sower went out to sow."
MATTHEW 13:3

Mary is bent over one of the flower beds in her front garden as I drive up. We are going to the gym, but I am not sure she needs any more exercise today: she has been weeding, workout enough for anyone. They come up overnight, we agree: after the fourth or fifth straight day of weeding the same bed, there is only one logical conclusion to reach: someone is coming in here at night and planting weeds next to my daisies.

Me, I forget where I've planted things sometimes, and then I can't distinguish between the early life of a plant that is new to me and the early life of a weed. I know most of my garden's weeds, but there are always interlopers, friends of theirs from out of town, who arrive like unwelcome in-laws and decide to stay. If they squat next to a plant with which I am unfamiliar, I don't always know who's who.

All you can do at times like this is wait. Let them both come up, and they will declare themselves: the weed will eventually look different from the plant I want, and its relatives will also pop up elsewhere in the garden, in places where I didn't plant the strange new bulbs. Then I'll know. But I'll only know if I wait.

I suppose I could be more meticulous—I could scarcely be less so—and precisely mark each spot where a bulb has gone. Then I would know which was which, and could pull out anything that I didn't put there. But then I would have cut off any initiative on the part of the garden itself. I would never allow it to surprise me. I would only have what I already knew.

A weed is nothing more than a native plant. They are not weeds to their mothers. Sometimes I end up liking both the planned plant and the weed equally well, and they both stay. And sometimes I find I was mistaken about that, that the weed in maturity really is a wretched thing and I don't want it, and out it goes.

You just don't know in advance, that's all. And you can't always tell by looking. People and plants are a lot alike: it isn't over until it's over.

⋁TUESDAY IN EASTER VI

Pss 78:1–39 * 78:40–72
Leviticus 26:1–20
1 Timothy 2:1–6
Matthew 13:18–23

*I urge that supplications, prayers, intercessions,
and thanksgivings be made for everyone, for kings and all
who are in high positions, so that we may lead a quiet
and peaceable life in all godliness and dignity.*
1 TIMOTHY 2:1–2

We pray for the president at every worship service. We do it every time, no matter who the president is. We do it, whether we agree with this particular president's policies or not. Whoever occupies that position of tremendous power and equal responsibility needs all the prayers he or she can get.

I think it's especially important to pray for a leader with whom you do not agree, but it can be difficult if your emotions run high. You find yourself praying against him, and that's not leading you into anything like a quiet and peaceable life. It's just giving you an ulcer. So you'd better slow down in your prayer, and back off a little: this may be one of those times when you're better off if words fail you a bit.

So just say his name and leave it at that. You don't have to spell it out for God, and you don't have to have a plan for what the president should do before you can pray for him. Prayer isn't strategizing. Or worry. Or a political speech with an "Amen" at the end of it. You don't need to say anything *about* the president at all, and you may be better off if you don't.

It is easy to demonize a public figure with whom you disagree if you care passionately about politics. Doing so is dangerous, though, because it locates all evil and error in one place, and the world is never that simple. Prayer protects us against doing that. I'm not sure it's possible to demonize someone for who you are praying every day.

So pray for him, whatever your politics or his. Then go ahead and work for better things.

⌄WEDNESDAY IN EASTER VI

Pss 119:97–120 * 68:1–20
Leviticus 26:27–42 * 2 Kings 2:1–15
Ephesians 1:1–10 * Revelation 5:1–14
Matthew 22:41–46

*. . . many angels surrounding the throne and the living
creatures and the elders; they numbered myriads of myriads
and thousands of thousands, singing with full voice, "Worthy
is the Lamb that was slaughtered to receive power and wealth
and wisdom and might and honor and glory and blessing!"*

REVELATION 5:11–12

I remember receiving a Methodist tract intended for children at
Bible school. It contained a series of good children, pictured
doing religious things. I remember in particular one of the pictures:
a very clean-cut boy sitting down at his desk with a Bible, a notepad,
and a pencil. The caption said, "Bill is determined to study Revelation carefully."

I was not about to let a boy, certainly not a *Methodist* boy, sur-
pass me in devotion and study. I went home and got out my Bible, a
notebook, and a pencil, just like the good boy in the picture. Barbara was determined to study Revelation carefully.

I had never even tried to read Revelation, preferring to read stories instead. I began to read. I cannot now recall how many chapters
I was able to choke down, but I know that I did not make a single
note. The Revelation to John was easily the weirdest thing I'd ever
seen in my life. I felt annoyed at myself for failing to do what Bill
the Good did, but I reminded myself that Bill *was* only a cartoon.

The tract itself was ridiculous: no child could study Revelation
by himself and hope to get anything out of it. Adults who mistake
it for a literal prediction of the future get tangled up enough. Its
psychedelic imagery and peculiar politics require a familiarity with
the ancient church that nobody today has; scholars painstakingly

piece it together, and churches read only the presentable snatches of it at worship.

But those presentable bits are well worth the trouble. They speak of Christ's victory over death, of the comfort and relief awaiting those who have suffered mightily during this life. They portray the ongoing life of the saints, a profound blessing to those who have lost someone dear.

I don't know how many angels there are in a myriad. I wouldn't want to meet any one of the Four Living Creatures in the dark. But I am eager for God to wipe away every tear from our eyes.

ASCENSION DAY

Pss 8, 47 * 24, 96
Daniel 7:9–14
Hebrews 2:5–18
Matthew 28:16–20

Now God did not subject the coming world,
about which we are speaking, to angels.
HEBREWS 2:5

Angels continue to be popular: any book, umbrella, hairpin, or wastebasket with an angel on it will sell. Victoria's Secret, purveyor of sexy underwear to the masses, undertook a truly surreal promotion a year or two ago, in which all the voluptuous models wore enormous white feathery wings with their thongs and push-up bras.

They are pre-Christian, these otherworldly helpers. Pre-Jewish, too, for that matter. Intermediate servants of God who do his bidding in heaven and on earth, imagined in a day of absolute monarchs and obsequious courtiers: surely God must have a court, like a great human king. Surely God is like us, only bigger. Surely God's courtiers have wings.

Well, probably not, anymore than they wear thong undies. Angels may be fun to imagine, but God's ways can't be imagined by the likes of us. We fall way short of that reality every time.

The Ascension is a little like the angels: an imagining of how it is that the risen Christ lives and reigns forever. Jesus isn't walking through walls and saying, "Peace be with you" any more. Hasn't for two thousand years. Well, where is he? Up there, we say, and look up at the sky.

Of course, there isn't really a "there." Not a place, like Omaha or even like Eden. Not up—and not down or anywhere else. We can use and enjoy our imaginings, for they have much to show us, but don't confuse them with the facts. God probably doesn't have facts; God *is* a fact. Beyond that, we can know nothing in the way we know other things. We're in completely unknown territory from the moment we begin to talk about God.

FRIDAY IN EASTER VI

Pss 85, 86 * 91, 92
1 Samuel 2:1–10
Ephesians 2:1–10
Matthew 7:22–27

*Everyone then who hears these words of mine
and acts on them will be like a wise man . . .*
MATTHEW 7:24

I don't know what she will say, the middle-aged mother says quietly. *But I have to tell her.*

Yeah, I say. *You do.*

Her daughter is terribly thin. Too thin. *Way too thin,* her mother says, *and her skin looks dull, and her hair isn't shiny. You should have seen the way she cut the fat off her steak—every last shred of it. It took her forever.* Her mom thinks she has an eating disorder.

Have you ever thought you might have an eating problem? she'll say sometime soon. And then she will wait to hear her daughter's response. It may be that the girl's illness will prevent her from hearing. But the truth must be pursued with tenacity: in this case, as in many, its opposite isn't just the lie—its opposite might be death. Every lie brings us closer to it, and part of becoming habituated to lies is that you don't know they're killing you until they almost have.

The fear of telling people the truth is usually worse than the actual telling. You just pray, open your mouth, and speak. They either listen or they don't: you don't control that part. They may become furious with you, and you don't control that, either. They may leave, and you really won't be able to stop them.

But somewhere inside them, they hear. If your truth is really truth for them, something inside them knows it, and files it away for a better—even if much harder—day.

SATURDAY IN EASTER VI

Pss 87, 90 * 136
Numbers 11:16–17, 24–29
Ephesians 2:11–22
Matthew 7:28–8:4

"... whoever is not against you is for you."
LUKE 9:50

You know, you shouldn't go to that gym, reads an e-mail. *The guy who owns it gives to all kinds of right-wing causes. Maybe you didn't know that.*

Actually, I did know.

Do I have a responsibility not to contribute to the bottom line of a business owned by someone who disagrees with my politics? I don't think so. He has the right to do as he wishes with the money he earns. I don't quiz the gas station owner about his opinions, or limit my grocery shopping to liberal supermarkets, if there are such things.

The good and useful things anyone does are, well, *good* and *useful*. Lasting contributions to our common life will *last*, regardless of who makes them. And we can join forces, on occasion, with those from whom we may differ profoundly, if a cause evokes commitment in both of us.

Meanwhile, we are free to live in society that is full of people who don't like us, or wouldn't, if they were really paying attention. I can't freely be myself unless I allow others the freedom to do the same, and probably can't accomplish much if I can only avail myself of the support of those who are like me.

At the gym, I lift and trot and stretch and bend. As we work out, my friend and I talk politics. *I don't think that lady liked what you had to say*, she says as we leave. *Oh, well*, I say. *I hope she at least enjoyed the music.*

SUNDAY, EASTER VII

Pss 66, 67 * 19, 46
Exodus 3:1–12
Hebrews 12:18–29
Luke 10:17–24

"I thank you, Father, Lord of heaven and earth,
because you have hidden these things from the wise and
the intelligent and have revealed them to infants. . . ."
LUKE 10:21

William Smith made the first geological map of England. Supervising the digging of many of the new canals that crisscrossed England in the eighteenth century, he noticed that the walls of the digs were in layers, different minerals striping the surface of the rock, and that the shells and fossilized animals in each layer were different from the ones below and above it. They had been laid down over time, he concluded. They showed the history of the world.

Of course, it was not possible simply to say so in eighteenth-century England. As cosmopolitan a society as London was, a discovery so contrary to the simple process of creation set forth in the first chapter of Genesis needed some serious spadework before it could burst upon the scene. So theology was a bit of a problem for Smith.

But he had a bigger problem than theology: Smith was not of noble birth. He was the son of a blacksmith, undoubtedly from a long line of blacksmiths—hence his surname. It was understood that superior birth produced superior minds. The Royal Academy of Science was composed of gentlemen scholars, and they intended to keep it just that way. Smith's birth discredited his research with them for a long time and, when its evidentiary weight was overwhelming, one of their number claimed credit for the work himself.

They couldn't believe that someone who was of humble origin could be so gifted. This idea seems quaint to us now, but how many times have we patronized someone because of her accent? Because of his race? Because she was old, or because he was young? We all think we can judge a book by its cover.

Puncturing this egotistical balloon was one of Jesus' favorite things; he did it a lot. We also know, in our heart of hearts, what he knew: that all good gifts come from God, and that God decides who gets them.

MONDAY IN EASTER VII

Pss 89:1–18 * 89:19–52
Joshua 1:1–9
Ephesians 3:1–13
Matthew 8:5–17

"For I also am a man under authority, with soldiers under me;
and I say to one, 'Go,' and he goes, and to another, 'Come,'
and he comes, and to my slave, 'Do this,' and he does it."

MATTHEW 8:9

This remark about a slave is matter-of-fact, innocent of any suggestion that the very existence of slavery is a moral issue. How you treat them is, though: who may be enslaved, how someone may be redeemed—all these things have rules. But slavery is basically okay. Hmmmn.

Don't try to live your life according to the letter of the law in scripture. It's not that simple. History has moved on, and we have moved on with it. The rules of one generation cannot govern another. The question with which scripture can help us is not always, "How can we live like the people in the Bible lived?" Sometimes it's "What will do for us, in our generation, what these words did for them in theirs?"

We don't hold slaves, not today. But we have a twenty-first-century equivalent, now that work and commerce are global realities. We maintain our prosperity on the backs of the poor, not just the poor in our own city, as was the case in biblical times, but poor people all the way across the world. We can have three pairs of expensive sneakers because they think two dollars a day is a good salary. And it's a good salary there because they are so poor. If they made more money, our sneakers would either cost more or the people who market them would make a smaller profit, and neither of those is not on the table.

It needs to be on the table. Somehow we have gotten from where they were—countenancing slavery—to where we are—not having slaves at all. And maybe someday we will summon the moral courage to tell the truth about where our prosperity comes from, and travel the rest of the way.

TUESDAY IN EASTER VII

Pss 97, 99, (100) * 94, (95)
1 Samuel 16:1–13a
Ephesians 3:14–21
Matthew 8:18–27

"Foxes have holes, and birds of the air have nests. . . ."
MATTHEW 8:20

Foxes. Birds. Sheep, of course, lots of sheep. And goats. There are lots of animals in the Bible. But here is a little poem, shaped like a psalm, about two animals, one nowhere to be found in scripture and one grievously misunderstood by our ancient writers.

A Psalm of Cats and Dogs
O God! Why are there no cats in scripture?
    And why no kindly dogs?
The ancient writers scorn your dogs
    They will not let them in the house.
But you have made the dog of love,
    The same way you created me;
You have given her a loyal spirit:
    She is truer than I have ever been.
In youth she glories in her strength
    And smells with interest all that you have made.
She holds back her mouth from biting your servant;
    she lies on the rug and bites a bone instead.
From room to room she follows me, securing the perimeter
    of her house,

she scolds away the intruder.
In age, she walks slowly, and sometimes not at all,
  Only her tail signals her joy at our approach.
She sighs in her sleep, her old legs move together,
  As if to run, a puppy still.
O! Praise God for this faithful friend,
  Make us half as good as she esteems us,
And give us grace to care for her with courage
  when the end of her days is upon her.
And O God! What happened to all the cats?

WEDNESDAY IN EASTER VII

Pss 101, 109:1–4 (5–19) 20–30 * 119:121–144
Isaiah 4:2–6
Ephesians 4:1–16
Matthew 8:28–34

When [Jesus] came to the other side, to the country of the
Gadarenes, two demoniacs coming out of the tombs met him.
MATTHEW 8:28

Not one demoniac: two of them. They lived among the tombs, the most unclean place the writer of Matthew could think of to situate them, and also a place that lets us know that they existed in a state of living death. Two unfortunate people, possessed by urges they could not control, behavior they did not author.

So was it the *demons* who enjoyed each other's company, out there among the tombs? Did they hang out together, egging on each other's illness and rage? Or was it their tragic *hosts* who sought one another out in their mutual loneliness, ostracized by their own behavior from other society, the only two people in town who knew what it was to be so terribly different? Or was it both?

Often people in recovery from addiction must give up the friends they drank with—old friends. Sometimes, people they've know for years and years. This is usually not understood very well by those they leave behind: they are insulted and hurt. But it is necessary: being with their old drinking buddies is just too dangerous to their shaky new sobriety. New friends take their place, other people struggling with the same demon and winning each day, one day at a time.

With their last ounce of strength, the two who lived in the tombs did that for each other: they knew that Jesus could command the demons against whom they were so utterly helpless, and they came to him together for help. They must have encouraged each other along the way: *I'm scared, too, but we've got to ask him. He's our only chance. We'll ask him together. We'll just do it!*

Together they asked for help and together they were delivered. "*I* get drunk, *we* get sober," is how the alcoholics put it.

THURSDAY IN EASTER VII

Pss 105:1–22 * 105:23–45
Zechariah 4:1–14
Ephesians 4:17–32
Matthew 9:1–8

Be angry but do not sin.
EPHESIANS 4:26

The man steadfastly insisted that he was not angry. This was odd, for he was dashing about the kitchen like a bat out of hell, slamming cabinet doors and banging pots onto the stove. His voice was clipped, and he refused to make eye contact. *Would you get out of the way, please?* he asked angrily, and the "please" sounded like a rebuke.

He couldn't own his anger at all, not then and not later. Asked about it later, he remembered the scene quite differently. *I just asked her please to move, because I wanted to get to the sink.* He didn't remember the banging doors or the clattering pots.

He had a strong commitment to kindness. He wanted to be a good man, and he was. He wanted it so much that he couldn't admit it when he became angry; he felt anger was wrong, that he shouldn't ever feel it. And so he denied that he ever did, denied it to himself and to everybody else.

But you can't do that forever. In a thousand ways, he telegraphed the anger he would not acknowledge, showed it to anyone who happened to be within range, frightening people who didn't understand what could possibly be wrong. This roundabout anger is much worse than anger directly expressed. It appears to come from nowhere, and the people around you are hurt by it: they don't know what they did to make you so angry, and you can't tell them.

It is a strange thing, that the attempt to refuse one's own anger creates the poison of sin where only anger existed before. Anger doesn't poison: it snarls and then gets over it. Try to smother it, though, and you get the reverse of what you want: it bursts into deadly flame, and injures the very people you are trying to protect.

FRIDAY IN EASTER VII

Pss 102 * 107:1–32
Jeremiah 31:27–34
Ephesians 5:1–20
Matthew 9:9–17

*"Those who are well have no need of a physician,
but those who are sick."*
MATTHEW 9:12

I was a student chaplain, and he was a heart patient. He had been very ill and had almost died. We sat and talked about the miracle of his healing.

He was struggling to understand it. *I don't go to church*, he said. *I haven't gone in years. I've done some things I wish I hadn't. I'm not like you,* he said then, turning to look at me. *People like you, who visit strangers in hospitals. I mean, you don't even know me and here you are. You're the kind of person who would deserve to be saved from death, not me. I'm not like that.*

Young as I was, I knew enough to know that made no sense. He was right about one thing, though: we didn't know each other. I'd done a few things I wished I hadn't, too. He talked on for a long time, about his life and his regrets. I left thinking he was *exactly* the kind of person who gets saved from death.

It is twenty-five years later, maybe a little more. Now I am a heart patient, and I have been saved from death a few times myself. By now, I've done even *more* things I wish I hadn't, so there is even less reason than there was then to think I am the kind of person who deserves it.

What kind of person does Jesus save? The ones who deserve it because of all the good things they've done? Nope. He saves the kind of person who needs saving.

SATURDAY IN EASTER VII (EVE OF PENTECOST)

Pss 107:33–43, 108:1–6 (7–13) * 33
Ezekiel 36:22–27 * Exodus 19:3–8a, 16–20
Ephesians 6:10–24 * 1 Peter 2:4–10
Matthew 9:18–26

"If I only touch his cloak, I will be made well."
MATTHEW 9:21

It was my first visit to Italy. We were in Assisi, the holy city of St. Francis. We had spent a lot of time in his basilica, soaking in the Cimabue frescoes depicting his life, and before going over to the Basilica of St. Clare, we stopped into the museum.

His tunic was in a glass case. It was of such rough cloth, much rougher than burlap; it looked awfully scratchy. And there were his shoes, flat and shapeless. And his hood. That was all. I stared at them for a long time. I wished I could touch them. Tears stung my eyes: Francis wore this garment, and I am here within two feet of it. *Just the hem of his cloak. Just a touch.*

I was quiet as we left the museum. The Basilica of St. Clare was lovely, too, its exterior stripes of pink and white marble. We saw Francis's childhood home, the courtyard in front where he must have played. *It is a holy city,* I told Q, and he nodded.

A couple of days later we saw another tunic that had belonged to St. Francis. And we saw another, in another town. Wait a minute— how many tunics did he have? I began to waver, and confided my fears to Q. He smiled gently and covered my hand with his. The important thing was what the tunics did for the people, he said, not so much whether or not they were genuine.

I bet there are fifty of Francis's robes in Italy. Somebody is making them still, for all I know. And the humble monk who stripped off all his clothes and left them at his father's feet, walking naked out of town to found his monastery, may not have worn any of them.

But people have stood before them and imagined him for centuries. Tears have filled their eyes, as they filled mine that day. They have felt holiness emanating from the very cloth, like the woman who pushed her way through the crown to touch the hem of Jesus' cloak. Who is to say how her healing occurred? What role the hem of Jesus' garment played in it? *Great is your faith,* he told her, and he called her "daughter." I guess it wasn't the garment. I guess it was him.

THE DAY OF PENTECOST

Pss 118 * 145
Deuteronomy 16:9–12
Acts 4:18–21, 23–33
John 4:19–26

God is spirit, and those who worship him
must worship in spirit and truth.
JOHN 4:24

Ask people to picture a church and they picture a building. When we say that Pentecost is the birthday of the church, then, most people connect that thought with the church they picture, with the institution itself, all its hardware and its history and its hierarchy. Some parishes observe the day with a birthday cake at coffee hour.

But the great gift of Pentecost isn't so much the birth of an institution as it is the celebration of the Spirit's *portability*: the freedom of the Spirit from the physical and geographical constraints of place and time, language and history. That day was the day those closest to Jesus accepted the freedom of the spirit of Jesus to move freely throughout the world. They spoke languages they had not known before, symbolizing the reach of the spirit throughout the earth, a clear message that what God was doing was not just for the people of a tiny Middle Eastern country.

Nothing could have been more important. As long as God is tied to a place in the minds of the faithful, they cannot move beyond a nostalgic effort to remain in that place. The life of faith can encompass the present and the past, but not the unknowable future. It can only do what it has always done, in the place where it has always done it, and its days are surely numbered.

Chain your worship to a particular place and time and you must remain there. Worship God in spirit and you can worship anywhere at all.

The Season
after Pentecost

⋁TRINITY SUNDAY

Pss 146, 147 * 111, 112, 113
Job 38:1–11; 42:1–5
Revelation 19:4–16
John 1:29–34

"Where were you when I laid the foundation of the earth?"

JOB 38:4

Well, we were nowhere. And now we are part of the long parade of its history, the cycle of living and dying that gives life to life. We are smarter than a paramecium or a housefly, but in comparison with the author of everything, we are so small.

I suppose the writer intended that question to put Job's suffering into perspective: it is small, in the grand scheme of things. So is mine, and so is yours. Our lives are so short anyhow: how much does it really matter what happens in them?

Yes, we're pretty small, that's for sure. But—small as it is—this is the only life we have here. We don't see the grand scheme of things. We are like caterpillars on a leaf: we can only see a short distance. Does considering the grand scheme of things do us any good in this life?

I think it can, if we think about what it has meant to us to have been created, rather than to have just *happened*. What it has meant that the foundation of the earth was *laid*, rather than just appearing out of nowhere. This is not to weigh in on the creationism/evolution debate: the presence of God in the majesty of plate tectonics and evolution seems like ample divine involvement to me.

But it introduces the positive element of love into our existence: we are created unnecessarily. For delight, our own and the delight of others. God's delight. Against the backdrop of our natural delight, our suffering makes some sense: it isn't *our lot*. It's aberrant. We're not built for suffering but for joy. We measure even our pain by its distance from our joy.

Is it possible that the only joy left in your life is the loving care of others? It is not only possible, it is inevitable: none of us are getting out of here alive, and suffering is the usual preamble to our departure. Off we go from the bed of that pain and weakness, helped on our way by those who love us, full of longing for that help if we do not have it, a longing shaped by what we know love to be. Off we go, into the life of the God who laid our foundation, leaving our earthly home for the heavenly one that first brought it into being.

MONDAY IN PROPER I

Pss 106:1–18 * 106:19–48
Ezekiel 33:1–11
1 John 1:1–10
Matthew 9:27–34

If we say that we have no sin, we deceive ourselves,
and the truth is not in us.

1 JOHN 1:8

Why on earth would anybody even think it *possible* to claim sinlessness? That's the same thing as denying human status altogether; nobody does everything right. The only reason I can think of would be to escape punishment: people who stoutly defend their innocence against all evidence do so because they're afraid of what's coming.

So what *is* it that's coming? Some of us haven't gotten the message about forgiveness: there is nothing we can do that will separate us from God. We can break God's heart, and we do it all the time, but God no more stops loving us than we stop loving our children when they misbehave.

Small children think that doing something bad is okay if their parents don't find out. That's a toddler stage of moral development. They sometimes hide something they have broken, and then it feels to them as if it didn't happen. We get older, and we know it *did* happen, whether we can hide it or not. We can't talk ourselves out of responsibility for the things we do. It is squarely ours.

The parents teach the child the value of honesty: compliment his courage in bringing his misdeed to their attention, help him make restitution if that is possible. They do not separate themselves from him. In fact, they come closer, as they help him make it right.

Just so, with all of us, no matter our age. It is courageous to tell the truth about ourselves when it is a truth of which we are not proud. But God commends the courage it takes, and God will help us get things straightened out.

TUESDAY IN PROPER 1

Pss (120), 121, 122, 123 * 124, 125, 126, (127)
Ezekiel 33:21–33
1 John 2:1–11
Matthew 9:35–10:4

. . . they were harassed and helpless,
like sheep without a shepherd.
MATTHEW 9:36

"Harassed" is such a good word for us. We are plagued, besieged, life swarms over us like bees, and we swat at it without result. Exhausted in the evening, we ask ourselves what we did all day. What did I accomplish? Where am I going? Am I any closer to getting there?

We can't live without direction, and sometimes we can't lead ourselves. We don't always see the big picture of life, so oppressed are we by the small stuff, and we need someone to lead us, someone who can see beyond what we see. Which is what a shepherd does.

It was like herding cats, a friend reported about a meeting that simply could not rise above its initial chaos. Harassed and helpless, we are, but stubborn, too: we refuse to admit that we need guidance, *any* guidance, human or divine. *I can do this myself*, we snarl, all evidence pointing to the contrary, and we are willing to sacrifice a success we truly desire to that questionable principle.

Some things we can do on our own and some we can't. Get help with the ones you need help with, and don't think you are diminished in any way by doing so. On the contrary, your maturity is showing, and it's very becoming.

WEDNESDAY IN PROPER 1

Pss 119:145–176 * 128, 129, 130
Ezekiel 34:1–16
1 John 2:12–17
Matthew 10:5–15

And the world and its desire are passing away . . .
1 JOHN 2:17

Ileen was diagnosed with ovarian cancer fifteen years ago. She died last night—that's a long life for someone with that disease. It's been only the last two years or so that she's been ill again. She got thirteen good years and two beautiful children she would not have had.

Nobody wanted to live more than Ileen did, and I've never known anybody who tried harder. Asked about where her courage came from, she had a matter-of-fact answer: *I have a lot to live for.*

Her husband wanted her to spend her last day in a beautiful place, not in ICU. So they moved her up to the twelfth floor of St. Vincent's, where she could look out at the city. Airplanes crisscrossed the sky in front of the window, and the moon shone. Friends came and went, and her children came for a cuddle. Ileen herself came and went, too, in and out of a delirium that functioned as a gentle natural buffer against her pain and sorrow at leaving. Seeing her sinking, Mark leaned close, kissed her, told her that she could trust him to take good care of the kids, and she took one final breath. That was it.

She wanted so much to live, but now she is dead. In the last hours of her life, she was very much in the moment: glad to have love surrounding her, glad that whoever was in the room was there, glad to have Mark holding her hand. Glad the sky was there, even when she could no longer see it. The keen edge of grief was missing from that room: there will be plenty of time for it in the days to come. But yesterday, the last day, she had everything she needed, and she pined for nothing. Even the man who would gladly have given his own life for hers felt it, and noted the absence of furrows in her brow, for the first time in two years or more.

THURSDAY IN PROPER 1

Pss 131, 132, (133) * 134, 135
Ezekiel 37:21b–28
1 John 2:18–29
Matthew 10:16–23

". . . be wise as serpents and innocent as doves."
MATTHEW 10:16

We work hard on our conflicts. We prepare for war at great expense, and we use it as a metaphor for aspects of life unrelated to it: we have advertising *campaigns*, for instance, and tell ourselves that *all is fair in love and war*, as if they were not opposites. We *fight* disease, focusing on the disease exclusively as intruder, rather than equally on the body's efficient maintenance of its own wellness and growth.

So we think that war takes brains and planning, but that peace just *happens*. The world would be a better place if the reverse were true, but such a thing is unlikely to happen anytime soon.

How does one walk in Jesus' way in such a violent world? How can we be wise and innocent at once, when the cunning we see in the world is so often employed in the service of the shabbiest of causes?

Faith is counter-cultural. Nobody *decides* on violence for us. We are the ones who decide how we live. We can wage peace, just as we wage war. We can also decide to forego the economic benefits violence carries with it, even in a world that becomes angry at the mere suggestion that there are any.

And will the world change if we do that? We are not in charge of the world, whatever we do. Sometimes it surprises us, and reminds us that we really can't predict much. But we can decide who we will be in the only earthly life we will ever have.

FRIDAY IN PROPER 1

Pss 140, 142 * Psalm 141, 143:1–11 (12)
Exekiel 39:21–29
1 John 3:1–10
Matthew 10:24–33

"Are not two sparrows sold for a penny?
Yet not one of them will fall to the ground apart
from your Father. And even the hairs of your
head are all counted. So do not be afraid;
you are of more worth than many sparrows."
MATTHEW 10:29–31

Notice something right away: sparrows are small and fragile, and God's intense regard for them doesn't make them big and powerful. Sparrows are not impervious to harm just because God loves them. They don't live forever. Their lives are risky: a hawk might get them, or a snake might eat their eggs. Sparrows fall to the ground.

So when Jesus tells us not to be afraid, one thing he is most assuredly not telling us is that we don't have to be afraid because life is perfectly safe. It isn't. We are only a little less fragile than a sparrow.

Faith is not an amulet—a magic something you carry around with you to protect you from harm. The cross around your neck is not an amulet: it doesn't protect you from harm. It helps you to understand the place of harm in the overall scheme of your life, to discern the measures of bane and blessing that come your way and see them each for what it is. Faith is what lives in you no matter what harm befalls. It is the assurance of the presence of God through the worst of it.

It is a dangerous world. It seems, to those of us who have been here a while, to be growing more and more dangerous each day—novel dangers, things we didn't have before. Some of them will get us, and one of them will definitely get each of us before we're through: we don't know which one it will be, but nobody lives forever.

But nobody lives outside the presence of God, either. None of us is unaccompanied through life. Whether you acknowledge or love God or you don't, God loves you, and stands with you when the chips are way down. What might that mean? Lift your head and listen for a moment, lift your eyes, and see around you, look at what might be there, something you didn't notice before, an avenue toward higher ground opening amid the wreckage of all your hopes. It may not look like much, but it may be the only avenue open, and so you start out on it. You and your Friend, the Friend who saw everything that happened to you and now comes closer to you than ever.

SATURDAY IN PROPER 1

Pss 137:1–6 (7–9), 144 * 104
Ezekiel 47:1–12
1 John 3:11–18
Matthew 10:34–42

*[Jesus said,] "Do not think that I have come to bring peace
to the earth; I have not come to bring peace, but a sword."*
MATTHEW 10:34

There is a cost to spiritual and moral integrity. Nobody else can pay it for you, and those closest to you may be fearful of your willingness to pay it yourself: you might suffer for what you believe, and they don't want that for you. We see Mary, the mother of our Lord, trying to get in between him and his destiny a couple of times: once when he was twelve on the way home from the temple, another time when he was a grown man, healing and preaching, and she came with his siblings to try to talk him into coming home. Where it was safe.

Faith is too important a thing to allow anyone else to decide it for you, even someone who loves you. We can raise our children in our faith, but they will, in the end, decide how to live it on their own. How, or even *whether* to live it—the choice is theirs, not ours.

No wonder a sword is what comes to Jesus' mind as he speaks about the cost of discipleship. The very fact of love can hold us back from following. Real anger might confront us, anger from people we don't want ever to lose.

But love never ends, and it is stronger than hate. What remains between people who love but disagree remains, and the anger of it fades eventually, to be replaced by respect. It may be grudging at first, but blood really is thicker than water.

Sometimes we are parted by death before this healing can happen. That hurts mightily: *Now I'll never get a chance to make things right with my mom.* Oh yes, you will. The dead are in Christ now, and understand a lot more than they used to. A lot more than we do, come to think of it.

MONDAY IN PROPER 2

Pss 1, 2, 3 * 4, 7
Proverbs 3:11–20
1 John 3:18–4:6
Matthew 11:1–6

Little children, let us love, not in word or speech,
but in truth and action.
1 JOHN 3:18

You *know I'll always love you.* The very thought that love might end is inconceivable to people preparing for marriage. But "I'll always love you" must remain a theoretical statement until you've walked the walk. In the beginning, you may say it, but you don't know what it means.

I won't always feel sexy. I won't always be nice. I won't always be able to overlook your faults, and I won't always be able to keep from sliding into my own, again and again. I may not always even talk the talk. I may snarl or snap instead. No wonder new couples never say things like that, and find it difficult to believe them: they'd scare each other away.

But you will be the one whose welfare I consult in all things. That's the walk. You don't know for sure you're going to be able to do that until you've done it. So love is always a risk.

But then, so is walking. Watch a baby learn: he edges around the furniture for a long time before he sets out for the middle of the room, and he falls immediately. Then he falls again, and again—countless times. And he gets up each time and keeps trying until he gets it. He has never walked the walk before. This is his first time.

So I guess there is *one* thing newlywed couples get right: they often call each other "Baby."

TUESDAY IN PROPER 2

Pss 5, 6 * 10, 11
Proverbs 4:1–27
1 John 4:7–21
Matthew 11:7–15

*Those who say "I love God," and hate their
brothers and sisters, are liars. . . .*
1 JOHN 4:20

We're not going to be able to get away from one another. When there is a breach among us, we're not going to be able to sweep it under the rug and present ourselves to God as clean and unwrinkled. No matter how many good things we've done in the rest of our life.

Why? Because God doesn't love us if we hold a grudge? No, God loves us, no matter what. It's only because our hearts are finite, not limitless, and the parts of them taken up with the grudge are not available for any of the things of God, who wants to fill every last inch.

The most recognizable figure of our era is also the most bizarre: the figure of the religious fanatic who believes he serves God by killing people he understands to be God's enemies. The most recognizable figure in the early church was the martyr: the one who gave his life for his faith. The terrorist often calls himself a martyr, if he should die committing his act of violence. But he is not a martyr. Martyrs don't take other people with them.

Hatred is never of God. If you think God is telling you that you're justified in perpetuating a state of estrangement, hang up and dial again. You have the wrong number.

WEDNESDAY IN PROPER 2

Pss 119:1–24 * 12, 13, 14
Proverbs 6:1–19
1 John 5:1–12
Matthew 11:16–24

*Go to the ant, you lazybones; consider its ways, and be wise.
Without having any chief or officer or ruler, it prepares its food
in summer, and gathers its sustenance in harvest.*

PROVERBS 6:6

Whatever their faults, it must be said that ants aren't afraid of hard work. Sit down at the picnic table and pretty soon one will walk along with a crumb several times her own size on her back. I'm not sure where she's going with it—back home to make supper for her little ants, I guess.

Actually, no. Ants have complex communities—more complex than the biblical writer apparently knew—but seem not to have families. If you're an ant, you have no particular relationship with the ant who laid the egg that became you, or with any of your brother or sisters. Those relationships are not important to ants. We might say that ants have no family values.

But they have *community* values in abundance. They share food. They collaborate on tasks that benefit the whole hill. They collaborate on the hill itself, building it and renovating it as needed. They appear to domesticate and herd aphids, milking them as if they were cows. They live in a group as if the group were one body, and they were all parts of it.

Which is exactly how the early Church thought of itself: it was a *body*. Not a family, no matter how many Sundays your rector stands in the crossing and tells newcomers they are welcome to "our parish family." It was closer than a family, more seamless. No member could be fully himself unless all others were able to be themselves, too.

THURSDAY IN PROPER 2

Pss 18:1–20 * 18:21–50
Proverbs 7:1–27
1 John 5:13–21
Matthew 11:25–30

"Come to me, all you that are weary and are carrying heavy burdens, and I will give you rest."
MATTHEW 11:28

I can't remember not knowing this verse—which is strange, because I carried no heavy burdens as a child and was only tired at night. But my mother was often tired, so I associated weariness with adulthood. I liked the kindness of Jesus' invitation to the weary. I was glad my mother would have somewhere to go for some rest.

I do know firsthand about burdens now, of course. Carrying them is part of growing up, and gaining the strength to carry them is the necessary first project for all of us. We've got to become people who can get along in the world, and the world can be a heavy place.

Most ancient people carried most of their own burdens. Poor people didn't have an ox or a cart; if something needed to get from one place to another, is usually had to be carried there on foot. Today it is the same: in poor neighborhoods, people in the street carry large boxes and bundles, two people carry a couch, a woman who has no stroller or carriage carries her toddler. Nobody has a car or a truck, or money to rent one. They just have their own strong arms. Or, especially in the case of women, their own strong necks: down the street they walk, with a carriage that can only be described as regal, perfect posture under a burden so heavy it seems impossible that they can carry it on their heads. But they do. I have seen women in India carrying enormous baskets filled with stones in this manner. Each basket must certainly have weighed a hundred pounds.

At some point, night comes. The sun leaves the sky and it is cooler. Everyone has eaten what there was to eat and now you can go to bed. You lie down, your neck aching from carrying the heavy stones all day, even though you are very used to it after all these years. Tomorrow you will carry them again, and the next day. But tonight, right now, there is rest.

FRIDAY IN PROPER 2

Pss 16, 17 * 22
Proverbs 8:1–21
2 John 1–13
Matthew 12:1–14

. . . those who seek me diligently find me.
PROVERBS 8:17

Somewhere in the course of your schooling—or maybe long after it is over—you get it: you're not there in order to "complete your education." You're *never* going to complete your education. You're there to learn how to learn, so that your education can continue throughout your whole life. *Knowing how to learn* is what wisdom is: the growing of a tough, flexible mind that knows what it doesn't know and thirsts to find out more and more.

You can lose your money and your home and your family and your health and everything else you have. Your world can change so profoundly it is no longer recognizable as your world. But if you know how to learn, you can find your way—perhaps not back to what you had, but to something new.

We hope that our personalities survive us after our deaths. We want those we love to be able to recognize us. We hope still to be ourselves. We want to know then what we know now, in that new world about which we know nothing at all.

One thing that we do know is that all life responds adaptively to the reality in which it lives. It learns its own medium: we have learned air and water, the sun, love, war, peace, and everything else we know, and we will learn what the larger life teaches, too, when it is ours. We'll become able to seek the wisdom it carries, so different from our own, large enough to contain our present life but never contained by it.

Not something we'll ever "complete."

⤵ SATURDAY IN PROPER 2

Pss 20, 21:1–7 (8–14) * 110:1–5 (6–7), 116, 117
Proverbs 8:22–36
3 John 1–15
Matthew 12:15–21

Greet the friends there, each by name.
3 JOHN 15

There are churches small enough so that everybody knows everybody else. They feel like extensions of the members' households, and members often speak of the church as being "like family." So it wouldn't be hard to greet each member of such a church by name.

But suppose it grew larger? What then? Would they still have that family feeling they cherish? Sometimes small churches take steps of which they may be unaware to make sure they do not grow: they do not advertise service times, do not greet newcomers or take any steps to encourage them to return, do not behave as if they wanted new people to come. They may articulate the desire to increase in size, but only slowly enough not to disturb the family feeling. And they may be very particular about what kinds of visitors they encourage: they want people who will fit in with them. People like them.

One of the things people often really love in such a church is that the priest uses their names when he gives them the communion bread. *Mary*, he says softly, *the Body of Christ. June, the Body of Christ. Frank, the Body of Christ.* So you certainly know you're a member of the church: the priest calls you by name.

But if you're new, the practice may feel very different to you. *All these people belong here*, you might find yourself thinking, *and I guess maybe I don't. I wonder how long you have to come before the priest says your name?*

Can you give up something that comfortable for the sake of a stranger? Can you even discuss it? Are newcomers welcome only after all the old timers have gotten what they needed, only if the things they want are only the things we also want? Hospitality to the stranger was the bedrock of the Jewish heritage from which Jesus emerged. It was worth real sacrifices on the part of the family. Have we also inherited it, or are we something else now, a "family" suspicious of those who are not members?

No offense. Just asking.

SUNDAY, PROPER 3

Pss 148, 149, 150 * 114, 115
Proverbs 9:1–12
Acts 8:14–25
Luke 10:25–28, 38–42

*"Lord, do you not care that my sister has
left me to do all the work by myself?"*
LUKE 10:40

It seems that Martha has only two scenarios available to her imagination: either Mary helps her or she does all the work herself. But there are other possibilities: Martha could have stopped working to listen, too, and everyone could have eaten a little later. She could have asked Mary for some *help*, for heaven's sake; we don't hear her doing *that* in the story. She just waits for Mary to volunteer and then feels hurt and angry when she doesn't, which is exactly the way that strategy works out when *I* try it.

It's one thing to *have* a right—surely Martha must have had the same right to listen to their visitor as her sister did—but your right to something is only half of what you need to get it. You must also *assert* your right. Probably no one's going to hand it to you. You must take it.

Commentators have always talked about Martha modeling the active life and Mary the contemplative. But maybe *Mary* is the activist here, breaking some new ground in her household and in the history that remembers her through the centuries that have passed since that ancient afternoon. And maybe *Martha* is the passive one, accepting what has always been as what must always be. Women always prepared the food and men always talked. But it didn't happen quite that way on that particular day.

And later on? Who knows—maybe the liberating words of their guest went to everybody's head a little, and the men began to help set out dishes of olives and goat cheese, cut the flat loaves of bread into triangles, arrange figs and dates on plates while the conversation went on and on into the night. Maybe whoever noticed they were running dry, man or woman, got up and got some more wine. Who knows? It might have been an even more unusual visit than we remember.

MONDAY IN PROPER 3

Pss 25 * 9, 15
Proverbs 10:1–12
1 Timothy 1:1–17
Matthew 12:22–32

*"If I cast out demons by Beelzebul, by whom
do your own exorcists cast them out?"*
MATTHEW 12:27

A senator campaigns on budget cuts as if his opponent had invented the pork barrel, but indignantly refuses even to discuss federal cuts for his own state. An Irish-American politician campaigns on an anti-immigration platform and never stops to consider how her own forebears got here. A man opposes abortion out of reverence for life, but enthusiastically supports the death penalty. Whoever said you can't have your cake and eat it too must not have been in politics.

It is always said that a negative political campaign means that there are no substantive issues differentiating one candidate from another. You can't really criticize your opponent's positions without indicting your own, so you go after him personally. Here, the Pharisees are mounting a negative campaign against Jesus: might it be because he is more like them than they wish to think? Both Jesus and the Pharisees look to eternal life. They both look to a renewed fidelity to the law in everyday life. Both reject the occupation of Israel by the Romans, and view it as related to moral decay in their society. The Pharisees long for holiness above all else, and a critique of those around them forms an important part of their self-under-standing. I imagine they regard the obvious holiness of Jesus with something like envy.

He exorcises demons, and so do some of them. He heals people, and there were other itinerant healers around Israel in those days. He performs miracles, and stories of other miracle workers circu-lated at the time. They attack him for bringing the kingdom closer, when the kingdom coming closer is exactly what they want.

TUESDAY IN PROPER 3

Pss 26, 28 * 36, 39
Proverbs 15:16–33
1 Timothy 1:18–2:8
Matthew 12:33–42

*. . . so that we may lead a quiet and peaceable
life in all godliness and dignity.*
1 TIMOTHY 2:2

My father's life in retirement was such a life—home and church, basically. Visits to the hospital and nursing home to help the local rector out. Walks in the morning, conversation with the neigh-bors every evening, all of them in the front yard on lawn chairs: they called it "solving the problems of the world." Unhurried trips to the grocery store and to the bank, chats with the people he met there, then a slow drive home in the car.

My life is so different, so *un*-deliberate: I seem to attract dead-lines and commitments like a picnic attracts flies. My schedule is much lighter than it was in the past, but it is still more frantic than that of almost everyone I know. The element of choice seems so hard to come by. Everything feels like an obligation, and when I run out of obligations a whole crop of new ones arrives to take their place.

It feels as if this frenetic life *happens* to me, as if I were not its author. But that cannot be true. Nobody imposes it on me. I impose it on myself. Not a single task I set myself comes from anyone else: I accept them all.

In my heart of hearts, I know that I *could* accept something else. I could ask God for a life that makes sense, for the courage to say "no," and then use that courage and the brain God gave me to do some common-sense triage of all my "obligations." That I don't do this—and have never managed to do it for long—is evidence that original sin is alive and well in me: I still behave as if I thought my own will a safer bet for me than the will of God. Afraid of the answer I might get, I just don't ask God for help. I just go ahead and do it myself.

The results are what one might expect.

⩔ WEDNESDAY IN PROPER 3

Pss 38 * 119:25–48
Proverbs 17:1–20
1 Timothy 3:1–16
Matthew 12:43–50

"Then it goes and brings along seven other spirits more evil than itself, and they enter and live there; and the last state of that person is worse than the first."
MATTHEW 12:45

Before I quit smoking for good, I stopped many times. Once I stopped for the better part of a year, only to pick one up one day for no apparent reason: at a social gathering, someone just offered me one and I took it. *Hey, that wasn't so bad,* I said to myself when I had finished it. It really was no big deal. I didn't ask for another one, and congratulated myself on my newfound self-control. *Maybe I can be a social smoker now,* I thought to myself. *Just have one once in a while.* I certainly didn't feel out of control.

But within a week I was smoking every day. And within a month I was back up to my previous level of consumption. In two months, I had doubled it. *And the last state of that person is worse than the first.*

The demons are stronger than we are—that we know. Stronger and smarter. But Jesus is stronger and smarter than they are. A power higher than our own can deliver us from their deadly grip, but we will not ask for help from that power as long as we think it's no big deal, that we're in control, that we've got it covered. Nobody is as good a liar as an addict, and we lie to nobody as successfully as we lie to ourselves: we truly believe our nonsense. And so the demon settles in for a long and comfortable stay.

He stays as long as we live in our lies. But when the truth is spoken and we hear it, he knows he must leave. He puts up a fight, but his death-dealing is no match for the Lord of Life. And we end up in a different place, not congratulating ourselves on our own power but struck with awe and gratitude at the power that has set us free.

This wasn't me, we say. *I didn't do this. I tried so many times and failed, but now I am free. I don't know how it happened, but I do know it wasn't me.*

No, it wasn't. It was God working in me. My only task was to ask for God's help.

ᐯTHURSDAY IN PROPER 3

Pss 37:1–18 * 37:19–42
Proverbs 21:30–22:6
1 Timothy 4:1–6
Matthew 13:24–30

"Master, did you not sow good seed in your field?
Where, then, did these weeds come from?"
He answered, "An enemy has done this."
MATTHEW 13:27–28

I open the door of Rosie's room and close it again quickly—it's just too frightening a sight for someone with heart trouble. We have had family meeting after family meeting about the very few rules of living here, and one of them is Keeping One's Room Clean.

Not Martha Stewart clean: Q and I are not unreasonable people. Just Centers for Disease Control clean. Just clean enough not to be a health hazard.

At the meetings, there is always grudging agreement about this—the *it's-my-room-yeah-but-it's-our-house* kind of detente which is often the best one achieves with very young adults. The meetings end up with a plan that the minimal cleaning we require will take place. Always. And it rarely does.

Meanwhile, she has cleaned my office to within an inch of its life without being asked. I hardly recognize the place.

I do not understand her.

Some of them are so easy and some of them are so hard. Some of them say yes and then do what they say, and others do all sorts of other things. We look at those others with a clutch of fear in our hearts, because we know fifty-year-olds, sixty-year-olds who have *never* gotten it, who have lived irresponsible and unhappy lives and have blamed everyone else for everything that happened in them, and we are so afraid they will end up like that.

And maybe they will. But most of them will get it, even if it takes them longer than we wish it did. Life will teach most of them what can and can't happen, and they will come to understand that nobody on earth has nearly as much to do with what happens to them as they themselves do.

FRIDAY IN PROPER 3

Pss 31 * 35
Proverbs 23:19–21, 29–24:2
1 Timothy 5:17–22 (23–25)
Matthew 13:31–35

"The kingdom of heaven is like yeast that a
woman took and mixed in with three measures
of flour until all of it was leavened."
MATTHEW 13:33

Usually you soften the yeast first in some warm water and add it with the other liquids. Sometimes, though, you mix it in with the flour. Whichever you do, you can't help but notice how much flour there is—and how little yeast. This is all right, though, because you know the yeast will grow: it will permeate the whole batch, and the loaves you form will rise into lovely rounded domes.

You have a role in helping this happen: you are the one who must knead the bread. You fold it over and over upon itself and then flatten it out so you can fold it again, dozens and dozens of times, trapping air in between the layers each time you fold. The yeast will enlarge every pocket of air as the dough rises, and then it will die when you bake the bread, leaving behind the cavities where it was, full of air again.

So the kingdom of heaven starts small and grows. And it grows by dying.

The march of our lives toward their end is usually seen by us as tragic. It is the great mystery of life, and it is life's great sadness. We wish we could stay here forever, and none of us can. But it is only through the leaving of this life that we can awaken to the next.

Next? What is *next* like? What's wrong with this life? Nothing, except that it ends. Perhaps it is small and heavy, like a leaden ball of unrisen bread dough. And perhaps, in the end, it combines with the stuff of life and becomes light, elastic, large, and so full of energy you can feel its life in your hands.

SATURDAY IN PROPER 3

Pss 30, 32 * 42, 43
Proverbs 25:15–28
1 Timothy 6:6–21
Matthew 13:36–43

For the love of money is a root of all kinds of evil . . .
1 TIMOTHY 6:10

Afrer the basic needs for food and shelter are met, moneymaking becomes a slippery slope. There is always something new to acquire, and the engine of moneymaking has no brake. Maybe you should make more money. And then maybe you should make more.

To people without money, it seems that life would hold no problems if only there were enough cash. Claims to the contrary by rich people anger them: "Oh, but money can't buy happiness!" someone will say, and a poor person who chances to hear it feels the knife of his need twist in his side. *Maybe not*, he thinks, *but it can keep you from starving to death. It can get you to the doctor when you get sick. It can get you an education. I'll trade places with you in your quest for happiness any time.*

But what money does is insert itself into the place where love should go. We transfer the sharp ache of our need in poverty to our more prosperous lives, treat our new luxuries as if they were the bare necessities. We try to extract from money things it does not contain, hoping against all the evidence that having more of it will change us into someone else and, unlike an addiction drugs or alcohol, this one is an addiction society wholeheartedly approves.

ᴠSUNDAY, PROPER 4

Pss 63:1–8 (9–11), 98 * 103
Ecclesiastes 1:1–11
Acts 8:26–40
Luke 11:1–13

The sun rises and the sun goes down,
and hurries to the place where it rises.
ECCLESIASTES 1:5

How can something have been so long ago and also be so *recent*? Today the tapes of firefighters and police responding on 9/11 were released to the public, and they are playing fragments of them on the radio as I work. Firefighters unable to believe their eyes, dispatchers in remote locations unable to believe their ears. *WHAT?* one of the dispatchers says in the last moment of her innocence. The second plane approaching. Both buildings, incredibly, on fire. *WHAT?* The first tower falling. The second building falling.

But I am fine, almost four years later. I had some respiratory difficulty in the months immediately following the bombing, but nothing compared to what other people had, and I am fine now. I still will not read a murder mystery: I, who used to read at least one a day and usually two. I just haven't the heart: living human beings hurtled through the air and hit the pavement, still conscious. Others just exploded and disappeared forever. And it was all done on purpose.

Was the bombing of the World Trade Center the worst thing that ever happened in the world? No, of course not. Competitors for that prize are numerous, and I can't imagine many of us would have the stomach to try and choose one of them. But it is a terrible thing that happened, one that continues to haunt us, and we can't undo its effect. We can only go on with life.

Hiroshima and Nagasaki, flattened and poisoned sixty years ago, have gone on with life. The memorials to the thousands who perished are among only a few traces of the terrible things that happened there. Those who remember it can't believe it's been sixty years. At certain moments—in certain lights—it feels so recent.

MONDAY IN PROPER 4

Pss 41, 52 * 44
Ecclesiastes 2:1–15
Galatians 1:1–17
Matthew 13:44–52

*"Therefore every scribe who has been trained for the
kingdom of heaven is like the master of a household who
brings out of his treasure what is new and what is old."*
MATTHEW 13:52

We usually assume that *tradition* means customs and ways the community inherits from the past, written down for the use of generations to come. Tradition is why we even *have* scribes: we can't be guided by the past it if we don't even know what it is.

But of course, part of what the scribe is recording isn't old. Not to him: it's what is happening right at that very moment. Most of it, maybe: the witness of the people around him to what happens and what it means. What he produces is a blend of the history he knows and the things he sees—what is old and what is new.

Tradition is not, by itself, a conclusive argument against change, because it is itself a *record* of change: Christian tradition contains things not found in scripture, responses to later situations in later times. Including our own times, right now. By definition, then, tradition is *new stuff*.

The life of faith would be a lot simpler if it were simply the project of doing what has always been done. If life in Christ just meant living like the people in the Bible lived. *And* if we knew which people in the Bible we meant.

Instead, the treasure of tradition turns out to be as alive as we are. It brings those long dead forward to our own age, and joins us to them. And it brings us back to them as the fruit of their work: *we* are where they ended up.

But we are not *them*. We know some things of which they never dreamed, and have forgotten some things they took for granted.

What we leave behind us will move on into history without us, and future generations will use them as they see fit: what we inherited and what we fashioned ourselves.

TUESDAY IN PROPER 4

Pss 45 * 47, 48
Ecclesiastes 2:16–26
Galatians 1:18–2:10
Matthew 13:53–58

They asked only one thing, that we remember the poor,
which was actually what I was eager to do.
GALATIANS 2:10

The laconic tone of Paul's account of how the resolution of the bitterest controversy in the early church was resolved fails to do justice to just how bitter it was: the question of how the church would relate to its Jewish roots was divisive and emotional. Would Gentile converts have to become Jews first? Should there even *be* any Gentile converts? Would men have to accept adult circumcision? *That* cannot have been a small consideration.

Perhaps it will be relevant to us now to remember that the resolution Paul worked out with the Jerusalem Christians was an interim one. Interim and very local: they would maintain their Jewishness, and he would expand the faith into Gentile culture in ways that Gentile culture could receive it. History would unfold as it would, but here was a solution that would work for now. It honored the perspective of both parties, and it allowed the future to judge.

And it did one more thing: it focused everyone's attention on the poor. We could do that, too. It would be nice if we focused less on our divisions and more on service in Christ's name to those in need. Because the very poor don't keep themselves awake at night with theological or ecclesiastical worries.

No. Not at all. It's their hunger that keeps them awake.

WEDNESDAY IN PROPER 4

Pss 119:49–72 * 49, (53)
Ecclesiastes 3:1–15
Galatians 2:11–21
Matthew 14:1–12

. . . a time to be born, and a time to die.
ECCLESIASTES 3:2

I understand we're going to live to be 120 years old, some of us. Not me personally, I mean, but certain hardy specimens of the current generation. Certainly centenarians are nowhere near the rarity they once were, and they are certain to grow more numerous still. Sixty is the new fifty, as everyone knows, and seventy is now parked squarely in middle age. We're all supposed to be as toned and vigorous as ever, for decades after the moment has come and gone when we would heretofore have expected to be dead.

I will not attend. I don't want my children to have to wait until they're eighty or ninety to experience the emancipation that will come to them upon my death. Every generation deserves the chance to be the senior one. As much as we miss our parents, their departure is an important part of our independence. And this is true even if they haven't taken care of us for years and years, even if it has been we who cared for them in the end. We need them, but we also need them to leave: one generation must yield to the next, so that the vigor it gave the world can flourish in a new era.

Besides, I believe in heaven. Don't know what it *is*, of course, but I'm eager to find out and ready to go, and you can't go to heaven unless you die, no matter *who* you are. Life is beautiful, but it is also hard work. I'm looking forward to some rest.

THURSDAY IN PROPER 4

Ps 50 * (59, 60) or 8, 84
Ecclesiastes 3:16–4:3
Galatians 3:1–14
Matthew 14:13–21

*Now when Jesus heard [that John had been
beheaded by Herod], he withdrew from there
in a boat to a deserted place by himself.*
MATTHEW 14:13

Here, we see something unusual in the gospel of Matthew: Jesus in mourning. He knows just what he needs—some time by himself. Time to think and feel and *not talk to people.* A splint is a device that surrounds a broken bone so it has a chance to begin to heal without moving. Solitude is a splint for the broken soul: we need the silence and the stillness to begin our healing.

Those who love you gather round, and you appreciate their presence. You pick, with gratitude but not much appetite, at the casseroles and cakes people bring, but their love and concern is palpable, and you are glad to have them with you. You see people you haven't seen for a while, and they tell you how much the person you have loved and lost meant to them, too, and every kind word is music to your ears. But there are other moments in bereavement when you just need silence, with nobody in sight, when you need to weep and need to do it alone.

Sometimes people who love you worry when you do this. *She's isolating herself,* they tell each other. *Let's see if we can't get her out somewhere.* And you *do* go out, after a while, and you *do* have fun. But you also need to be by yourself sometimes: the soul needs time to absorb the shock of what has happened, of its new loneliness, of what exactly has been lost. Shock isn't always fast. Sometimes it's slow.

Jesus is wise to allow himself some silent time to feel it. I am sure the people around him were disconcerted by his desire to get away:

they were shaken by John's death, too, frightened about what it might mean for them, sorrowful. They probably needed him to lead, to be himself, his old self, the Jesus they counted on.

And he *was* still that Jesus. But he couldn't lead, not right then: he needed to mourn. He would be back in his place very quickly— probably too quickly to suit him, but then, mourning is like that.

FRIDAY IN PROPER 4

Pss 40, 54 * 51
Ecclesiastes 5:1–7
Galatians 3:15–22
Matthew 14:22–36

"Take heart. It is I; do not be afraid."
MATTHEW 14:27

*S*o how was it? Ugh. Draining. I'm exhausted and so is he.* My friend and her husband have just returned from the couples' therapist I suggested they see.

Sounds about right. You feel a whole lot worse before you feel a whole lot better in therapy, as you bring item after item into the light and lay it on the table for everyone to see. *Ugh. Why am I doing this?* you ask yourself. You were fine when you were just pretending those things weren't there. Or, if they were there, that they didn't affect you.

But you *weren't* fine. Unprocessed angers and sorrows and fears find a voice, even if you won't give them one, and the voice they find usually does you more harm than good.

Recently, several movie stars who are also Scientologists have flown into televised rages about psychotherapy on national television, screaming at interviewers who have suggested that it might not always be such a bad thing. *It's evil,* they say. *You don't know anything about it, you haven't studied it like I have.*

Hmmn. Of course, their study was supervised by people who believed shrinks were evil, so it might not have been, as we say, "fair and balanced." I'm always a little skeptical of convictions that must be expressed in a scream. I've known many people who have benefited from psychotherapy and have benefited from it myself, so I have a somewhat different view.

Scary? Oh, yeah. But Jesus is present in scary places, too. *It is I; do not be afraid.*

SATURDAY IN PROPER 4

Pss 55 * 138, 139:1–17 (18–23)
Ecclesiastes 5:8–20
Galatians 3:23–4:11
Matthew 15:1–20

As they came from their mother's womb, so they
shall go again, naked as they came . . .
ECCLESIASTES 5:15

What *should she wear?* my sister-in-law asked, and we went upstairs to look in my mother's clothes cupboard for the right outfit.

Hmmn. The bottle green silk suit with the lime green lapels and matching blouse I made her? No, it no longer fit her. The wool plaid skirt and brown sweater she always wore? No, too wintry for early May. The black and white party dress she had saved from when she was a young woman, a dress I always loved? What a silly idea.

We settled on a light knit blue suit with a blue striped mock turtleneck top. She looked nice in blue, with her blue eyes. But of course, her eyes would be closed now.

Oh, they do not see us! They don't speak! They look like themselves, but different somehow, and we don't like it. And yet we clothe them, and we look and look, memorizing the body their spirits lived in, through which we loved them and they loved us. Sometime people take pictures of them, lying so still in their satin nests. Already the voice and the movement are gone, and soon everything physical will go. We will take their clothes and divide them up, give them to the poor. Wear some of them ourselves, and derive some comfort from being surrounded by them.

And they won't need them at all. Naked we come and naked we go, and we are fine with that. Other things absorb us, in that new life we can only enter through that one door.

SUNDAY, PROPER 5

Pss 24, 29 * 8, 84
Ecclesiastes 6:1–12
Acts 10:9–23
Luke 12:32–40

All human toil is for the mouth,
yet the appetite is not satisfied.
ECCLESIASTES 6:7

I suppose you could keep a food diary, I say. *I don't want to be compulsive about it*, my friend says. *I got that way with exercise once, years ago, and I was running off to the gym after every meal to work it off. That was so crazy.*

Yeah.

We talk about what a struggle it is, finding strategies that work. How bizarre it is to be Americans, obese and fretting about it, in a world starving to death. To desire something and yet do its opposite, over and over again. To reach for food as a response to everything that happens, happy or sad, to celebrate *and* mourn by eating.

The way to begin to live in another way is just to *begin*. You don't have to *end*, not on the first day. You just make a start, and then you do it again the next day. You add to it as you are able, and you don't worry whether you're going to be able to do the same thing in the future. You don't worry about the future at all: we may all be dead in the future, and *none* of us will be eating cookies then.

Every healthy choice you make is a healthy choice you made. It *counts*. The more you celebrate it, the more healthy choices you will make. To the extent that compulsive behavior like overeating is a way of calming a spirit unaware of its own anxieties, the purposeful celebration of health is itself therapeutic: it contradicts the harsh voice within. Very few permanent improvements have been made in anybody's life by listening to that harsh voice.

MONDAY IN PROPER 5

Pss 56, 57, (58) * 64, 65
Ecclesiastes 7:1–14
Galatians 4:12–20
Matthew 15:21–28

"Yes, Lord, yet even the dogs eat the crumbs
that fall from their masters' table."
MATTHEW 15:27

The woman just wouldn't give up—and she won! Jesus was mean to her, and she corrected him and he listened and learned from her. From a woman. A *Canaanite* woman.

If we can't wrap our minds around the idea that this story begins with Jesus behaving badly, because we spent our childhoods hearing that he never did anything wrong, we will miss the majesty of it. No unnaturally good Baby Jesus who never cried could come close to the profound holiness of the Son of God allowing himself to be corrected and instructed by a wretched, half-hysterical woman. She confesses his power by making her request, and he affirms her humanity by engaging her in an argument as an equal.

But the first two unlovely exchanges with her came straight from his culture. He articulated the insularity of his community, and he didn't question its justice until she did. He was open to conversion, and he converted. Became larger when the woman called him on his smallness.

Keep your perfect Jesus if you feel you need him. But remember that "truly human and truly God" really means truly both, and Christians can't get away from the paradox of that impossible pairing. But imagine, for a moment, what it might mean to have a Jesus who learned from life the same way we learn from it: by making mistakes and growing from having made them.

TUESDAY IN PROPER 5

Pss 61, 62 * 68:1–20 (21–23) 24–36
Ecclesiastes 8:14–9:10
Galatians 4:21–31
Matthew 15:29–39

"How many loaves have you?"
They said, "Seven, and a few small fish."
MATTHEW 15:34

What are we doing out here? I can't believe this—we've been here all day long in the heat, night is falling, and nobody has made any preparation for feeding all these people.

I was so busy with crowd control myself that I didn't get to eat my lunch. Not that it was such a spread. My wife says I'm getting fat, and now she never packs me enough food. I could eat double what I brought. I could eat a camel.

But I guess I'm not going to eat any of it, because he's just asked for all our food! What next? But that's okay: I couldn't eat my lunch in front of all these hungry people anyway, so I might as well hand it over. I do think we should have sent them into town to spend the evening and get a good meal. Let them come back tomorrow. Would that have been so terrible?

Maybe the miracle of the loaves and fishes is more nuanced than just the astounding multiplication of food. Maybe it contains other, less spectacular wonders, like the disciples' willingness to follow an irrational request in utter puzzlement but complete trust. Like the willingness to deny the self in solidarity with everyone else's hunger. Like a crowd of thousands of hungry people responding to a request to sit down on the ground by—well, by sitting down on the ground. A like-in-the-movies miracle happened that day, for sure, but the readiness people displayed for the miracle was also miraculous.

We focus on the multiplication of food and forget about the role people play in their own miracles. They show up. They go out on a limb. And they risk looking really, really foolish.

WEDNESDAY IN PROPER 5

Pss 72 * 119:73–96
Ecclesiastes 9:11–18
Galatians 5:1–15
Matthew 16:1–12

I wish those who unsettle you would castrate themselves!
GALATIANS 5:12

This is as good a place as any to remember just how, um, *frank* a person Paul could be. Not a diplomat, our Paul. It was a time when everything about the new faith was up for discussion. There were no Christian scriptures. Paul himself did not know the term "Christian."

His considerably evangelistic approach to the faith was not the only one around. Others favored a much more local way of being the church, one that would have included the understanding that being a Christian was a better, more genuine way of being a Jew, a way that would leave intact all the obligations of being Jewish— circumcision, for sure, but hundreds of others as well. The whole observant lifestyle.

The diverse presence of the church in the world shows how thoroughly Paul's vision prevailed. It could live within the boundaries of any culture in which it found itself, and every age, and it has. Its orthodoxies have always inveighed against the challenges of change and foreignness, but—slowly, painfully—the faith has always found ways to embrace what was necessary to remain alive.

The mechanism for accomplishing this embrace is often conflict. People argue and fight and leave, and begin new institutional churches with new names. The churches they leave behind are hurt and angry, and so are they: centuries can pass before a rapprochement begins. They vary widely, and believe many different things about the itinerant preacher who was also the Son of God, who sometimes seems very far away from these struggles.

THURSDAY IN PROPER 5

Pss (70), 71 * 74
Ecclesiastes 11:1–8
Galatians 5:16–24
Matthew 16:13–20

"You are Peter, and on this rock I will build my church."
MATTHEW 16:18

You can't tell it in English, but this is a pun: the Greek word *petrus* means "rock." So Simon's new name was "Rocky." I like that.

Most Americans don't understand ancient Greek; modern Greeks don't even understand it. But *wait* a minute—neither did Jesus. His language was Aramaic. Oh, dear.

This text, so important to those who care deeply about the Apostolic Succession, the proof text of the papacy, is probably not an authentic saying of Jesus. We might have suspected it anyway, even if we didn't know about the pun, because of the use of the word *church*. There's not much evidence that Jesus understood himself to be founding a *church*; he does not use that word elsewhere. Jesus was proclaiming the kingdom, not starting an institution.

This is not to say it's not very old: it certainly is. It appears here so that the segment of the church faithful to Peter's leadership could locate itself in the mind of Jesus, attributing its primacy to him. While it fails to do that to our satisfaction, it certainly shows anybody who cares to inquire that the continuous leadership Peter begins is very ancient and important. No damage is done to any Pope, I think, by this little investigation.

And a certain good is accomplished: it reminds us that the church is not eternal. It is a contingent structure, scaffolding for the building of the kingdom of God. Its earthly arrangements, ancient and valuable and beloved though they may be, will all pass away like everything else. It points to God, but does not contain or limit God. Because the kingdom of God is among us already, and it is also coming. At the same time.

FRIDAY IN PROPER 5

Pss 69:1–23 (24–30) 31–38 * 73
Ecclesiastes 11:9–12:14
Galatians 5:25–6:10
Matthew 16:21–28

My friends, if anyone is detected in a transgression,
you who have received the Spirit should restore
such a one in a spirit of gentleness.
GALATIANS 6:1

So many transgressions in church news in recent years: horrid stories of child sexual abuse by priests, some going on for decades while bishops looked the other way. Priests *in flagrante* in the newspaper, dealing drugs from the rectory. Embezzlements of donated money by trusted church treasurers. Ugh.

The priest was God to us, a middle-aged man says tightly. *You didn't tell him 'No.' You'd jump out the window if he told you to.* "Gentleness" is not the word for the feelings of those injured by church officials. They are furious, with the sting of their betrayal still fresh in their memories, bitterly aware that the damage that has been done them cannot be reversed. They demand accountability and punishment; in so many of their cases, restitution is not an option.

How is one "restored in a spirit of gentleness" if he must also be deposed from the ordained ministry? If she is convicted of a crime and must go to prison? What does "restored" mean, if it cannot provide actual restoration of presence?

Actually, *restoration* is never possible, in any situation. Things can never again be as they used to be: nothing is as it used to be. Even if the terrible thing had not happened, things still would not be as they were before. What can be restored is not the past; that is gone already. It is the future that must be restored.

And that is something we *can* do. The future is open, waiting for us in the hand of God. We who cannot change what has happened can still make the future a place of possibility and grace by remembering that those who have survived injury in the past have a claim on it. And that those who have inflicted injury in the past are still beloved children of God, even though they must pay the debt to society that they have incurred. Even if, for reasons of safety, they can never return to live in community, they will always be part of the body of Christ.

SATURDAY IN PROPER 5

Pss 75, 76 * 23, 27
Numbers 3:1–13
Galatians 6:11–18
Matthew 17:1–13

*See what large letters I make when
I am writing in my own hand!*
GALATIANS 6:11

Is it just me, or do you find this thrilling, too: an ancient voice so personally present, a moment of direct communication, no scribe in between us and Paul? If I were to see the original letter and beheld these words, large and dark and impatient, so markedly different from the well-mannered script of the scribe, I think I might just fall over with excitement.

Paul felt it, too, right then. I can see him grabbing the pen from the hand of his scribe and bending over the parchment himself, scrawling out something he wanted people to read and understand, to make no mistake about it, understand just how important it was. *This is me talking*, his big dark letters tell those first readers. *You'd better mark my words because I really mean them!*

The autograph of someone we admire feels to us like a small piece of the person himself. That's the idea behind all signature requirements: it's *you*, when you sign in your own hand, no one else. Your signature is as good as your very presence.

Scripture contains so many layers of writing: translation after translation, scribe after scribe after scribe. It can be hard to sort out all the different voices that comprise it. But this one is not hard: Paul bursts through the door, and we cannot not mistake him for anybody but himself. He makes sure of that: *See what large letters I make when I am writing in my own hand!*

√SUNDAY, PROPER 6

Pss 93, 96 * 34
Numbers 6:22–27
Acts 13:1–12
Luke 12:41–48

"From everyone to whom much has been given,
much will be required. . . ."
LUKE 12:48

At the time of the World Trade Center bombing, it seemed that we would be in for a long and difficult era of self-sacrifice. We talked about it a lot then; I remember Carol Towt worrying out loud about how this generation would handle it, as we stood and talked outside the post office one morning late that September. *We had the Depression to make us strong, but they've never had to struggle for anything,* she said. *I'm afraid they don't know how.*

In New York, we responded with a unanimous and willing spirit that surprised us and must have stunned the many visitors who soon descended upon the city to help out. We reached into ourselves and into the hearts of our neighborhoods and found there the same spirit that sustained men, women, and children through all our country's darkest days. War is about aggression and failed politics, but a city's response to war is always local: neighborhoods, local kids gone overseas, a communal belt-tightening in the service of something greater than ourselves.

But very soon, it seemed, this one would be different. The patriotic thing to do, it appeared, would be to shop more. And go out to eat. This made sense in our part of town, a street in Hell's Kitchen christened "Restaurant Row," hit hard by the abrupt drop in business: the bombing immediately and directly injured the owners, the suppliers, the waiters, and kitchen people. Many places closed. I made the rounds of the local eateries.

But it turned out that we were *all* supposed to shop and eat out more, not just New Yorkers. Buy more cars: we began to buy Hummers, enormous vehicles that imitated the all-terrain conveyances the troops were using in Afghanistan and Iraq, as if by buying cars that were like their cars we were somehow partaking in their terrible daily risks. How odd—our most serious spiritual vices, the very things that were making us weaker, more soft and corpulent and less useful every year were the things we were supposed to do to win the war against terror. Why was it that in other times of national trial we were expected to do without things and in this one we are expected to acquire more of them?

There are potent economic forces in the world that will do very well regardless of what happens to us: wealth that knows no national boundaries, wealth with a mission to enlarge itself, whatever the cost; wealth that goes where the money is, that would just as soon take it from you as from me and would prefer to take it from us both; wealth whose short-term prospects are so dazzling that nothing long-term matters. But shopping and acquisition can't win a war or govern a people. No one can prosper safely on a foundation of self-indulgence alone.

MONDAY IN PROPER 6

Pss 80 * 77, (79)
Numbers 9:15–23; 10:29–36
Romans 1:1–15
Matthew 17:14–21

" . . . if you have faith the size of a mustard seed,
you will say to this mountain, 'Move from here to there,'
and it will move; and nothing will be impossible for you."
MATTHEW 17:21

This promise comes about because the disciples have failed in a healing they tried to perform, that of an epileptic boy. *Why couldn't we do it?* they ask Jesus plaintively. Not enough faith, he tells them.

This idea troubles most of us. Is faith something we need to *come up with*, something we need to produce ourselves, and when we have enough of it, God—who otherwise would stand idly by—will instead act in our behalf? Is it a ticket we must buy in order to gain entry into the love of God?

No. Faith is not a ticket. It's not even something *we do*. Faith is a relationship with God, completely a gift of God in our lives. We don't give it to God; God gives it to us. If we live in longing for God's presence in our lives, soon we begin to see the signs that it is a trustworthy presence. We lean more and more of that presence, whatever happens to us.

But what about the mountain? What about the explicit promise that the laws of nature will bend to our will every time, if we have enough faith? Well, we don't know what the laws of nature will do, other than what they've always done. We don't control that. But living in the life of faith will certainly shape how we pray for healing, and it will inform our embrace of what happens in the course of a life. It will give us a longer view of our tragedies, one that includes the life that contains this life; we will become larger, as that life is larger than this one.

The boy was healed of his seizure disorder. But he died one day, later on, as did everyone else in this story. A day came when prayer didn't bring his illness grinding to a full stop. But perhaps he had been thinking about his miracle for years, ever since it happened, and perhaps it had made faith, that combination of longing and trust, more real in his life than it was before. If it was, his death was not a defeat for his faith. It completed it, and led him into the kingdom of God.

TUESDAY IN PROPER 6

Pss 78:1–39 * 78:40–72
Number 11:1–23
Romans 1:16–25
Matthew 17:22–27

*". . . take the first fish that comes up; and when
you open its mouth, you will find a coin . . ."*
MATTHEW 17:27

Here is an incident in the life of Jesus that we don't hear much about. It sounds like a folktale, does it not? A fish with a coin in its mouth comes up from the sea, and now Jesus has the money to pay his temple tax. He can even pay Peter's tax.

So it's not a famous Jesus story. I've never seen an ancient or medieval painting of this moment. Why is that, do you think?

Perhaps it's because it's not a very edifying story. Folk stories about amazing things that happen to the hero are just that—stories. This one doesn't give us a moral lesson to take away, nor does it tell us something we need to know about the kingdom. It might be a little like the time when Jesus cursed a fig tree whose only offense was that it wasn't bearing fruit out of season, and the poor thing withered and died. You don't see pictures of that one, either.

These stories just show us that, then as now, different people had very different ideas about what was important about Jesus. Jesus the teacher, Jesus the judge, Jesus the worker of wonders, Jesus the suffering servant, Jesus the new Moses, giving the law. And, once in a while, Jesus the shaman: not an image we kept, one later generations have found a little embarrassing. But there it is. Somebody, long ago, thought it enlarged his understanding of Christ.

Okay. We can't pick and choose our relatives or our history. We do, though, decide what *we* will emphasize in it, how *we* will receive it. The story of Jesus, the fish, and the coin is in my Bible. But it doesn't have to be on my Christmas cards.

WEDNESDAY IN PROPER 6

Pss 119:97–120 * 81, 82
Numbers 11:24–33 (34–35)
Romans 1:28–2:11
Matthew 18:1–9

*". . . unless you change and become like children,
you will never enter the kingdom of heaven."*
MATTHEW 18:3

Okay, what are children like, then? Jesus shows his hand in the next line. He's not talking this time about children's credulity or their spontaneity or even their innocence: it's their humility that makes them our spiritual models. They don't count for much. The only power they have so far is the love others feel for them. It is their only protection. Children are weak.

Most people with a vocation to life in a religious community will take vows of poverty, chastity, and obedience. Their friends and families are apt to be horrified, and it is the first two that shock them the most. *You mean you can't own anything at all? How can you promise never to get married?* They struggle to imagine such a life for themselves and their imagination fails them, a clue that monastic life is not their vocation.

But the ones for whom it is a vocation notice something very early on: neither poverty nor chastity is the big challenge. It's obedience. The humility a person in the religious life learns comes only with difficulty. The surrender of our own power and authority terrifies us to the bottoms of our souls; we correctly sense that we do not belong to ourselves. We suspect that we never have, that the shocking humility lived out in religious life is a sign of what life really is, for *everyone.*

They see that obedience really contains the other two, that possessions and sexuality are both intertwined with stature in the world, with the self-sufficiency the world assumes and admires. *You will be a wife, a husband, a mother or father, a lover. You will be a success; people will look to you. Then you will be an even greater success.*

The child knows nothing of these things. He is only himself. Your "only" self is that which relates to God; you have nothing else to recommend you, and that is perfectly fine: you need no other recommendation.

THURSDAY IN PROPER 6

Pss (83) or 34 * 85, 86
Numbers 12:1–16
Romans 2:12–24
Matthew 18:10–20

*"For where two or three are gathered in my name,
I am there among them."*
MATTHEW 18:20

We didn't exactly pack them in for daily Morning Prayer at St. Clement's. I always made sure that people who volunteered to officiate understood that it was quite likely that they would be the only people there. They needed to be people who didn't require an audience. *Your affirmation has to come from God on this one.*

Of course, a person praying the Daily Office is never praying it alone. The communion of saints is with you, all of them, the living and the dead. When you say, "The Lord be with you," they respond, "And also with you." You are in the presence of the famous and the unknowns, the faithful and those who forgot to pray today. You are in the presence of those who never pray and never will, as long as they live: if they are not at prayer, you are praying on their behalf, bringing them before the presence of God. You bring them with you.

So *of course* Christ is there. How could he stay away when all these people are gathered? Your two or three, or even your one— and the multitude of those whom God loves. Think of that throng, sitting close to you across miles and centuries, the next time you pray alone and feel isolated and ineffectual.

Once in a while I would get there early enough to pop in for Morning Prayer at the church instead of at home. The officiant was always surprised, and I sometimes thought I detected a certain disappointment. Maybe they were just nervous, hoping they did everything right.

Or maybe my physical presence interrupted their communion with the invisible saints.

FRIDAY IN PROPER 6

Pss 88 * 91, 92
Numbers 13:1–3, 21–30
Romans 2:25–3:8
Matthew 18:21–35

*"Lord, if another member of the church sins
against me, how often should I forgive?"*
MATTHEW 18:21

Jesus' answer would be a daunting one for anybody: not seven times. Seventy times seven. Well, this is not good, you think, since I have a hard time managing to forgive even once.

But maybe you have a hard time because you have some unrealistic ideas of what forgiveness is, ideas that need to change. It's easiest to begin by talking a bit about what forgiveness *isn't*.

Forgiveness is not acquittal. The person you need to forgive is guilty; that's not up for questioning. You don't *need* to forgive people who aren't guilty.

To forgive is not to say, *Oh, that's okay*. Whatever else the deed in question may be, it was not *okay*. You don't *need* to forgive things that are okay, right?

And to forgive is *not* to forget. That dumb equation has enjoyed such universal currency for so long that some people think it's in the Bible. It's not in the Bible. Forgiveness is not amnesia. You don't forget your own history. What has happened has happened.

If someone is forgiven, it doesn't mean he doesn't need to pay for his action. If it is possible, restitution must be made. If not, an appropriate penalty may be exacted. Forgiveness is not about "getting away" with anything. It's about rejoining the community you have violated.

Forgiveness does not necessarily mean restoration of presence. This is hard, because that's the dream: *He can come home again, and things will be like they used to be.* But sometimes that can't happen, as in many cases of domestic abuse: it may not be safe for anyone to restore presence. Sometimes forgiveness can't begin until the abuser is permanently at a safe distance; then it might be possible to see him as someone else's victim, before he became a victimizer.

There are some other things forgiveness isn't, too. But just clearing some of these away might make it easier to see what it really is: the decision to leave the past behind and move freely into the future. The choice to lives one's own life, rather than letting it be dominated by someone else. For unforgiveness rarely hurts the one you can't forgive anywhere near as much as it hurts you.

SATURDAY IN PROPER 6

Pss 87, 90 * 136
Numbers 13:31–14:25
Romans 3:9–20
Matthew 19:1–12

"It was because you were so hard-hearted that
Moses allowed you to divorce your wives. . . ."
MATTHEW 19:8

The fact that divorce is more possible now than in former times, and that it is administered more fairly and divorced people treated more kindly than used to be the case, might tempt one to think that it's not such a terrible thing. But it is a terrible thing; just ask anybody who's gone through it. Jesus is right: it is hard-hearted. There wouldn't be any divorces if it were not for the hardness of our hearts.

But it is never a simple hard-heartedness. The hard-heartedness of divorce begins long before it starts to show. And it is never one-sided: a thousand missed opportunities and tragic misreadings on both sides throttle a marriage until it has no breath left in its body. One or the other party may feel like the innocent one, and proclaim the argument for that belief loudly to anyone who will listen. But there are many ways of missing the boat in marriage, and most divorces are the product of more than one of them.

God takes us back when we are hard-hearted. God softens our hearts. Sometimes we won't let this happen until it's too late to save our situations, and we stumble forth from the wreckage of them, bruised and bleeding. But God doesn't turn away from that, either. We can be healed from the battering we give ourselves or from the one someone else gives us, and we can be healed from the battering that's a combination of both of these. We'll have scars, for sure. But we'll be healed enough to go on in life, healed enough to live again with a joy we could never have imagined finding.

SUNDAY, PROPER 7

Pss 66, 67 * 19, 46
Numbers 14:26–45
Acts 15:1–12
Luke 12:49–56

*"Do you think that I have come to bring peace to
the earth? No, I tell you, but rather division!"*
LUKE 12:51

We decry faction and dispute in the church as if it were a curse of modern times, but the fact is that there hasn't been an era in its history when there was none. This only makes sense: religion is about important things, essential things, and emotions about essential things will run high.

You can, and probably should, follow advice of experienced well-wishers about the nuts and bolts of life: manners and nutrition, dental care and the stock market, auto and home repair. But there are other important things, larger things, about which you simply must make up your own mind. Other people may form your values in childhood, but as time goes on, your final authority is yourself: you either do or do not certify your actions as good.

Decisions about faith are among those important things. Nobody can make them for you. You must claim what you claim on your own. It may emerge from your history, but only you can carry your history into your future.

What is true for you is also true for the ones you love, and this is hard for us. We long for our children to embrace our faith and values, but they must appropriate their own, and they may not be ours. We cannot make them choose our way: the same freedom to accept life's formation that we enjoyed is also their birthright. Some decisions are too important to be left to others, even to the people who love us the most.

MONDAY IN PROPER 7

Pss 89:1–18 * 89:19–52
Numbers 16:1–19
Romans 3:21–31
Matthew 19:13–22

*"If you wish to be perfect, go, sell your possessions,
and give the money to the poor. . . ."*
MATTHEW 19:21

The French philosopher Blaise Pascal is said to have done this. So is the Russian writer Leo Tolstoy, although he can't have given it *all* away, as at least some of his 250 descendants remain wealthy today. Francis of Assisi did do it, stripping down to nothing and walking any from his hometown to found his monastic order.

If you wish to be perfect. The members of religious orders take this requirement seriously: I don't think they imagine themselves to be in much danger of becoming perfect, but they do understand the pull of material possessions. They need to peel themselves away from everything; what books and dishes and furniture the convent doesn't need go to friends on the outside or to charity. They will not own it again. They will own nothing at all.

You may not become perfect, but it is true that the more you give away, the better you feel. Lighter and much more free. Everything you own has an ongoing cost, not the just the cost of its purchase. It wants to be insured, or to be repaired, polished, or dusted, to be locked up in a safe or secured to the floor. The things you give away can turn into money that will buy food for hungry people to eat, and nobody has to dust.

It tells us in this story that Jesus loved the young man who couldn't be perfect. He must love us, too, then, we who can't manage to grasp the freedom of voluntary poverty either. After all, the quest for perfection was not Jesus' idea; it was the young man who brought it up.

TUESDAY IN PROPER 7

Pss 97, 99, (100) * 94, (95)
Numbers 16:20–35
Romans 4:1–12
Matthew 19:23–30

*". . . it is easier for a camel to go through the eye of a needle
than for someone who is rich to enter the kingdom of God."*
MATTHEW 19:24

This verse always distresses people, who want to find some other meaning to it. There was a narrow gate in the Jerusalem wall, they say, that was called the "eye of the needle." Maybe that's what they meant. Well, maybe. But I imagine Jesus was talking about a real needle, and that this is yet another example of his humor: he often taught by using exaggeration.

Because how can the camel get through the eye of the needle? He would have to shrink.

Well, yes. And that's just how a rich person enters the kingdom: we have to shrink. The more space we occupy in the world, the less room the spirit has to move within us. The more invested we are in our possessions, the less interested we are in anything else. And the more wealth insulates us from our own need, the less able we are to see the need of other people.

One thing this passage *cannot* mean is that God doesn't love rich people and wants to keep them out of heaven. No, God loves everyone. It's only that wealth makes it difficult to do and be the things one must do and be to live a complete spiritual life. It entices us to settle for much, much less.

Probably people laughed when Jesus conjured up the image of a camel struggling to squeeze through such a tiny opening; camels are pretty funny as it is. But probably they had been wondering, as we wonder now, how the relationship between us and our wealth fits into our spiritual lives. Most decent people know that wealth is a moral issue, and a spiritual one as well.

WEDNESDAY IN PROPER 7

Pss 101, 109:1–4 (5–19) 20–30 * 119:121–144
Numbers 16:36–50
Romans 4:13–25
Matthew 20:1–16

"'Or are you envious because I am generous?'"
MATTHEW 20:15

My four-year-old was inconsolable after nursery school. We made it into the car, and then she began to sob. *What's the matter?* I asked, taking her into my lap.

Kristy-Beth can make an R! she wailed. I held her and rocked her back and forth as she sat on the steering wheel. She would learn to make an R soon, too, because she had an R in her name, too. We'd work on Rs that very night. She did so many wonderful things. She was such a fine girl. She was Mommy's best friend.

She calmed down and we drove home. I suppose we worked on Rs that night; it was a long time ago. In her mid-thirties now, she seems to have no trouble with them. I recognized myself in her despair at her friend's good fortune, though. Oh, yes. I have felt that feeling more often than I wish I had.

Of all the Ten Commandments, the one against covetousness must be the only one virtually everyone has broken. Is there anyone who has ever lived who didn't feel angry and hurt because someone else had something he or she wanted? I can't imagine there has ever been such a person. Murder doesn't tempt many of us, and most of us refrain from stealing. But I don't think any of us are free from even a trace of envy.

But most of us learn how to rise above it. We have a better angel, and it helps us grow a more generous heart than the one we started out with.

THURSDAY IN PROPER 7

Pss 105:1–22 * 105:23–45
Numbers 17:1–11
Romans 5:1–11
Matthew 20:17–28

*But God proves his love for us in that while
we were still sinners Christ died for us.*
ROMANS 5:8

O h, you don't want *me* in church, the man tells me with a laugh.
The roof of the church would fall in if I showed up.

We hear again and again that Jesus forgives all our sins. But some of us keep thinking we can't visit him if we have any. We say a confession right before we celebrate the Eucharist, but some people still think they can't receive communion if they've done anything wrong.

Maybe it's not *Jesus'* forgiveness we don't believe in. Maybe it's our own. Maybe we just have trouble forgiving ourselves.

If we were able to live sinlessly, we would have no need of a savior. If we could do everything on our own, we'd be in fine shape, but we can't. You don't wait to call the doctor until you're in perfect health because you think you should be able to cure yourself; you call when you're ill.

Sometimes people resort to a campaign of falsehood to maintain the fiction that all is well with their souls and always has been. Others project their own guilt onto others: everything is someone else's fault. And some are like the man who made a joke about the roof falling in if he ever went to church. Anything to avoid the honest gaze of Christ into their hearts, as if it might punish them further than they have already punished themselves. Not knowing that accepting the forgiveness of Christ will end their refusal to forgive themselves as well.

FRIDAY IN PROPER 7

Pss 102 * 107:1–32
Numbers 20:1–13
Romans 5:12–21
Matthew 20:29–34

When they heard that Jesus was passing by, they shouted,
"Lord, have mercy on us, Son of David!"
MATTHEW 20:30

Both men were blind, joined by the disability they shared. They certainly knew what it was to be isolated in a culture that assumed physical disability mirrored some kind of moral defect. But they had each other. Maybe they sat in that spot by the side of the road often, maybe every day, hoping for alms from passersby. Maybe that's how they supported themselves.

They knew who Jesus was. This means that someone had told them. So people spoke to them. They lived in the community and shared in its events. As isolating as their disability was, it seems not to have stopped them for being a part of the group. They heard the gossip. They went to big events, like this visit from a famous preacher.

And they knew their tradition. Knew who David was, and that the Messiah would be the Son of David. Their disability didn't stop them from learning. This means someone taught them.

I can imagine that many people in their situation might have just stayed home that day. Not wanted to brave the crowd. Being in a crowd can be threatening when your mobility is compromised. But maybe they were well known by everybody in town. Maybe people they knew checked on them to see that they were okay. Maybe they knew people wouldn't let anything happen to them. Maybe this village took care of its own.

Their shout sounds self-confident to me. It sounds like they belonged, that they could speak out. They probably encouraged each other: *Go on, call out to him! No, you call out to him. All right, we'll both call. Ready? One, two, three: Lord, have mercy on us, Son of David!*

SATURDAY IN PROPER 7

Pss 107:33–43, 108:1–6 (7–13) * 33
Numbers 20:14–29
Romans 6:1–11
Matthew 21:1–11

*". . . immediately you will find a donkey tied, and a colt
with her; untie them and bring them to me."*
MATTHEW 21:2

This is one of those Bible bloopers that are so interesting. The gospel writers are often concerned to match up their narrative with prophecies from the Hebrew Scriptures, and this description of Jesus' preparation for his entry into Jerusalem is an example of that impulse. The passage in question is Zechariah 9:9, concerning the paradoxical arrival of a king in to Jerusalem:

Rejoice greatly, O daughter of Zion!
Shout in triumph, O daughter of Jerusalem!
Behold, your king is coming to you;
He is just and endowed with salvation,
Humble, and mounted on a donkey,
Even on a colt, the foal of a donkey.

Matthew is writing in Greek. He is at some distance, in culture and time, from the parallelism of Hebrew poetry, in which a thought or image is often originated in one line and repeated in the next. But he wants to include the Zechariah passage, since it is so apt: a king entering Jerusalem in unexpected humility. Perfect! It seems to him that there are *two* animals in the prophecy, though, the donkey and her foal, and so he sends the disciples off to fetch both of them. He does not tell us how Jesus planned to ride two donkeys at once.

A convoluted solution to a common dilemma: what to do with biblical passages that don't make sense to you. As far as Matthew is concerned, you *make* them make sense.

But they are richer if you don't try to do that. You learn more about the different societies that gave birth to the many perspectives we find in scripture, about the different authors and what they wanted to convey. Read carefully, respectfully, and you are almost there.

SUNDAY, PROPER 8

Pss 118 * 145
Numbers 21:4–9, 21–35
Acts 17:(12–21) 22–34
Luke 13:10–17

"Athenians, I see how extremely
religious you are in every way."
ACTS 17:22

With dozens of other foreigners and two native Athenians, I climbed up to the Acropolis. *I've never been up here*, one of them said, and we all laughed. This was not surprising to me; I myself have never been to the Statue of Liberty or to the Empire State Building.

The Parthenon was amazing, just as I have seen it in so many pictures. It is spectacularly lit at night, and is one of the loveliest sights I have seen. The caryatids who held its roof upon their heads have retired to live in the museum of the Acropolis, out of the polluted air: reproductions fill in for them now. Alongside the Acropolis is another, smaller hill: this is the Areopagus. "Here is the rock from which St. Paul spoke to the Athenians, Acts 17," said a sign next to an enormous flat stone.

My goodness, I said. This was the place. I could stand where Paul stood to preach. And, since there appeared to be no one bent on stopping me, I did. I looked down at the ground around the great rock, where two thousand years ago a crowd had gathered to listen the stranger. It was littered with the remains of old shrines and columns and little temples; Athens is squarely in earthquake country, and most of what was here is in pieces.

In my mind, they flew back together, all the stones and carvings back in order, each to its place, so that the landscape was as it was in those days. The shrine "To an Unknown God" that gave Paul his homiletical foothold was there. He was in my place on the rock, short and dark, kinetic, his arms waving, his fierce eyes and thick eyebrows expressive. He did not see me; none of them did. They were intent on what Paul was saying, weighing it, planning their argument against it when their turn came to speak. They loved to argue.

There was really nobody near the rock except my two friends and some Japanese tourists. I didn't preach.

MONDAY IN PROPER 8

Pss 106:1–18 * 106:19–48
Numbers 22:1–21
Romans 6:12–23
Matthew 21:12–22

"May no fruit ever come from you again!"
MATTHEW 21:19

Well, that seems a little harsh, no? I guess Jesus got crabby when he was hungry, like the rest of us. Truly human and truly God, we always remind ourselves about him, to cover just such puzzling situations.

There were other gospels written at the time ours were, gospels in which Jesus did a lot more things like this than he does in the four we have. They didn't make the cut, and so we don't hear them in church. Who knows, maybe it was things like this that kept them out. It shows a gratuitous use of power that sits uncomfortably with the humility we expect in our Jesus, a god a little more like the impulsive gods of the Greeks or the Vikings than we are accustomed to encountering in our God.

It's hard to think of Jesus cursing a tree: through him all things were created, we say. We see him angry, and we see him violent in the temple, earlier in this reading, but we don't see him kill, anywhere except here.

Wait a minute: might there be a link between the fig tree and Jesus' rampage in the temple? They are so close together in the text. Can that be an accident?

The temple was a house of prayer, and it had become a den of robbers. It was not as it should have been: worship there was no longer bearing *good fruit*. It was like the fig tree.

Matthew is writing after the temple has been destroyed. Such a thing was unthinkable before it happened, and people must have been grasping for a way to make sense of the tragedy. The new sect of Christians had a way: something new has come to take the place of what has been destroyed. The old way didn't work. It needed to wither away.

Hmmn. Maybe the fig tree *is* a figure of the temple, a kind of code. Maybe that's why a story that makes Jesus look so, well, *mean*, was transmitted in writing from generation to generation and retained in the canon of scripture. Maybe.

Or maybe he was just hungry and having a bad day.

TUESDAY IN PROPER 8

Pss (120), 121, 122, 123 * 124, 125, 126, (127)
Numbers 22:21–38
Romans 7:1–12
Matthew 21:23–32

Then the LORD opened the mouth of the donkey....
NUMBERS 22:28

I think this story of a talking donkey was my favorite Bible story when I was little. I already knew that animals had some special information: the dog would whimper when lightning was coming, and the cats would all come inside. The birds knew it was morning before anyone else did. Certain caterpillars wore special fuzzy, striped coats as autumn approached.

And this donkey could see angels! I wondered if any of the other animals I knew possessed this talent, too: if angels were everywhere, with important messages for me, warnings and instructions, and I just couldn't see them. I would ask them, sometimes, looking into my dog's kind brown eyes, searching there for a word only he could tell me. He could send only love back in response. Maybe that's what the angels told him.

Notice that when the angel finally got through to Balaam in person, he told him that he would have killed him if he had proceeded, and would have spared the donkey! He must have told the donkey the same thing, so the donkey knew his own life was not in danger. And yet he still sat down on the job, refusing to carry his master into harm's way. He still wanted to protect his friend. Even after he was struck three times.

He treated his master a lot better than his master treated him.

WEDNESDAY IN PROPER 8

Pss 119:145–176 * 128, 129, 130
Numbers 22:41–23:12
Romans 7:13–25
Matthew 21:33–46

*For I do not do the good I want, but the
evil I do not want is what I do.*
ROMANS 7:19

I know, I know. Don't remind me. So many things that I know would be good and helpful, and I just sit and look at them. And I do so many, many things I know I should stay away from.

So Paul had that problem, too. I wonder if he counted his hot temper as one of the things he did against his better moral judgment.

He gives no sign of regretting it in any of the writings we have of his, so maybe he meant something else. And so did St. Augustine; I wrote my thesis on him in college. Chastity was very important to him, and even in old age he found it frustratingly difficult to maintain it, even as a mental state. A lot of important people find themselves doing things they really don't want to be doing, it seems. Everybody, maybe. We know good and well what we ought to do. We even *want* to do it—want the good feeling one gets from doing a good thing. And then we go and do something else.

We don't ever get too grown up to need guidance. Left to our own devices, we'll backslide at least as often as we do not. So, if we are wise, we set ourselves up with structures that will support us in doing the things we want to do. Join an exercise class, for instance, instead of just relying on your resolve to get you out to the gym. Don't carry your cigarettes with you. Have your savings taken out of your paycheck before you ever even see the money. Find someone else trying to do the same thing and agree to support each other in weak moments.

The church did that in Paul's day. Almost as many of his letters deal with behavior as with belief, and he expected people to keep each other in line. He viewed it as a kindness. It was interior and exterior, personal and communal, this impulse toward chaos, and he used his own struggles against it as a model for others to be similarly honest. Two millennia later, he could be sitting on any modern psychotherapist's office or in any twelve-step meeting. He would be saying the same thing. And everyone at the meeting would nod.

THURSDAY IN PROPER 8

Pss 131, 132, (133) * 134, 135
Numbers 23:11–26
Romans 8:1–11
Matthew 22:1–14

*"I brought you to curse my enemies, but now
you have done nothing but bless them."*
NUMBERS 23:11

B e careful when you bring in a consultant. He might not tell you what you want to hear.

Prophets were like consultants in ancient Israel. Kings kept them in their employ, to advise them and tell them God's will about matters of state. Naturally, God's will was usually exactly what the king wanted to do. A royal prophet who didn't do that would soon find it hard to get work. But none of the house prophets' names are remembered in scripture. We don't know a single one. The only ones we remember deviated from the script and told the truth as they saw it.

Having an enemy is energizing if you can get others to join in your hostilities. A common enemy is an important bond, and it can define a relationship to the exclusion of any other factor. The perverse delight the two take in hating the same person makes even discussing the possibility of peace seem like an act of disloyalty to the friendship. This is a toxic thing: those who are united only in their dislike of something have a thin reed upon which to lean, and should not count on each other's loyalty.

Balak wanted God on his side against his enemies, and thought a prophet could accomplish this for him, much as the right person can get a celebrity to attend your party. But Balaam, a true prophet—if not a perfect person—by the end of the story, knows that God doesn't work for us.

FRIDAY IN PROPER 8

Pss 140, 142 * 141, 143:1–11 (12)
Numbers 24:1–13
Romans 8:12–17
Matthew 22:15–22

"Abba! Father!"
ROMANS 8:15

You shouldn't use masculine pronouns for God, a woman told me. *Some people have been abused by their fathers and just the word "Father" has terrible associations.*

I know. And of course, *father* isn't accurate when applied to God. And neither is *mother*. All religious language is metaphor. None of it is accurate. I spent some time bending over backward not to say "he" when I was first ordained, but I gave it up, for several reasons.

I was not sure that the best way to approach pain in people's past is to skirt the issue. Never mentioning the concept of father struck me as doing just that. People who have been injured by their fathers need to know that they have another Father, who will never abuse them or betray their trust. I also have had parishioners who were abused by their mothers, for that matter. It seemed to me that the same argument applied.

I noticed that African-American women did not share the skittishness of their white sisters about the use of the male pronoun applied to God. I reasoned that they knew more about prejudice than I ever would and have been sitting with that thought ever since.

I noticed that my use of a feminine pronoun for God diverted the attention of my audience to itself, no matter what I was talking about. I don't lecture people about whether God is a boy or a girl, and I don't want all my preaching to turn into that issue. I just don't find it very interesting.

Where I can get away with it, I don't use a pronoun at all. But I don't wish to write sentences like "God said to Godself that God would take a walk in the garden of Eden to visit God's creation," and so I sometimes wander into a reactionary usage.

I regret it, a little. But I'm a writer, and I love the English language. I think it's suffered enough.

SATURDAY IN PROPER 8

Pss 137:1–6 (7–9), 144 * 104
Numbers 24:12–25
Romans 8:18–25
Matthew 22:23–40

I consider that the sufferings of this present time are not worth comparing with the glory about to be revealed to us.

ROMANS 8:18

I wonder what it is like. We all wonder. Our imaginations fail us, or they make things up, like in the Bible: golden streets, angels with wings, lots of clouds, and legions of dignified smiling people in white.

And yet when we are deep in prayer, the kind of silent, centering prayer that leaves intercession and all narrative behind, we have an experience that contains none of these special effects. I don't see or hear anything in those moments; it would be hard to describe what I do experience. Perhaps the best I can say is that I am right *next to* God. Or *in* Christ. I am in a place that is not a place, seeing something that is like nothing and everything. I am behind my own senses, and it is more real than anything my senses have ever shown me.

Can we go there when the sufferings of this present time grow too heavy to bear? Taste heaven, just a bit, in the midst of all the bitterness we must also taste? Through the practice of centering prayer, we do. It is oddly difficult to peel ourselves away from our woes. We cling absurdly to them, unwilling, somehow, to allow the relief centering prayer will bring. So we refuse to go to heaven at the very times we need it most.

Paul had an experience of heaven, too. His description of it is hard to understand, which is how I can tell that's what it is. It helped him arrive at the attitude he displays here: whatever happens, it's nothing compared to that.

SUNDAY, PROPER 9

Pss 146, 147 * 111, 112, 113
Numbers 27:12–23
Acts 19:11–20
Mark 1:14–20

A number of those who practiced magic collected
their books and burned them publicly. . . .
ACTS 19:19

The preachers of the new faith looked to some like other itinerant wonder workers who peopled the spiritual landscape of the ancient Near East: stories of such healers and miracle workers abounded at the time, a combination of rumor and legend. Here is an account of a series of encounters with a few of them, in which the Christians clearly win, scaring their Jewish and pagan rivals so badly that they are willing to part with $50,000 worth of magic books.

The writer wishes us to recognize a clear difference between magic and miracle. Miracle was a revelation of God's power in the world, and a sign of relationship with God. It was the difference between holiness and celebrity: miracle points to God, not to the miracle worker—that's why Jesus was always so reticent about his miracles. He was not a magician.

Most modern people are not as willing to believe in magic as the people in the Bible were. This is a good thing, of course, but it also makes it hard for us to register miracle when we see it: we're afraid of seeming gullible. We are the poorer for this. But if we think of miracle as the hand of God, and allow ourselves to be willing to see it everywhere, we will not miss what it has to teach us.

MONDAY IN PROPER 9

Pss 1, 2, 3 * 4, 7
Numbers 32:1–6, 16–27
Romans 8:26–30
Matthew 23:1–12

". . . do whatever they teach you and follow it; but do not do
as they do, for they do not practice what they teach."
MATTHEW 23:2

Do as I say, not as I do, my ballet teacher used to groan when she was unable to demonstrate a step to her satisfaction. She was in her early fifties, and her body was not what it had been when she was young and a Rockette.

Her rueful instruction to us was not an example of hypocrisy, though; she was trying her best. Jesus' scorn is reserved for those who place demands on others that they are unwilling to accept for themselves, a different thing entirely. People do this knowingly, in which case they're *really* rotters, or they do it without really being aware of it, in which they're more like all the rest of us.

I care about the environment but drive a car the size of an ambulance.

I worry about my children constantly, but smoke in front of them. I'm afraid they'll become involved with drugs, but they see me having a couple of drinks every night.

I complain about the president, but didn't vote in the last election.

I want good schools and other services from the government, but believe taxes are evil.

We aren't hypocrites, but sometimes we fail to think things through, to explore fully the implications of our actions. We settle too quickly for our own good intentions, and convince ourselves that we have implemented them merely by intending them. Nope. You have to talk the talk *and* walk the walk.

TUESDAY IN PROPER 9

Pss 5, 6 * 10, 11
Numbers 35:1–3, 9–15, 30–34
Romans 8:31–39
Matthew 23:13–26

For I am convinced that neither death, nor life,
nor angels, nor rulers, nor things present,
nor things to come, nor powers, nor height, nor depth,
nor anything else in all creation, will be able to separate
us from the love of God in Christ Jesus our Lord.
ROMANS 8:38–39

I just want someone who will love me unconditionally, she said, her voice quivering a little. A love affair upon which she had pinned all her hope had ended, and it wasn't her idea. *I've never had that.*

This was not the time, but someday it would be good for her to come to terms with the fact that no one else has had it, either, not from a fellow human being: people don't love each other unconditionally. The purest human-to-human love in the world has strings attached: we have needs, and we expect to get some of them met from those we love. We invest, and we want investment back. That's far from unconditional. Many things can rip human love from us.

The divine love is different. It completely defines us: we can no more be unloved by God than we can cease to be human. It was out of love for us—before there was an "us" to love—that we came into being. Whether we are good or bad, our very existence is what the love of God means. Even death, our greatest defeat, the thing we fear and thus deny our whole lives long, does not make us cease to be. We still live in the love of God, even after the world has lost us.

Before we have spent some time—I mean years, not a few hours on an afternoon—thinking and praying about this idea, it seems manifestly untrue. We feel separated from God frequently, by our own shortcomings, by our sorrows, by our moods, certainly by death. But something grows in us as we think and pray: an awareness of a steady something within us that remains, while we dart about on the winds of a thousand problems. Remains, no matter what. It is not a feeling: they come and go like streetcars. It doesn't come and go. It stays. And it is not an "it": it is living.

I am not describing it well, but I doubt anyone else could do it better. We are only now learning to speak the language of God.

WEDNESDAY IN PROPER 9

Pss 119:1–24 * 12, 13, 14
Deuteronomy 1:1–18
Romans 9:1–18
Matthew 23:27–39

For I could wish that I myself were accursed and cut off from Christ for the sake of my own people, my kindred according to the flesh.
ROMANS 9:3

People seldom preach on this verse. It is a far cry from the every-man-for-himself approach to faith that typifies American Christian thought and behavior, so let's be clear about what Paul is saying: *He would give up his own salvation for the salvation of his fellow Jews.* Paul's faith isn't about him and his Jesus and the heck with everyone else. It isn't even about talking other people into a faith that's about them and their Jesus. It is something else entirely.

It is about oneness before our creator and our redeemer. It is about the blossoming of an ancient tradition, and the blossom isn't the same as the root or the stem. It can be expected to look different.

A powerful conversion experience is not an end: it is a beginning. It inaugurates a life lived in expectation of God's continuing action, which includes God's capacity and freedom to bring ancient things to flower in blossoms that look different from their roots. A powerful conversion experience like Paul had does not substitute spiritual self-absorption for material selfishness. It introduces us, rather, to a life lived without anxiety about what we will wear or what we will eat or how many cars we will have.

Our life in Christ is no longer our own. More than anything else, conversion introduces us into a community whose hallmark is its diversity. Christ goes everywhere, touches everyone, lives in every culture, is not dependent on cultural certification for any of his power to enter human lives and change them.

THURSDAY IN PROPER 9

Pss 18:1–20 * 18:21–50
Deuteronomy 3:18–28
Romans 9:19–33
Matthew 24:1–14

". . . wars and rumors of wars . . ."
MATTHEW 24:6

It was thirty years ago that the last helicopter left Saigon, leaving us with a final terrible photograph of that terrible war: the helicopter lifting off from atop the American embassy, seemingly tethered to the roof by a chain of human beings desperate to get out. Declare victory and leave: I guess that's how you end a modern war. No North Vietnamese delegation in formal attire came to sign instruments of surrender on an American battleship. I guess that was because Communists don't wear formal attire. And because everybody knew they hadn't lost.

A silence about the war settled on all of us. The last of the three presidents who presided over it resigned amid the flames of his own disgrace; his kindly successor, in pardoning him, referred to him as "the man who brought peace to millions," and we all had to stop for a moment to remember what he meant. It took twenty years for us to understand how callous we had been to the soldiers returning from that war, whose presence among us reminded us of something we wanted to forget. Something strangely like relief sprang up when Desert Shield turned into Desert Storm and our smart bombs shot through the air, flying low and unseen toward their targets with deadly precision: we would shower these young soldiers with the love we had withheld from their Vietnam-era counterparts, we would make up for it all now. Yellow ribbons appeared everywhere. Our exit strategy triumphed: quick, clean, out. Our losses were gratifyingly modest: from hostile fire, 122 dead. From friendly fire, 35. Non-combat fatalities, 31. And, as always, we did not count the enemy dead. That would be their concern.

Immediately upon our departure from Saigon, the Vietcong took control of the government; Saigon was now Ho Chi Minh City. There was a border war with China, even bloodier than the ten-year engagement with the Americans.

Thirty years later, Vietnam is at peace and Americans visit as tourists. Once in a while, even now, a group of American MIAs is returned to us: something to bury, at last. Black flags with the silhouette of a POW, his head bowed in discouragement, continue to hang from the flagpoles of American firehouses and police stations, marking the survival of a civic myth that persists thirty years after the war: *They are still being held. They still wait for us to come.*

But I wonder if we don't cling to the POWs for another reason, something besides the obvious longing for the return of loved ones. If we admitted that they were gone, then we would be finished. Then there would be nothing more to do. Not even one more chance to change something—anything—about what happened thirty years ago.

FRIDAY IN PROPER 9

Pss 16, 17 * 22
Deuteronomy 31:7–13, 24–32:4
Romans 10:1–13
Matthew 24:15–31

*The scripture says, "No one who believes
in him will be put to shame."*
ROMANS 10:11

The church is often in the news these days. We are on television and in the paper, so noisily denouncing one another's morals that an outside observer might be forgiven for believing that arguing is mainly what churches do and that sex is the centerpiece of our belief system.

And I suppose arguing *is* what churches do, in part. Ethics is part of any religious faith, and ethics always involves debate over competing values. The presence of disagreement is not by itself a sign that something is wrong. It's actually a sign that something is right: people are awake and thinking, they care about what they do, they want a better church and a better world.

But no human activity can be the centerpiece of faith. Not sex, for sure, but not war, either, and not economics, as important as these things are. All our ethical conundrums are important, but faith is about God, too, not just about us, and God transcends us. We have the values we have because of our relationship with God, not the other way around. We don't check God's references to see if he qualifies and then begin a relationship with him. We have the relationship first. We had it before we knew we had it: before we could talk, before we could read, before we'd ever heard of God or Jesus or anything else in scripture, God was loving us and calling us to love back.

We look to ourselves as children of God in communion with each other. Period. After we know that primary identity to be primary, we are free to discuss, argue, write, and study, theorize and conclude, change our minds, all under the umbrella of God's love. That is our first principle.

It will govern how we disagree. It will recognize and respect an opponent, and will not descend to a level of spiritual violence that must brand him an enemy. It will include a healthy suspicion of our own virtue based upon that most orthodox of Christian doctrines, Original Sin: humanity's ancient tendency to substitute our will and understanding for the will and wisdom of God. God is good, but *we* can be bought, and we often are, trading our godly freedom for peer approval, for proximity to power, for comfortable moral certitude, for insulation from the daunting task of ethical discernment, even for money, sometimes.

What a state of affairs! We shame each other, confident in our own rightness. In the gospels, it was the scribes and Pharisees who claimed that confidence.

SATURDAY IN PROPER 9

Pss 20, 21:1–7 (8–14) * 110:1–5 (6–7), 116, 117
Deuteronomy 34:1–12
Romans 10:14–21
Matthew 24:32–51

*Moses went up . . . and the LORD
showed him the whole land. . . .*
DEUTERONOMY 34:1

The picture in the morning paper is heartbreaking: a little boy in a yarmulke, tears streaming down his cheek as he pushes with all his might against the massive chest of a young Israeli soldier. Other soldiers strive with other settlers, and their young faces clearly show the misery of their position: *We are arrayed against our own. We are forcing our own people out their homes. My grandfather was forced out of his home in Germany: how can I be doing this?* One covers his face with both hands in a vain attempt to hide his own tears.

The little boy is no match for the soldier. The settlers are all leaving: they can choose to leave under their own power or to be physically carried out. What they can't choose is to stay. Some set fire to their homes as they leave, watching numbly as the black smoke climbs up into the blue sky, even though they know that all their homes will be razed to the ground anyway, after they are gone.

Most Israelis think that this painful event, and the others like it playing out throughout Gaza, is something that should have happened long ago. Most hope that it will begin a new chapter in the decades-long agony that has been Israeli-Palestinian relations. Most hope that it will bring peace a little closer. Most think that the most extreme of the settlers have become the victims of their own religious ideology, that the potent biblical image of the promised land must have meaning for modern Jews beyond the literal promise of a land unaltered from ancient times. Painfully, born of loss and the self-examination that always comes with loss, something new has become thinkable to many Israelis.

This, too, is a loss: an old dream is dying, and a new day is in sight. It is very possible that it will not dawn, that the old darkness will descend again. If it does, it will not be the first time a Jew has glimpsed the Promised Land and been unable to cross over into it. It was a land of figs and dates. It was a land running with milk and honey. And the old man Moses looked upon it from afar, knowing he would never reach it himself, that he would die before the people reached it.

But he died trying to get there. We may not see peace in the Holy Land. We may die before we get there. But we may not, and it is worth the journey.

Ⅴ SUNDAY, PROPER 10

Pss 148, 149, 150 * 114, 115
Joshua 1:1–18
Acts 21:3–15
Mark 1:21–27

"What are you doing, weeping and breaking my heart?"
ACTS 21:13

Well, that's a bit strong. All Paul's friends were trying to do was save his life. Who among us would not have given someone we loved the same advice? *Jerusalem?! Now?! Are you crazy?!*

Sometimes the people you love do foolish things for no good reason, and you will move heaven and earth to try and stop them. In the end, you may not be *able* to stop them, and you will have to watch them reap what they have sown. In the end, the best you can hope for may be that the whole experience has been an unforgettable lesson.

And sometimes, someone you love takes a terrible risk for something very important, fully aware of what might happen. Again, perhaps, you move heaven and earth, and again you may not be able to stop it. And so you must watch as actions you have warned against yield to their consequences.

This time, though, the watching is very different. This time, the one doing most of the learning is probably you. You learn how brave he is, something you may not have known before. And you learn—again—that even the most potent love does not empower you to control the actions of another, that the really important things in life are far too important to entrust to another's decision. Even yours.

You want life with your beloved to go on forever, but it will not. If you try to protect your world as it is, to the exclusion of all else, you will lose all the joy of it while you are doing so. And, in the end, you will lose your world anyway.

We cannot cling to safety. We cannot make our whole life about being safe. We cannot clutch it to our chests. If we do, we will not have our arms free to embrace the world for the little time we have to live in it and love its life. It will be over. And we will have missed it.

MONDAY IN PROPER 10

Pss 25 * 9, 15
Joshua 2:1–14
Romans 11:1–12
Matthew 25:1–13

*So they went, and entered the house of a prostitute
whose name was Rahab, and spent the night there.*
JOSHUA 2:1

I wonder if a prostitute's house was readily identifiable; perhaps our two stopped there for some pleasure before business. However the first part of their visit went, the second half was exciting enough: armed men came to the door demanding Rahab's guests, and she hid them up on the roof and lied about their whereabouts, sending their pursuers on a very long wild goose chase.

She knew that they would destroy her city. She knew this because of the rumors she had heard about the Israelites, that God was with them in battle. Her first thought was for her own family; by saving the lives of these two visitors, she could perhaps establish an indebtedness to her. And her plan worked, as far as we know. Her family would be dealt with kindly and faithfully when the invasion came.

I wonder how kindly and faithfully her family dealt with *her*? Her profession, earth's oldest, is held in scorn in most places. Perhaps her family was ashamed of her. Perhaps they had cut her off: she lived alone, an unusual thing for a woman. If the men had showed up at *their* house, would they have thought to bargain for her safety as she bargained for theirs? We do not know and we never hear from her again, except in one place: she appears among the ancestors of Jesus in Matthew's genealogy. Not bad.

Rahab reminds us never to judge a book by its cover. Because you know *what* I am, do not think you know *who* I am.

TUESDAY IN PROPER 10

Pss 26, 28 * 36, 39
Joshua 2:15–24
Romans 11:13–24
Matthew 25:14–30

"Master, I knew that you were a harsh man . . . so I was afraid, and I went and hid your talent in the ground."
MATTHEW 25:24, 25

When President Roosevelt spoke the words for which we remember him best—*We have nothing to fear but fear itself* most people who weren't around then assume he was talking about the Second World War. But he wasn't. He spoke those words before the war. He was talking about the Great Depression.

People were so beaten down by the terrible grind of unemployment and want in which they lived, year after year, that confidence in any future at all had mostly disappeared. Even the weather seemed to conspire against humanity: terrible drought in the agricultural heartland, raising the specter of a great nation unable even to feed itself. Closed factories, idled workers, no cash anywhere. None of the usual economic fixes seemed at all relevant to the ongoing economic disaster. It took a radical solution: the forced closing of the banks for three days, the creation of a massive federal works employment program, the inauguration of the Social Security safety net for the elderly and the disabled. And it took a leader who wasn't afraid to move, to help everyone else not to be afraid.

Most spiritual paralysis—which looks like laziness to others—actually arises from fear. *How can you just sit there and not try?* somebody close to you asks in exasperation, and does not know that it is not because you set low standards for yourself. That it's actually the opposite: you have set your standards too high. *I must succeed. But I'm afraid I might not. So if I never begin, I can't fail. And failure is unacceptable.* And you do not move.

But every beginning of every enterprise involves an acceptance of the possibility of failure. *I may have gotten this all wrong. If that is the case, it will be clear soon enough. But in order to change anything at all, I must be willing to risk failing. So I will step out in faith, and then, well, I guess we'll see, won't we?*

Refusing to begin conquering the lonely spirit of perfectionism allows whoever taught you so harshly to demand it of yourself to win every time, even if that person has been dead for many years. It strangles your own judgment in its cradle, substituting that person's judgment instead.

Such a state: inability to move, to begin things, to trust one's own judgment, substituting instead the judgment of an authority outside the self—that's what depression is. FDR combated an economic depression with the courage to try something new, not knowing if it would succeed or fail. Maybe a spiritual one can yield to the same thing.

WEDNESDAY ON PROPER 10

Pss 38 * 119:25–48
Joshua 3:1–13
Romans 11:25–36
Matthew 25:31–46

"He will separate people one from another as a
shepherd separates the sheep from the goats . . ."
MATTHEW 25:32

The goats call out loudly: sometimes they sound like a terrified woman. The sheep call out, too, but they seem to have a more limited vocabulary. The sheep are much easier to herd. They're more docile, not as mischievous. They eat more normal food, like grass; goats will eat anything that isn't nailed down. They'll even eat the nails.

The righteous are more like the sheep, but the unrighteous are usually more interesting. Tabloid newspapers know this: the front page is always some celebrity's adultery or drunken rampage. Very seldom is it somebody's good deed. And they do this for a reason: the bad guys sell papers. We like to look at what they do. They get away with things we wouldn't get away with. We like to watch them do it.

As universal as this prurience is, nobody could claim it is us at our best. To borrow the sin of others as a spectator sport is to encourage more of the same, and the world would not be a happy place if everyone in it were an adulterer or a thief. We wouldn't like living in it.

None of us can really know the heart of another, which is why we don't get to do the sorting—Jesus does. But we do know there's such a thing as right or wrong behavior. We sometimes disagree about what they are, but we know there is such a thing as a moral perspective, and we possess the capacity to activate our own.

THURSDAY IN PROPER 10

Pss 37:1–18 * 37:19–42
Joshua 3:14–4:7
Romans 12:1–8
Matthew 26:1–16

*Now while Jesus was at Bethany in the house of Simon the leper,
a woman came to him with an alabaster jar of very costly
ointment, and she poured it on his head as he sat at the table.*

MATTHEW 26:6–7

The nameless woman is, in another place, called "a woman of the street," and most have thought that meant that she was a prostitute. It makes some sense: she approaches Jesus so boldly, and she touches him, something a more proper woman might not have done.

And there's another thing: they are both in the home of Simon the leper.

I don't imagine everyone in town wanted to go to Simon's house. Hanson's disease is a very slow disabler and killer of its victims, but it was and is a scourge of that part of the world. Lepers were ostracized from society as unclean, and most were required to live outside their towns, alone or with other lepers. They had to raise a loud noise whenever they encountered someone, so that people could avoid their touch. People assumed their disfigurement corresponded to a moral deformity; illness was the result of sin in those days.

But the woman with the alabaster jar was already a conspicuous sinner. She could visit Simon the leper with impunity. What more did she have to lose? Both of them were outcasts, she for her reason and he for his.

There were other people at the dinner party, people who complained about the expense of the exotic ointment she used. So other people visited Simon, too, then, with Jesus. I wonder what kind of persuasion he had to use to get them to come. Probably it was the last straw when the prostitute with the ointment showed up: somebody had to *say* something.

But their protest was turned back upon them, as was usual when people tried to enlist Jesus in their hardness of heart. A lot of things would need to be rethought, because a whole new life was dawning, one with no room for any of the hierarchies people had thought were so important—up until now.

FRIDAY IN PROPER 10

Pss 31 * 35
Joshua 4:19–5:1, 10–15
Romans 12:9–21
Matthew 26:17–25

*"Remove the sandals from your feet,
for the place where you stand is holy."*
JOSHUA 5:15

I forgot to bring black shoes to the beach and didn't even think about it until Sunday morning. It promised to be hot as Hades again, and things are a little looser in church when it's hot, but still—nobody in seminary ever said anything about the celebrant wearing pink flip-flops in the summer.

I remembered another August Sunday years ago: summer youth work in a seaside church. A handsome boy showed up for church in blue blazer and khaki trousers, the preppy summer uniform. From the ankles up, that is. I couldn't help noticing that he wore no shoes. But I was thrilled to see him: he had not yet joined in any of the youth activities that season. He was visiting his grandmother for the summer, and didn't know the other kids very well. Still, I had been hopeful; my exchanges with him had been brief and careful, but pleasant, and now here he was. Good. I hoped to see him at the picnic after church, I said, and he nodded and smiled a little.

His grandmother descended upon me like Grant through Richmond. Had I noticed that he was wearing *no shoes?!* Hadn't I *said* anything to him? She'd never seen such a thing in all her life. She shook her head, her mouth a thin, straight line, and sat down in her pew, her back stiff as a poker.

I imagined the conversation in the house getting ready to come to church. *Time to get ready.*

Coming.

Now, please.

The thunder of feet on the stairs. A pause. *You are not wearing those sneakers to church. Now go up and change, please, and I'll see you there.*

An answering pause. *Okay.* More feet, back up the stairs. And he didn't wear the sneakers to church. He didn't wear any shoes at all.

I thought of him as I layered my vestments on over my clothes. In procession, I tried not to let my pink sandals flap against my heels. But they hit smartly with every step I took: up the aisle, to the pulpit, up to the altar, back and forth across the communion rail. My pink toes peeked out at the faithful from under the crisp white hem of my alb. Ah, well. It's holy ground anyway.

SATURDAY IN PROPER 10

Pss 30, 32 * 42, 43
Joshua 6: 1–14
Romans 13:1–7
Matthew 26:26–35

Jesus took a loaf of bread . . .
MATTHEW 26:26

Naturally, one of the hottest and most humid days we've had so far was also the day we found ourselves almost out of bread. If I start early enough, I told myself, it'll all be done by the time it really gets hot. But there was an eMo to write, and yesterday genius did not burn: it just smoldered sullenly, never quite catching fire.

Hot and humid is good bread rising weather; it's just that then you have to bake it in a hot oven and heat up your kitchen. You can't wait until it's cooler, once it's riz (an honest-to-goodness word that spell-check doesn't seem to recognize). If you do, it'll fall and you won't have lovely rounded loaves. You'll have something more like rectangular bricks. Tasty but demoralizing.

And so the loaves went in at high noon. Our old oven is a little cranky, and you have to turn things around in there during the course of the cooking time, so I was stuck in the hot kitchen with the bread while it baked.

This is an old house. People have baked bread in it for a long time. Women in long skirts and long-sleeved, high-necked blouses, who managed the fire in the stove themselves, putting in just the right number of small logs, expertly keeping the fire evenly hot. Warm work. Strong women.

With the right combination of attitude and necessity, heat goes away if you just stay in it for a while. You drink a glass of water and notice its coolness, sit by the window and feel a momentary breeze, think of the dough changing into bread behind the oven door, and soon it's done. Then you bring out the fragrant loaves and lay them on their sides to cool, and you invent a reason to go outside.

SUNDAY, PROPER 11

Pss 63:1–8 (9–11), 98 * 103
Joshua 6:15–27
Acts 22:30–23:11
Mark 2:1–12

Then some people came, bringing to him
a paralyzed man, carried by four of them.
MARK 2:3

How good a friend could someone so disabled be? A pretty good one, judging from the lengths to which his friends were willing to go to get help for him: carrying him down the street, arguing with the people who blocked their entrance, and, failing to move them, hoisting him up on the roof and climbing up after him, either finding or cutting a hole through which to lower him into the living room.

Was he paralyzed his whole life long? It's hard to believe he could have survived into adulthood were that the case, but who knows? Or maybe he had been paralyzed in a terrible accident, a fall from a roof or from a horse. Maybe he knew what it was to have strong arms and legs, to run up a flight of stairs, to work with his hands for a living, to toss his toddler up in the air. Maybe he surveyed his current state and wished he had been killed outright. But he wasn't killed. He was alive.

His courage and the courage of his friends is already miraculous, before Jesus has laid eyes on him. The courage to live a life you once would have thought unlivable. The courage to make a fool of yourself for the sake of a friend's need. The courage to hope.

You don't see many paintings of this miracle. I would paint one, if I could: the hole in the roof, the faces of the four friends looking down at the man on the pallet, who grasps Jesus firmly by the wrist as he struggles to his feet; the owner of the house, dumbfounded, off to the side, wondering who's going to fix his ceiling.

I would paint the light in a special way, if I could: a nimbus of gentle silvery white that included Jesus and the paralytic, and the four friends. A cloud of collegial blessing.

MONDAY IN PROPER 11

Pss 41, 52 * 44
Joshua 7:1–13
Romans 13:8–14
Matthew 26:36–46

Love your neighbor as yourself.
ROMANS 13:9

The Golden Rule presupposes self-love. We have needs and long-ings, and it is appropriate for us to seek after them. It isn't self-ish to desire happiness: it is normal. There is no room, in this simple equation, for prettily insisting, in Christian love with saccharin on top, that you don't matter.

There are those whose natural self-love has been scolded out of them by parents who confused good manners with theology, using a flawed if-one-pill-is-good-eight-must-be-even-better application of that misguided principle. It *is* polite to allow someone else to precede you, but it's crazy to think you should never be first in any-thing. It *is* impolite and boorish to brag about what you have and what you do well; it isn't rude to affirm your own gifts. It *is* more blessed to give than to receive, but it is sometimes also easier: if you never permit yourself to be on the receiving end, you deny people close to you the honor and delight of doing you a service.

The attempt to deny one's own self-love never works: the spirit itself insists on it. Those who consciously refuse its promptings will unconsciously seek to follow them: if we fail to take care of our own needs in a good way, we will take care of them in a bad way.

But what about self-denial? What about sacrifice? What about holy martyrdom?

Paradoxically, such acts are really not acts of holy love *without* the ingredient of self-love: giving my life means nothing if I refused to love my life in the first place. That's not martyrdom, it's just sui-cide. It arises from illness, not from love. Giving up something I didn't feel entitled to anyway is not much of a sacrifice, either: it's like giving away something that belongs to someone else. Neither is much like the self-giving love of Christ, a healthy young man with everything to live for, one who loved life and parties and friends. And laid it all down for the sake of people he loved and people he would never meet. People like us.

TUESDAY IN PROPER 11

Pss 45 * 47, 48
Joshua 8:1–22
Romans 14:1–12
Matthew 26:47–56

*Welcome those who are weak in faith, but not
for the purpose of quarreling over opinions.*
ROMANS 14:1

It has become the practice in many churches to raise the bar very high where the sacraments of baptism and marriage are concerned. The argument is a good one: we're not a sacrament machine, here to help you meet your social obligations, a pretty church for your wedding and nothing more. The Christian sacraments are sacraments, not social rites of passage, and they should be offered only to committed Christians.

Well, okay.

But unchurched people have to start somewhere, and I think a rite of passage is a good place to start. It's a teachable moment with a motivated student, one who might go decades longer without coming to Christ on his own. Marry them or baptize their child, and you have a chance to tell the good news and to assure them that it is good news *for them.* Refuse unless they sign on the dotted line, and there could be consequences you do not intend.

Even the most distracted bride and groom or new parents will remember you and your church. The friendliness of the altar guild and the organist, the kindness of the sexton, everything. Everyone at the wedding will hope and pray for good things for the couple, of course, but it is certain that trouble will come into their lives, sooner or later. Who will they turn to: the son-of-a-gun who chased them out of his office because they weren't Christian enough, or the one who welcomed them as they were and offered them sacraments that, after all, never were only about their readiness. The spirit is active in a sacrament, regardless of who administers it or who receives it. It isn't solely a function of our commitment, or want of it.

WEDNESDAY IN PROPER 11

Pss 119:49–72 * 49, (53)
Joshua 8:30–35
Romans 14:13–23
Matthew 26:57–68

. . . and some slapped him. . . .
MATTHEW 26:67

There are many ways to injure someone. You could speak harshly. You could throw something. Heck, you could take out a gun and blow him away, if you're made like that.

But the most humiliating way I know to injure someone is also the most casual: you can slap him.

A slap is contempt itself. It is administered only to an inferior. A slap is suffered, and there is no response to it: the victim stands there, stunned: she didn't see it coming. There was no windup, no threatening preparation, just the flat palm of a hand, whipping out from nowhere to brand your cheek and whipping back again. The rest of the person's body doesn't even move. Just that hand.

The slap stings after it is over. It was so fast, so off-handed, almost bored: you mattered so little to the one who slapped you. Anyone who witnessed it could see how little you mattered. You stand there, still, with your burning cheek: what do you do now?

Run away and cry, showing the one who slapped you how weak you are? No. You stand there in humiliated silence.

Some of the soldiers slapped Jesus like that, to show him how little he mattered. How he wasn't *their* king, that was for sure. How he was just a Jew and they were Romans, and they could do what they liked to him because he was going to be dead soon anyway. I know his cheek stung where they slapped him.

THURSDAY IN PROPER 11

Pss 50 * (59, 60) or 66, 67
Joshua 9:3–21
Romans 15:1–13
Matthew 26:69–75

*We who are strong ought to put up
with the failings of the weak . . .*
ROMANS 15:1

As we head toward the car, What's-Her-Name sails in a sudden leap from the driver's seat window and into the peonies, startling us.

Will you look at that—she was trying to steal our car! Q says. "Unauthorized use," that would be, I think, instead of car theft. I think there's a separate offense they can use for family members. But maybe I'm wrong; I'm not a lawyer.

She probably *was* trying to steal it, though. I know that cat: if she'd known how to drive a stick, we'd be carless and she'd be in Buffalo.

What's-Her-Name is changing, though. She's six years old, now, and has civilized just a bit in middle age: she comes downstairs from the third floor when she hears us get up in the morning and heads for the kitchen, expecting the nice breakfast she receives. If she has spent the night outside, which she doesn't do nearly as often, she frequently comes when called. She talks to us when we set her food before her. Once in a while she presents her chin to be stroked. Then the moment is over, and she is gone.

She is like an aging convict: not as wild any more, not as convinced she doesn't need anyone or anything. The prisons are full of them: old men who did terrible things in their youth but are now just old men, who have problems with their feet like other old men have, whose backs and knees hurt, who tire easily. Couldn't rob a bank or assault someone if they tried, but also couldn't do much else. Frozen in one place by choices they made long ago, frozen in their own lives.

Every pastor has noticed that visiting someone in prison feels much the same as visiting someone in a nursing home. *This is odd,* you think at first, noticing that you're saying the same things to a convicted murderer that you said yesterday to a sweet, ancient lady with a broken hip: looking at family photographs, chatting about the food, about how they pass the time, about the past, carefully about the future. But no, it's not odd. Neither of them can leave. Each has lost the life he knew, the life she knew. Each is learning the hard way what it means to live one day at a time.

And then you remember that there really is no easy way to learn that.

FRIDAY IN PROPER 11

Pss 40, 54 * 51
Joshua 9:22–10:15
Romans 15:14–24
Matthew 27:1–10

And the sun stood still . . .
JOSHUA 10:13

The cats have it right: find something flat and lie down on it until evening, when it's bound to be at least a little cooler. Gypsy has staked her claim on the bathroom's cool tile floor. Noodle, not as experienced, has chosen the wool rug in our room. What's-Her-Name is outside under the picnic table. I join Noodle in the bedroom and log a full two hours of oblivion. Q claims the couch downstairs and does the same. With a pang—but only a slight one—I think of friends in their offices or on the train, friends descending the subway stairs to the airless platform. It is not fair that I get to take a nap in the middle of the hot day and they do not. But, on the other hand, would my staying awake out here make it any better for them? No, it would not.

I alternate my naps with brief showers. I do not dry myself off: I let the water evaporate on me and I am downright cool.

What shall we have for dinner? Q asks. Something cool, I reply immediately, and we settled on cold poached salmon with dill, cucumbers in yogurt, sliced yellow squash (steamed just a bit), and strawberries for dessert.

The general store in our town was not air-conditioned—nothing was, in those days. At the front of the store there was a large red chest cooler for soft drinks. Icy water, the coldest water I'd ever encountered, kept them cold. We'd lift the metal lid and reach down into the water as far as we could, and we would stand there like that until the storekeeper told us to get out of there if we weren't going to buy something. We would mop our faces with the drops of water as we left the store. Then we would walk halfway home and sit on the little stone wall surrounding the storm drain, looking up at the sky through the lace that the leaves of the trees made.

Heat is only a moment. You can take care of it in that moment, and then you can take care of it in the next one. You can nap or splash your face with water or take a shower or be still and gaze at the blue sky through a tracery of leaves. Panic about how hot it is or how hot it's going to get makes you hotter, and you don't notice the tiny breeze that whispers over you now and then, don't notice how efficient a cooling mechanism your own sweat is, don't notice how cooling even a tepid glass of water is as it washes down your esophagus, softening it as it goes.

Beautiful things and hard things are the same in that respect: they are lived moment to moment. You can't bank them, nor can you evade them. We can't really stop the sun. So enjoy or endure the moment. And note its brevity: for good or ill, you will not prolong it.

SATURDAY IN PROPER 11

Pss 55 * 138, 139:1–17 (18–23)
Joshua 23:1–16
Romans 15:25–33
Matthew 27:11–23

I will set out by way of you to Spain . . .
ROMANS 15:28

Paul mentions several times that he hoped to go to Spain, but he never got there. He was arrested and taken to Rome first, and he was martyred there. Someone else would have to make that trip.

What will you leave unfinished? What half-completed projects will people scratch their head over when they're going through your things: *What on earth was she going to do with this?* What won't they understand? I wander through my house sometimes and think about this: of the dozens of baskets I have, will my children know which one is a real Gullah basket from South Carolina? I think of putting a note on the bottom of it: *You're making a big mistake if you throw this out! Love, Mom.* Then I get distracted by something else and forget all about it.

Maybe I'll go around the house with colored dots and sort things out for them, I think. Or maybe I'll die suddenly, and there will have been no time to go around with dots. Then they'll be on their own. What matters to me may not matter to them. They may not know or care who the Gullah are.

Somebody else went to Spain. It wasn't Paul, but somebody went and strengthened the church there. Knowing Paul as we do, we can assume that this person didn't do things quite as Paul would have done them. Didn't emphasize the teachings he would have emphasized. The people to whom the church is left never keep it as it was. They change it. Every time. Whether they know it or not.

SUNDAY, PROPER 12

Pss 24, 29 * 8, 84
Joshua 24:1–15
Acts 28:23–31
Mark 2:23–28

"But as for me and my household,
we will serve the Lord."
JOSHUA 24:15

Gods were personal in ancient Israel and environs: you made them yourself, sometimes, out of wood or stone. Then they were your personal gods, and the gods of your family, and you carried them with you wherever you went. Gods were of the family's place, but they also traveled. So the "God of Abraham, Isaac and Jacob" was exactly that: their family god.

Our God is a family god whose worship expanded. Abraham's family god became god of the entire human family.

It was the people and the culture who changed, of course, not God. We see a widening perspective unfolding throughout scripture, and we see the tensions it produced: the fierce jealousy of God against other gods of other tribes, the universalizing cadence of the first creation account in Genesis as against the folkloric individualism of the one in the second chapter. We see a triumphalist approach to the powerful idea of the chosen people in the promised land give way to the image of the suffering servant, when the political tide turns and Israel goes into exile. We see the early Christians, too, struggling to navigate between the parochial past and the universal future. None of these transitions were easy, not for anyone. They continue to be difficult.

We still want God to be our family God. We want God in our suitcase. The universalism of the divine love makes us anxious: can it be that we don't own God? That there is not a divine preference for us? Might it be that we really have no preferential edge and can't fix it so we can get one?

It sure can. That's exactly how things stand. The God of Abraham, Isaac, and Jacob, who pointed to the stars in the sky to demonstrate the numbers of Abraham's descendents, didn't mean just his blood descendents, no matter what Abraham and his chroniclers thought.

There are *a lot* of stars in the sky.

MONDAY IN PROPER 12

Pss 56, 57, (58) * 64, 65
Joshua 24:16–33
Romans 16:1–16
Matthew 27:24–31

*. . . he took some water and washed his hands before the
crowd, saying, "I am innocent of this man's blood. . . ."*
MATTHEW 27:24

Sometimes *not to decide* is to decide. Pilate was mistaken: a claim
of innocence erected upon a refusal to act is a fraudulent claim.
To refuse to help is to harm.

In the hot, dirty chaos of the convention center in New Orleans,
a young woman lay on the ground, her frantic brother and sister
vainly trying to help her drink, but the water trickled uselessly out
of the slack corner of her mouth. A row of National Guardsmen
stood nearby, their assignment to control the crowd in that area.
Aren't you going to help her? asked a reporter. *Uh, yes,* one of them
said, clearly frightened, *Let me check on that*—and he was gone. In
ten minutes or so a stretcher arrived, but ten minutes is too long
not to be breathing. The woman died. She was twenty years old.

Their orders were to control the crowd, and they were following
them. Something about their training, though, made them think
that following their original order was more important than saving
a life. Something about their training prevented them from thinking: they had ceded the thinking to their higher-ups. They were
good at following orders, but something prevented them from siz-
ing up a new situation and responding to it. It must have been the
chaos of the situation, but military training is all about keeping
your head in chaotic situations.

Chain of command is crucial in situations like this. But the duty
to save a life, if the opportunity presents itself, precedes it. There are
terrible moments in warfare when an order *is* given to disregard
that prior duty for the sake of the group, and no soldier who has

had to follow that order ever feels free of its stain, no matter how many times he washes his hands. He wears it the rest of his life. Decades later, he can hardly bear to talk about it.

Our guilt or innocence is not ours to declare. We can't abdicate responsibility halfway through the situations in which we have signed up to be responsible. The choices we make remain our choices, and they'd better be good—we will live forever after with their consequences.

TUESDAY IN PROPER 12

Pss 61, 62 * 68:1–20 (21–23) 24–36
Judges 2:1–5, 11–23
Romans 16:17–27
Matthew 27:32–44

. . . they came upon a man from Cyrene named Simon . . .
MATTHEW 27:32

Simon was from Cyrene, and he was the father of Alexander and Rufus, whom we don't know anything about either—except, of course, that their dad was Simon of Cyrene.

So we don't know what Simon's opinion of Jesus was. Was he a follower of his, and that's why he was in the crowd on what we would come to know as the Via Dolorosa that day? Was he just a visitor, out to see the sights on his first visit to the holy city for Passover? Or did he live there now, with his sons, a Jew with an out-of-town accent?

Did he come forward in kindness when he saw Jesus stumble and fall, distressed and wanting to help, and then did the guards grab him and force him to carry the heavy cross himself? Or did they just reach into the crowd and choose him, an unwilling participant? He was older than Jesus, this Simon—he had two grown sons. Or maybe he was not: maybe Alexander and Rufus were little at the time, or maybe they were not even born yet, and they grew up with the story of the day their father carried the cross of Jesus up to the Golgotha hill.

Whoever he was, and however it happened, Simon came closer to Jesus than anyone else during that walk. He shared in his humiliation. Simon walked back down the hill and back into his life, hot and dirty and exhausted, when the terrible deed was done. Did he stay to watch, or was he afraid of what else the Romans might do to him? We don't know. But we know he became part of the new community of Christians in some way: the writer mentions his name and his son's names, as if they might be familiar to people. So the terrible walk changed his life, and we remember him still.

Jesus didn't walk back down. He went back to his life, too, and returned in a different way.

WEDNESDAY IN PROPER 12

Pss 72 * 119:73–96
Judges 3:12–30
Acts 1:1–14
Matthew 27:45–54

*After his resurrection they came out of the tombs
and entered the holy city and appeared to many.*
MATTHEW 27:53

It does seem that someone besides Matthew would have mentioned such an unusual occurrence if it had really happened, and we don't hear about if from anyone else writing at the time, including Flavius Josephus, who makes one offhanded reference to Jesus and surely would have seen fit to mention it if dead people had arisen *en masse* after his death.

Most Christians are quick to say that an important difference between Christians and Jews is that Christians believe in resurrection and Jews don't. But this difference was not as simple then as it is now, after centuries of painful difference between Jews and Christians has made it a significant divide. Then as now, there were many opinions within Judaism, about everything. The Pharisees are reported in the gospels and by Paul as believing in the resurrection, as against the Sadducees, who did not. Even more importantly, there were expectations in some quarters about a general resurrection in connection with the coming of the Messiah, making it fairly obvious why Matthew would want to include this startling detail in his passion story.

In Christian legend of just a little while later, one of the saints who were "seen by many" was Simeon, the old man of the temple who first recognized the infant Jesus as the Messiah. He was old even then, so he must have been dead for a long time by the time of the crucifixion. Sweetly fitting, this little touch: he was peaceful about his own death, you recall, now that he had seen the Messiah, and his lovely words upon seeing the Christ are preserved liturgically for us in the canticle *Nunc dimitis*—"Lord, let your servant depart in peace, according to your word, for these eyes of mine have seen your salvation. . . ."

THURSDAY IN PROPER 12

Pss (70), 71 * 74
Judges 4:4–23
Acts 1:15–26
Matthew 27:55–66

But Jael wife of Heber took a tent peg, and took a hammer
in her hand, and went softly to him and drove the peg into
his temple, until it went down into the ground . . .
JUDGES 4:21

Well, *there*. Who says women are no good with tools? This chapter from the book of Judges is not remarkable for its bloodiness; it would be hard to pick a winner in that category. Nope, what sets it apart is that it is two women who move the violent action of the story: Deborah and Jael.

Deborah is the new judge of Israel, in the line of Joshua. The writer gives no sign that it is at all unusual for a woman to be in this position, but Deborah is the only female judge of Israel we hear about in scripture, so it can't have been all that common. She gives military men orders, and they follow them. They view her presence as a necessity for victory in battle, and carry her along with them into the fray, as if she were the Ark of the Covenant. Of course they win against 900 iron chariots, and kill every last one of the enemy soldiers, leaving the senior general Sisera on the run. And Jael, whose husband had a separate treaty with Israel's current enemy, invites his senior general into her house, feeds him and lets him get some sleep, tenderly covering him with a rug—and then she pounds a stake into his head. Right down into the ground. So much for the separate treaty. History does not record what Heber said about this when he got home.

All the tales of the judges of Israel have a folkloric flavor: brave heroes—and a couple of heroines—winning the day with their strength and cunning. The women's tales show a curious combination of leadership and subservience: Deborah is a judge, but she is also almost a mascot, carried here and there like a good luck charm. She never seems to go anywhere by herself. Jael's bloody deed is done in the midst of her excellent performance of all the traditional feminine duties of hospitality.

A moment in our ancient history when true partnership between men and women came a little closer. It didn't last. But this is very old literature, and it's nice to know that they even imagined such a thing.

FRIDAY IN PROPER 12

Pss 69:1–23 (24–30) 31–38 * 73
Judges 5:1–18
Acts 2:1–21
Matthew 28:1–10

And suddenly there was a great earthquake;
for an angel of the Lord, descending from heaven,
came and rolled back the stone and sat on it.

MATTHEW 28:2

Everybody seems to hear the earthquake, and the women are already at the tomb when the angel shows up and rolls away the stone. The soldiers see the angel and faint dead away. The women don't pass out, and so the angel can tell them what has happened. The tomb is already empty before any of this occurs. The women see the risen Jesus on their way out of the garden and back to town.

Jesus risen is like Jesus in his earthly life in one respect: he relies on people who are not at the top of the pecking order. He entrusts the news of his resurrection to women. Of course, they are also the only people available: only women came to visit his grave. The soldiers have fainted and the angel already knows. Who else is he going to tell?

The people God will use are the ones who show up. There's no one else available. Showing up is our primary contribution to God's saving and healing work in the world, whatever it is and wherever it is. We usually don't know in advance what the work will be; we have some plans and ideas ourselves, but sometimes it's something else entirely.

And only those who show up—no matter who they are—will know about it.

SATURDAY IN PROPER 12

Pss 75, 76 * 23, 27
Judges 5:19–31
Acts 2:22–36
Matthew 28:11–20

While [the women] were going [to tell the disciples],
some of the guard went into the city and told the
chief priests everything that had happened.
MATTHEW 28:11

This was after they regained consciousness, I guess. I wonder if they told the chief priest that they'd fainted? Maybe they left that part out.

When they reached the chief priest, he chaired a curious damage control meeting. From this little detour, we surmise that the body-snatching accusation was current: it was a reasonable explanation for a tomb without an occupant, much more so than the actual one.

With these two opposing efforts—the disciples, male and female, commencing their new life proclaiming the resurrection of Jesus and the members of the priestly hierarchy preparing their case for its denial—we leave the gospel of Matthew. It is so full of so many famous things, stories and teachings we usually hear in isolation, chopped into pieces small enough to swallow at a church service. But you have read the whole thing this year at Morning or Evening Prayer. Little by little, one verse has led to another in ways that make sense sometimes and at other times seem not to. You will read it many more times in your life, I think—two years from now, for sure, when we'll be in Year II again—as part of the daily gift of prayer God gives you every time you stop for it.

Perhaps you will drift away form the Daily Office for a period of time, and then perhaps you'll feel bad about having done that. Don't. There is nothing to be gained from berating yourself. Just know that it will always be here, the book waiting to be opened, glad to see you when you take it down off the shelf. And begin again.

SUNDAY, PROPER 13

Pss 93, 96 * 34
Judges 6:1–24
2 Corinthians 9:6–15
Mark 3:20–30

The point is this: the one who sows sparingly
will also reap sparingly, and the one who sows
bountifully will also reap bountifully.

2 CORINTHIANS 9:6

I mostly don't measure when I cook. I've been doing it a long time and know what a teaspoon looks like. And I like to make a little more than I think people will eat. I don't want to appear stingy; I want people to feel that there is plenty, that they can have as much as they want. I want there to be enough, in case an unexpected diner appears: I never want anyone to wonder if perhaps he should not have come.

I am that way in the garden, too. I plant more than I need. I like to have plants to give away. I like to put plants in places where there were no plants before. I know that some will die and I want to be prepared for that. Q is that way, too. This summer he has thirty tomato plants, and there are only two of us here.

I am that way about work, too, and it sometimes gets me into trouble. On balance, though, I would not change it. I attempt lots of things. Some of them don't work. But that leaves quite a few that do.

God seems to be this way, too. The creation is unstinting. God must not measure every time. So many things begin, in so many ways, with so many different results. Willing to take a chance on something that might not work.

Because if it does work, it will be so wonderful.

∖MONDAY IN PROPER 13

Pss 80 * 77, (79)
Judges 6:25–40
Acts 2:37–47
John 1:1–18

The light shines in the darkness,
and the darkness did not overcome it.

JOHN 1:5

The Meadowlands, that stretch of marshland just outside the Lincoln tunnel, is either aptly or utterly wrongly named, depending on how you look at it. The New Jersey Turnpike cuts right through them, and so do the train tracks into New York from the west. Decrepit factories ring the Meadowlands. The meandering streams are studded with discarded tires, oil tanks, parts of old industrial machinery.

But the Meadowlands are also acres of golden marsh grass, its silvery plumes waving gently in the breeze. Snowy egrets live there, their long necks gracefully curving downwards as they preen. I have seen a blue heron in the Meadowlands. Dozens of ducks swim in its pools, and dragonflies the size of birds, visible from the train window, skitter across the water and disappear into the tall grass. These animals are much more numerous than formerly; their presence is a sign that the industrial pollution of the wetlands is clearing. They are returning to the state God intended.

We have made the earth dark by living on it carelessly. For a time we did not know this could happen: it seemed so infinite. But the earth is small, smaller all the time, and now we know about our power to change the earth, for good and for ill. By the grace of God, its self-healing powers remain. The Meadowlands recovers, now, from our depredations, and now we know to leave it alone in future, so we never injure it again. We can begin to see the world as God sees us, if we try. When we do, we change. We become more Christlike, more in tune with the creation, of which we are only a part, that came to be through Christ.

At night, the Meadowlands are dark. The lights of the industrial areas surrounding it, invisible during the day for the ugly buildings to which they are attached, light the night like fairy lights. It is a lovely sight.

And the darkness does not overcome it.

ⅴTUESDAY IN PROPER 13

Pss 78:1–39 * 78:40–72
Judges 7:1–18
Acts 3:1–11
John 1:19–28

. . . walking and leaping and praising God.
ACTS 3:8

Nothing is quite like walking if you've ever been unable to walk. Simply to get up and run out for the paper, to bend down and pick something up from the floor, to have left something in the bedroom and pop upstairs to get it. Every time I must retrace my steps because I've left something somewhere, I praise God for the inefficiency of turning around and walking back the way I came. If I hadn't forgotten, I wouldn't have the chance to move. I wouldn't feel my legs responding to my intention. Let me be inefficient again, soon.

I am like a baby whose walking is a new skill: he is never too tired to try it again, never falls down so many times that he gets discouraged and stops trying. Loves the freedom of his new mobility, the possibilities it inaugurates. Attempts steps ridiculously high in proportion to his height, steps that are thigh-high, and eventually triumphs over all of them.

I must run down and answer the door. Oh, good, I think, even though I am up to my neck in something upstairs in my office. I can

get up. I can go down the stairs. I don't really *run* down them anymore, and I listen to my husband's thundering down the stair with
admiration. *How does he do that?* But I can walk. Oh, good. Another
chance to move.

The people who saw the formerly lame man walking and leaping were stunned. They asked one another what could have happened, how this could have come about. Not the man himself,
though. He was moving too fast.

WEDNESDAY IN PROPER 13

Pss 119:97–120 * 81, 82
Judges 7:19–8:12
Acts 3:12–26
John 1:29–42

*"Here is the Lamb of God who takes
away the sin of the world!"*

JOHN 1:29

The *Agnus Dei.* A little three-part hymn, sung after the breaking
of the bread and before it is consumed. And here is its modest
beginning: John the Baptist sings it first.

He is such a colorful figure that we forget how faithful he was.
How hopeful. Above all, how tender he is toward Jesus, and how
trusting. Whether the story of John leaping in his mother's womb
when visited by Jesus *in utero* Jesus is true or not, he knew who he
was when other people didn't. He trusted him and honored him.
When he is as good as dead, it is Jesus he thinks of: *Are you the one
who is to come,* he pleads, *or should we look for another?* John wouldn't
be around to look for anybody, and he knew it. But he wanted to
hear Jesus affirm that his lifetime of proclamation wasn't for nothing. That it was all true: the kingdom really was at hand.

We're not here for long. We're not famous. The world isn't very different after we leave from what it was before we came. But we want to know our lives had meaning, that there was a purpose—small, but *ours*—for our being here at all.

THURSDAY IN PROPER 13

Pss (83) or 145 * 85, 86
Judges 8:22–35
Acts 4:1–12
John 1:43–51

"Can anything good come out of Nazareth?"
JOHN 1:46

When Nathaniel slammed Jesus' home town like that, you'd think Jesus would have been offended. But he seems not to have been angry at all. He complimented Nathaniel on his bluntness.

Nazareth was not a power center of ancient Israel. The people from that part of the country were the hillbillies of their time: you could tell them by their accent and their appearance. They were expected not to be very smart.

We think we know about a person if we know where he's from. And we may know something about his general history that way, but we have next to nothing to go on about *him*.

The subtle evil of such assumptions carries with it its own unhappy result: if I dismiss someone because of what I think I know about him, I will be impoverished for want of what I would have learned from him. What he could have shown me, and how I might have entered a culture different from mine and come to love it.

The grosser evil is much more sinister: it is the preamble to a pogrom. Tell yourself someone is lower than you because he is different from you, and soon it doesn't matter what you do to him. Soon it begins to seem that he is more trouble than he is worth. It begins to seem that he is the *cause* of troubles that seem on the surface to have nothing to do with him. Soon it can seem no great matter to kill him.

Nathaniel began by dismissing Jesus. But, braver than Nathaniel, Jesus ignored his dismissive tone and moved closer to him. "A true Israelite," he called him. There might have been a gentle satire in that little compliment, something that Nathaniel didn't pick up. Maybe people from Nazareth weren't all that dumb, after all.

FRIDAY IN PROPER 13

Pss 88 * 91, 92
Judges 9:1–16, 19–21
Acts 4:13–31
John 2:1–12

On the third day there was a wedding in Cana of Galilee. . . .
JOHN 2:1

Our guide had a stack of elegant long envelopes in his hand, wrapped in a scarf to keep them fresh. It was important to deliver them by hand, he told us. It is rude to send them in the mail unless the addressee is far away. We stopped at a rug merchant's shop so he could deliver one; the two men talked happily as the invitation changed hands, and the merchant gave the odd upward/sideways turn of the head that means "okay" in India. He would be there. Our guide came back to the bus, one invitation lighter. He had promised his wife faithfully that he would distribute them all today. It was their daughter's wedding. It would be in two weeks: a far cry from the months of advance notice American wedding mavens sternly advise. All in all, it would last for several days, the wedding, and the wedding feast would feed hundreds of guests.

His demeanor was a combination of joy and gravity, befitting the momentousness of the occasion. This would be the greatest day of his life, much greater than his own long-ago wedding had been. It would certify his success as a father and as a businessman.

I hope the wedding went well. That there was enough food. If a miracle was needed, I hope it happened. Jesus performed his first miracle at a wedding that must have been a lot like this one: a happy but vigilant father, an anxious mother, a shy bride and groom. Lots of people eating and drinking for days. And—one way or another—plenty for everyone.

SATURDAY IN PROPER 13

Pss 87, 90 * 136
Judges 9:22–25, 50–57
Acts 4:32–5:11
John 2:13–25

. . . he fell down and died. . . . Immediately
she fell down at his feet and died.
ACTS 5:5, 10

Wow. I bet nobody else held back property from the common fund after *that*. I wonder why they don't read this one when it's time for people to pledge for the following year. Maybe people wouldn't treat the stewardship drive so off-handedly if they thought it might be a matter of life and death.

Are there other good reasons to give, even if you know you won't drop dead for not doing so? From the beginning of the church, we have thought so: several of Paul's letters are fund-raising appeals, and it seems he was successful at it.

The appeals were for the relief of widows and orphans in Jerusalem, widows and orphans whom most of the people Paul was encountering would never meet, in a place where most of them would never go. Both communities were Christian, but the Greek-speaking Corinthians and Ephesians and Galatians had next to nothing in common with the Jewish Christians in Jerusalem. That's exactly what giving is like today: I'm giving for the help of people I'll never meet in countries I'll never see, as well as for the mission of my own community at home. I benefit directly from some of what I give, but not from most of it: we give because we care about things beyond our own narrow self-interest.

And for another reason. Life has been a gift. We didn't earn it, nor did we earn the good fortune of being born in a prosperous country. We have made of it what we have made, and we have been free to do so—more gifts. Most of us should feel profoundly grateful, and happy to have something to give back.

SUNDAY, PROPER 14

Pss 66, 67 * 19, 46
Judges 11:1–11, 29–40
2 Corinthians 11:21b–31
Mark 4:35–41

"Alas, my daughter! You have brought me very low;
you have become the cause of great trouble to me."
JUDGES 11:35

I beg your pardon? Jephthah is about to sacrifice his only child to fulfill a foolish promise he never should have made, and he tells her she's caused *him* trouble? Somebody has indeed caused trouble in this story, but I don't think it's Jephthah's daughter.

Interesting, though—she does not agree with me. She willingly allows herself to be killed, just asking for two months to go with her girlfriends and bewail the fact that she will never marry, never have children, never have the chance to grow up and grow old. We find this unnecessary agony infuriating. But the people hearing it in ancient times found it noble, moving: *Jephthah is a man who keeps his vow to God, even if it means sacrificing his own child.*

But the ancients weren't stupid: they knew it was a silly vow, too. This story is also a warning: *Watch what you say.* It may lead you somewhere you really don't want to go. Think ahead with seriousness when you make a promise, so that your honor does not collide with itself and bear a bitter fruit.

Almost everyone has more than one sacred obligation. Handle them with care. To be forced to choose between them can be a terrible thing.

MONDAY IN PROPER 14

Pss 89:1–18 * 89:19–52
Judges 12:1–7
Acts 5:12–26
John 3:1–21

. . . born from above . . .
JOHN 3:7

The Massachusetts Bay Colony consisted of people who had been "born from above," and could point to the very moment when that happy event had occurred. Being born again, a dramatic shedding of the old life and embrace of the new, certified their membership in the blessed company of the elect, which was definitely the group to be in, since everyone else was going to hell.

As years went by, though, a problem arose: what about the children? What about the children of the elect, raised by the elect, who might not have experienced such a disjunction between the old life and the new? Who couldn't produce a definitive date and time with which to answer the question "Are you saved?" Were the saints' beloved children going to hell?

Love warred with theology. In the end love won out: they developed the idea of the "Halfway Covenant," an interim form of membership in the community in anticipation of a born-again event later on. So the children could remain in the church that was the only community they had ever known.

Are you born again? Can you supply a date and a time when you got that way? I cannot. There has never been a time when I did not know of God's love, and my decades of life in the world have been a steady lesson in it, increasing my awareness of it year by year.

Of my own elite status I have no knowledge. I only know the love of God, and it is enough.

◊ TUESDAY IN PROPER 14

Pss 97, 99, (100) * 94, (95)
Judges 13:1–15
Acts 5:27–42
John 3:22–36

No razor is to come on his head, for the boy
shall be a nazirite to God from birth.
JUDGES 13:5

Just why it was important that Samson not have a haircut is lost now: the explanation offered in the text—*he shall be a nazirite to God from birth*—doesn't help us much.

But it was crystal clear at the time: Samson's great physical strength resided in his long hair, the sign of his being pledged to God. There are other folktales about long hair—Rapunzel, for instance—tales in which long hair confers power, wealth, and sometimes a few problems. Samson's tale is the oldest we have. His is also a tale of blindness, and we knew other blind people with special stories: blind Homer, blind, ruined Oedipus, blind Paul, about to be converted.

Tales of cunning and trickery. Tales of superhuman power. Maybe the Samson story is older than Judaism itself, predating the history we know and inserted into it by a later hand. It is like other tales of women longing for children, rewarded with motherhood at last, but grimly obligated by the gift. Nothing is really free, they tell us over and over again. You must pay in some way for what you receive. If your gift is extraordinary, the price will be, also.

The folkloric bargains of these old stories are different from the free gift of grace in Christ—that really *is* free. It cannot be earned, nor can it be charmed into being. We cannot bargain or conjure with it. Like Samson's, Jesus' power arises from the ashes of his weakness. But this weakness is not the result of a trick; Jesus' strength is not stolen from him. His is a weakness he willingly assumes.

WEDNESDAY IN PROPER 14

Pss 101, 109:1–4 (5–19) 20–30 * 119:121–144
Judges 13:15–24
Acts 6:1–15
John 4:1–26

*"We have heard him speak blasphemous
words against Moses and God."*
ACTS 6:11

Well, there it is: Stephen is branded an underminer of the most basic, mom-and-apple-pie test there could be in his society. The custodians of the institution sense a threat and move to protect it. He's not just a danger to us, he's against *Moses*. He's even against *God*. Need we say more?

This sounds awfully familiar, and we know why: God is regularly enlisted as a partisan in American politics these days. Just now, his spokespersons have declared him opposed to the senate institution of the filibuster. Oppose them, and you're no longer just on a different page as regards parliamentary procedure: you're against "people of faith."

Well, I'm a person of faith, and I'm okay with the occasional senatorial soliloquy into the wee hours. I have a lot of friends who are also people of faith, and they are sprinkled over the entire wide spectrum of political persuasions. And some of my POF friends agree politically with other friends who have no faith at all—the non-POFs, I guess you'd call them.

What would Jesus do? It's a good thing to ask that question of ourselves as we ponder an ethical dilemma, but it's dangerous to imagine that we know. Certainty, in the New Testament, belongs to the scribes and the Pharisees, to the chief priests; the followers of Jesus are often puzzled, and Jesus himself is often enigmatic. Uncertainty births the church; the oldest accounts of the resurrection appearances are full of ambiguity and painful doubt. These people struggle for clarity, and put everything they have into the fight. The last thing we need to do is foreclose on such struggles in our own day.

THURSDAY IN PROPER 14

Pss 105:1–22 * 105:23–45
Judges 14:1–19
Acts 6:15–7:16
John 4:27–42

*"Is there not a woman among our kin, or among
all our people, that you must go to take a wife
from the uncircumcised Philistines?"*
JUDGES 14:3

Don't you know any nice Jewish girls? Orry Shackney's mother would have nothing to do with Grace at first: didn't come to the wedding, wouldn't visit the young couple in their home, wouldn't invite her new Roman Catholic daughter-in-law to her own home. Orry should visit her by himself, she said. He refused: *I don't come without my wife.* His mother couldn't hold out against that for very long: she softened, got to know the woman her son loved, who would become the mother of her grandsons. They became very close. The handful that Orry's mother was, Grace loved her as a second mom. At the end of her life, it was Grace who cared for her in her final illness.

People shake their heads at stories like this. How could a mother be so hard-hearted? So narrow-minded? Of course, nobody sent six million Anglicans to the gas chambers in the space of five years, so I don't have a sense of what it is to feel your tribe disappearing from the face of the earth.

As it turned out, Samson's marriage wasn't as happy as the Shackneys'. He should have listened to his mom. As far as the author is concerned, the whole thing was God's plan. If Samson *had* listened to his mom, there would have been no story of deliverance from the Philistines. Just another happy Jewish family.

⋎ FRIDAY IN PROPER 14

Pss 102 * 107:1–32
Judges 14:20–15:20
Acts 7:17–29
John 4:43–54

Samson's wife was given to his companion,
who had been his best man.
JUDGES 14:20

As difficult as the whole thing must have been for Samson, read what it was like for his nameless Philistine wife! She is passed from man to man like a sack of flour, with not a word to say about it herself. Then when Samson wants to get back together and her father refuses to allow it—she being married now to the guy who was best man at her wedding, someone she didn't know at all before their marriage—he burns the place down, and the entire agricultural structure of the Philistines as well. Angry about all the destruction, the rest of the Philistines blame her and her dad, and burn them to death.

At the wedding rehearsal, I always take the time to acquaint the bridal party with some of the hidden history of the marriage rite.

In the beginning of the service, I spell out what the church thinks marriage is and tell the congregation that the couple understands this and agrees with it. Then a stern warning, first to the congregation and then to the couple themselves, that any secrets that would invalidate the marriage if they were known, be confessed: protection for each against being discarded on trumped up legal grounds later on, when the going gets tough. Having determined that they are free to marry, we move on to determine whether or not they both really want to: the Consents, asked of the woman first, in memory of other marriages, like that of Samson's wife, when the bride had no say at all in who she married. The father of the bride often still presents her, but it is a presentation, not a "giving away," and often the mother of the bride joins him in it, and often the groom is similarly presented by his family. It is asked of both bride and groom in exactly the same language: the same things apply to the man as to the woman. That seems not to have been the case for this Philistine wife .

The Marriage Vows themselves are also the same for each; *obey* has disappeared from the rite. With the exchange of rings—and almost all ceremonies are double-ring today—each pledges to honor the other, "with all that I am and all that I have." Then the marriage is declared and a final warning given: "What God has joined together let no one put asunder."

A prayer, a blessing, and a kiss, and they are married.

Safer, at least for the woman, than the arrangement into which Samson and his Philistine bride entered. But serious, nonetheless. Whatever else marriage is, it's not for sissies.

SATURDAY IN PROPER 14

Pss 107:33–43, 108:1–6 (7–13) * 33
Judges 16:1–14
Acts 7:30–43
John 5:1–18

". . . while I am making my way,
someone else steps down ahead of me."
JOHN 5:7

Years after being struck by a car, I remain unsteady on my feet. Walking down the subway steps is a shaky thing for me: I must hold onto the railing, and I cannot go very fast. I do remember that once I could run down a flight of stairs, but I no longer remember what that was like.

Sometimes I begin my descent into the 110th Street station, and hear the train doors opening to the platform below. There is not much time. Other people rush by me down the stairs, and I hold the handrail tight: I am afraid of being knocked down. I cling to the rail and walk down, one step at a time. Once down, I cross more quickly to the turnstiles and slide my Metrocard through the slot. Then across the platform. Still, I am often the last one to reach the train itself. Many times, the door slides maddeningly shut just as I reach it, leaving me with no choice but to hope the next train comes soon.

The man by the pool experienced this disappointment regularly. The pool was a miraculous one: sometimes the waters began to churn, and the first one to get in the pool when it began to churn would be healed: that was why sick people stayed around it all day, why the man who had been ill for thirty-eight years was there.

But he was slow. He had no one to help him move. Other sick people were faster and surer than he was. In all these years, he was never the first one in the churning water.

He needed his Lord. The stock miracles, too much like magic, weren't working for him. His illness was his own and his healing would have to be his own, too, not someone else's. Not a lottery biased toward the strong.

SUNDAY, PROPER 15

Pss 118 * 145
Judges 16:15–31
2 Corinthians 13:1–11
Mark 5:25–34

There was a woman who had been suffering
from hemorrhages for twelve years.
MARK 5:25

We don't know her age, this nameless woman, and so we don't know if it was, as the Bible would put it, "still with her after the manner of women." Maybe she was young and had this unnatural bleeding, weakened by it while she tried to care for her children and her husband and her animals and her vegetable garden and her house. Or maybe she was well past the change of life, and this bleeding was a sign of something very wrong, a slow death she carried with her everywhere she went.

Her condition is interesting to the evangelist, I suppose, because it rendered her persistently unclean, contagious in that uncleanness. And that must certainly have added to her wretchedness: her husband and even her children, for instance, couldn't touch her if she had an issue of blood. But to me, it is the twelve years that stands out: twelve years is a long time to be ill. The woman must have tried every remedy she could think of, to no avail.

A person with a chronic illness gets good and tired of doctoring. Tired of friends' recommendations of this or that miracle-worker, this or that new vitamin, new drug, new operation. Well-meant suggestions begin to feel like unfair demands: You want me to what? Go to the hospital your cousin went to? Go see your doctor instead of mine? Try the medicine you read about in the paper? Hey, I've got an idea: how about you just leave me alone? The sheer boredom of illness and pain set in long before twelve years has passed. I am impressed at the energy of the woman's approach to Jesus, pressing forward in the crowd to touch the hem of his garment. Many people would have been too discouraged by too many false starts even to try one more time.

With all that her illness must have taken from her, it seems not to have taken away her hope. Hope of something better helped her hang on for all those years, until the day came when her hope was rewarded.

MONDAY IN PROPER 15

Pss 106:1–18 * 106:19–48
Judges 17:1–13
Acts 7:44–8:1a
John 5:19–29

*"... the hour is coming when all who are
in their graves will hear his voice ..."*
JOHN 5:28

A favorite professor has died: eminent in his field, internationally known, and universally respected. Although his health had been failing for several years, he died in the best possible way: at his computer terminal working on his next scholarly article.

The news of his death traveled fast over the Internet: the seminary, the bishop's office, all the clergy, the network of old students and former colleagues. We will keep you informed about funeral plans, the bishop's office said. But no word came that week, and no word the second week, either. He was an elderly bachelor; equally elderly cousins were all that remained of his family, and it was hard to find them. And so this eminent man's body remained in the hospital morgue for more than a week.

It's a disgrace, we all said. It seemed so cold and cruel that he was there among the unknowns, when there were so many waiting to pay public tribute to him.

But of course, he was already in heaven, with the unknowns and the famous and everyone else. Where his earthly body was did not concern him. Disgrace was not a meaningful concept to him any more, and neither was honor. We are the only ones who feel those things: our professor was fine. He has other things with which to occupy his new timelessness, new music to sing, new words beyond the words that had formed so much of what he was to us. And the clear voice of God, audible in a new way that leaves no room for doubt.

⅄TUESDAY IN PROPER 15

Pss (120), 121, 122, 123 * 124, 125, 126, (127)
Judges 18:1–15
Acts 8:1–13
John 5:30–47

"Come, let us go up against them. . . .
When you go, you will come to an unsuspecting people."
JUDGES 18:9, 10

What seemed clear to the Israelites back then isn't so clear to us: they seem untroubled by embarking upon a series of wars of naked conquest, taking the land from the people who live there and killing as many of them as they can. They understand the rightness of this to consist in the land having been promised to them by God. There seems to be no ethical dilemma in this matter. So much suffering inflicted on the people whose land they will enter and win seems not to be a concern.

Whatever its uses may have been in biblical times, the idea of the promised land hasn't aged well. "A land without people for a people without a land" early Zionists enthused about Palestine, seeming not to notice that, actually, there were people living there, that they had lived there for centuries. Arguing for a Jewish state of Israel on the basis of biblical promises about the promised land and the chosen people made about as much sense as giving Manhattan back to the Native Americans. There are compelling arguments for Muslims, Jews, and Christians to share the Holy Land and its sacred sites, but the notion of a promised land isn't one of them. In modern times, it has caused nothing but pain and misunderstanding.

The chosen-ness of the chosen people has meant different things to different ages. When these texts were new, it meant that God was on their side, and so they were certain to triumph against all odds. Later, they weren't so sure: sometimes they wondered if their suffering itself were not the sign of their chosen-ness, showing fidelity to God in the face of overwhelming temptation to despair. Since the Holocaust, most people would agree that the example of Jewish courage and resilience in rising from the very ashes of genocide has been a light to the nations.

But righteousness in one generation does not confer it upon the next. You don't inherit it. I may have done wonderful things yesterday, but that doesn't mean that everything I do from then on will be wonderful. The relationship between the chosen people and God is new every morning, full of blessed possibility but also full of moral risk, and how they will live out their chosen-ness will determine their tomorrows.

WEDNESDAY IN PROPER 15

Pss 119:145–176 * 128, 129, 130
Judges 18:16–31
Acts 8:14–25
John 6:1–15

When Jesus realized that they were about
to come and take him by force to make him king,
he withdrew again to the mountain by himself.

JOHN 6:15

There are enough people who mistakenly believe themselves called to positions of power and fame, with disastrous results, that one who knows he is not ought to be respected in that opinion. But the crowd will not take no for an answer; Jesus can't be among them as an equal. They won't allow it.

It is equality for which he longs, this man who is like no other man. He must not lean on any power on earth, in order to make it clear to us all where his power is from. Otherwise, we will think we can become him through our political astuteness, our strong intellect, our sheer guts. If Jesus' power derives from the world, like all our other powers, he can add nothing to what we already have. He'll be just another king—an extraordinary one, perhaps, but different only in degree from other kings. He will not be God and man. He will not be a savior.

Later, he tells a perplexed Pontius Pilate that his kingdom is not of this world. We always take that to mean that he will reign in heaven, but it could just as well mean that he understands the true source of earthly power. None of it is really from us. It's all from God.

We think we want God to be in charge, but that usually means we want God to appoint us regent over the things within our grasp. We talk about a kingdom that is not of this world, but hope that somehow God will hand us a slice of the earthly power we secretly crave. We worship a crucified God, but somehow still think that our faith will always save us from harm. For all that we know about Jesus, we haven't gotten too far beyond Pilate, or the enthusiastic would-be king-makers in this story.

The human ego is such that we all want to be king, although few will own up to it. Perhaps it is Jesus' refusal of a crown, more than anything else, that marks him as distinct from us in his god-ness. Earthly dominion can't take him home to the right hand of the Father. Only a crown of thorns will do that.

THURSDAY IN PROPER 15

Pss 131, 132, (133) * 134, 135
Job 1:1–22
Acts 8:26–40
John 6:16–27

"I alone have escaped to tell you."
JOB 1:19

This phrase becomes full of foreboding as it is repeated, four times in quick succession, while Job's tragedies pile on top of one another, transforming his serene, sensible, prosperous, and seemingly safe life into an insane contest of escalating pain. We learn by the second appearance of the messenger to dread his coming. We know what he will say: *I alone have escaped to tell you.*

Surviving a devastation changes your world. It was charmed, before: bad things happened to people, but they didn't happen to you. But now you live somewhere new, a fearsome place forested with sharp things pointed straight at your eye, of things that might at any moment burst into flame, of dangerous heights, collapsing floors. Before, disaster seemed remote: now, it seems likely.

No wonder people who have suffered are sorely tempted to hide themselves away. It takes no courage to lead a charmed life: you just accept the things that come to you, and you accept them as your due. You don't know any better. But to take full pleasure in the goodness of life is brave, is brave in one who has suffered greatly. His temptation is always to brace himself against further loss, and in bracing himself against pain he also becomes impermeable to joy.

How do they survive? we ask ourselves when we read of terrible things: people who lose their whole families, who lose their limbs, all their money. I couldn't live through that, we say. But you could if you had to. The ending of the book of Job as we have it today, with everything returned to him a hundredfold, is spurious: it wasn't part of the earliest versions of the story. The original ends with Job and God facing each other, God almighty and Job all alone. There is nothing in the end but God; Job loses it all, as we will surely lose it all. There he stands, stripped of all his imagined entitlements, but still, in the oldest versions of this old story, a person to whom God speaks.

FRIDAY IN PROPER 15

Pss 140, 142 * 141, 143:1–11 (12)
Job 2:1–13
Acts 9:1–9
John 6:27–40

"Skin for skin!"
JOB 2:4

Ouch! Stern and bloody, the idea that our suffering is retribution for our sin. And attractive, too: it encourages us to think that there is a way out of the inevitability of pain, that we can govern our behavior in such a way as to avoid it altogether.

When my stepson was killed by a drunken driver, a friend of my husband's called to express his condolences. He didn't know anything about the particulars of the accident. *So, was he on a motorcycle?* he wanted to know.

That was odd: Ross didn't have a motorcycle, and the friend had no reason on earth to think he had ever ridden one. But still he asked: *Was he on a motorcycle?*

I know what he was really asking: If I keep my own son off motorcycles, can I ensure that I will never be in your shoes? Tell me what I must do to keep your tragedy far away from my door, and I will do it, no matter what it is. Tell me there was something Ross did that he shouldn't have done that caused his death, tell me that he was unwise or foolish in some way, so I can instruct my own son not to do that foolish thing and thereby preserve his life. What must I do to save him?

It was only temporarily hurtful, this strange and hidden plea, because the fear behind it was so obvious and so real. No, there was no motorcycle. Just a chance encounter with another driver who'd been drinking for a day and a half. Just the wrong place at the wrong time. Nothing more.

No, there is nothing you can do or avoid doing that will ensure that you will never know such a sorrow. The future is a mystery, and the past does not control it. Some things that happen in life have causes that are easy to see; others strike from a sunny sky. Be as careful as you can, and as wise. Evade what sorrow you can evade. But none of us knows what the future will hold, for good or ill, and none of us can orchestrate it.

SATURDAY IN PROPER 15

Pss 137:1–6 (7–9), 144 * 104
Job 3:1–26
Acts 9:10–19a
John 6:41–51

Then he got up and was baptized, and after
taking some food, he regained his strength.
ACTS 9:18–19

This conversion took a lot out of Paul. No wonder he needed nourishment.

Still, eating wasn't the most important thing—and he must have been hungry, not having eaten for three days. Baptism came first. They must have all trooped down to the river and Paul must have waded in with a few of his new Christian friends, and they must have lowered him backwards into the water until he was completely immersed and then righted him again, and then they must have waded back out and put a blanket around him and walked him back to their house. And only then was it time to eat.

Paul was already accustomed to making sacrifices for his faith. He'd been doing that in his relentless pursuit of Christians for some time now, had little else in his life besides his crusade. The hardship of his new life wouldn't be much different from the hardship of his old one; Paul was a creature of extremes, and put his whole self into everything he did. He already knew there was a cost, and he already knew himself to be equal to it.

There's a cost to everything we want. We say no to something every time we say yes to something else. There are turning points in life that close off one road to us forever, so that we can journey further down the road we truly long to travel. So we'd better choose well, and honor our best desires: we could be left, someday, with nothing else.

SUNDAY, PROPER 16

Pss 146, 147 * 111, 112, 113
Job 4:1–6, 12–21
Revelation 4:1–11
Mark 6:1–6a

And immediately I was in the spirit . . .
REVELATION 4:2

Don't make your prayer a job. It's a gift. Don't make it a grim and costly ticket you must buy in order to gain admittance to the divine love; you're already there.

When you begin to exercise it's hard. You don't feel well. You don't like to sweat. Moving hurts. Everyone else is stronger and faster and looks better. You know that years of not moving have been bad for you, and now you feel like you're being punished for it. But you keep going.

And soon you begin to feel different. Wonderful. Soon you love to move, even love to sweat, soon your body loves it: it's what your body's made to do. Soon you feel strong. Soon you don't care what other people look like. Soon you don't feel guilty any more. You're doing good things for the body God gave you, and you're being blessed every time you do them.

Spiritual discipline is just like that. It can be hard at first. You can feel guilty and inadequate at first. I should have been praying and reading scripture already, you think. I don't do this right. Other people do it better.

But prayer's what you're created to do. You are naturally good at it: God made you that way. Soon you don't care what other people do, how long they've been doing it, whether they're better at it than you are. Soon you just love it for its own sake. Soon you hardly remember what made you feel guilty about it.

If you have trouble with the word "discipline," you won't later on, not after you get going in a routine that blesses you. In the meantime, use the word "practice." It's the same thing.

MONDAY IN PROPER 16

Pss 1, 2, 3 * 4, 7
Job 4:1; 5:1–11, 17–21, 26–27
Acts 9:19b–31
John 6:52–59

*. . . human beings are born to trouble
just as sparks fly upward.*
JOB 5:7

Once I get over this hump, you tell yourself, things'll be fine. But then something else happens, and something else. After enough time passes, you grasp something important about life: it's never going to be smooth. It will never be problem-free. It's a series of challenges. The only thing that stops it is death: then you have no more challenges and can just lie in your box and get some rest for a change. But not until then.

So if we're going to be all right, we'd better find a way to do it that doesn't depend on life being trouble-free. Eliphaz the Temanite—who hasn't had the trials Job has had, not yet anyway—at least knows where to go with them: we don't have anywhere to take our troubles but God. We can't lift them ourselves, and nobody else we know can, either. Everyone else has his own heavy weights to carry. Even those who love us dearly can't take our burdens away, although their love does help us bear them better.

We need to be in relationship, conversation, even argument with God constantly—before things go wrong, as well as after they have. Unlike other knowledge, which is something we can acquire, we come to know God by seeking God. It is in the process of searching for God itself that God lives. Then we have a matrix in which to experience everything good and everything bad, an abiding presence that we learn to know and even *feel* over time.

Knowing that trouble is a constant saves us from many pointless activities, such as keeping score to see who's getting off easier than we are, or trying to fix things so that nothing bad ever happens to us. Being angry at God because we have trouble in our lives. Thinking that our woes are worse than everyone else's. Living in fear of adversity. Trouble is not an aberration. It's normal to have it.

But we will never have it without God beside us. We never face it alone.

ⱽTUESDAY IN PROPER 16

Pss 5, 6 * 10, 11
Job 6:1–4, 8–15, 21
Acts 9:32–43
John 6:60–71

All the widows stood beside him, weeping
and showing tunics and other garments
that Dorcas had made when she was with them.
ACTS 9:39

My brother John walked through the lobby of our brother David's apartment building and out the front door. *Hi, Dave,* somebody said from across the room. John started when he heard it, and then he remembered: he was wearing David's leather hat. Our brother had just died, and not everyone had gotten the word. Somebody saw the hat go by, and it was Dave.

When someone wonderful dies, the people who loved them cling to the things they used every day: drink from her favorite teacup, wear his hat, her sweater, read from his Bible instead of their own. I prefer my father's prayer book to the one I received for my ordination: it has his marginal notes in it, old bulletins from long-ago church services, funeral cards from the funerals of people who've been in heaven for years.

Dorcas's friends were all widows. They knew all about bereavement and loss. They knew about going to bed with a shirt, as if it still contained the one who wore it. They knew about talking to an empty chair, about moving around a silent house, about breakfast alone.

They already knew about the odd comfort inanimate objects can give, and so they got out all the lovely things Dorcas had made. Her spirit inhabited them, for those who loved her. They had become holy.

In a drawer, I have sheaves of my father's sermons. Sermons and sermons and sermons, for every Sunday of the year and every feast day. He could not have been a more different preacher from me; we were not at all alike in the pulpit. I will never use them.

But I will never throw them out.

WEDNESDAY IN PROPER 16

Pss 119:1–24 *12, 13,14
Job 6:1; 7:1–21
Acts 10:1–16
John 7:1–13

When I say, "My bed will comfort me, my couch will ease my complaint," then you scare me with dreams . . .
JOB 7:13–14

aggh. I awaken suddenly with a syllable of no language I know in my throat. It was a terrible dream: married to Q but somehow still connected to an old boyfriend who couldn't let go, desperately trying to get back home, full of guilt, unable to explain, unable to understand how all this had come about, hating all of it.

It takes me a moment to calm down. I am here in our house, in our bed. Q is next to me sleeping. None of this has really happened. It was just a dream.

Why *that* old boyfriend? What was he doing in my dreams? Does this mean he's died or something? Could be—he's no spring chicken. There was a time when I dreamed delightfully of him, but that was a long time ago.

Your life shows up in your dreams in so many odd ways: disguised as something else, people out of place and out of time, people who don't belong, doing things they would never do in real life.

And each one is a code, a message from your spirit to your mind—a vague one, but not without meaning.

The careful editing of conscious life does not go on in dreams: they are wild and free, and will do anything to get their point across. They offend us with their images: *I don't think about sex like that!* you say, embarrassed, when you wake from one. *I'm not violent like that!*

They are only dreams. If we do not study them, they will fade from memory. If we do, we will tease out important strands of meaning and be the better for it. Either way, they will do us no harm.

THURSDAY IN PROPER 16

Pss 18:1–20 * 18:21–50
Job 8:1–10, 20–22
Acts 10:17–33
John 7:14–36

"How does this man have such learning,
when he has never been taught?"
JOHN 7:15

In India one morning, walking through a large and busy temple complex filled with people carrying flowers and coconuts filled with milk as morning offerings to the god, people coming to pray, Hindu priests walking back and forth, a quiet scene in one corner caught my eye: a young boy and a priest, sitting cross-legged on the floor, facing each other. The boy was reading from a scroll; the priest listened intently. Someday the boy would be a priest. This was how he studied to become one, at the feet of his teacher, who gives him the gift of the wisdom and lore he has received.

This was in 2001, but the scene was ancient, this apprenticeship between the boy and the priest. That was how priests and scribes studied in Jesus' time, too: a student under a master. Often the student lived with the master from a young age. In the Bible, we see the young Samuel living such a life, under the tutelage of old Eli.

It seems informal to us, but it must have been a very complete education for its purpose. And it was an education Jesus didn't have: he hadn't come up under the direction of a master people knew, to whose prestige he could refer skeptics.

Credentials symbolize knowledge: if you've been to such-and-such a school and gotten a diploma, you must know what you needed to know to get it. The diploma stands for the work you did. People have some idea of what you can do even before they meet you.

Of course, the reverse isn't true: if a credential proves competence, the absence of one doesn't prove incompetence. It doesn't prove anything, only that you didn't go to school. Someone who wants to know what you know can't use the shorthand of a diploma to find out. He must inquire.

Faith in Jesus required that people listen to him and watch him. He lacked credentials. There was no shortcut to knowing him, and no substitute. Theological schooling has certainly changed—at least here it has!—but that part hasn't.

FRIDAY IN PROPER 16

Pss 16, 17 * 22
Job 9:1–15, 32–35
Acts 10:34–48
John 7:37–52

"Have any one of the authorities or of the Pharisees believed in him?"
JOHN 7:48

At least one of them had: Nicodemus did. There were probably others. We hear council member Gamaliel, in the book of Acts, arguing in favor of caution in persecuting the early Christians. And, still later, Paul the Pharisee, who becomes the apostle of the new faith to the Gentiles.

The Pharisees suffer from their commitment to group-think. *Does the boss agree? Is it like other things we do? Did we invent it? Does it fit into our system, allowing most of it to remain unchanged?* It is hard for any group to embrace something new if the answer to any of those questions is "no"; it can refuse its only hope for survival and not see it.

Of course, the Pharisees did not become extinct. They just didn't embrace Christ. They continue to the present day: the deeply observant Jewish Hasidim are their spiritual descendants. They were the sect of first-century Judaism that could survive into modern times, whose commitment to the law was the only thing they could carry out of Jerusalem. Their faith was portable, as was Christianity. You could be a good Jew anywhere, as it is also true for Christians. They didn't need the temple in Jerusalem and its rituals, as we did not. The two were never far apart.

SATURDAY IN PROPER 16

Pss 20, 21:1–7 (8–14) * 110:1–5 (6–7), 116, 117
Job 9:1; 10:1–9, 16–22
Acts 11:1–18
John 8:12–20

Let me alone . . .
JOB 10:20

After a hard day that was even harder than you thought it would be. After you've shaken five hundred hands. After ten hours without having seen or spoken with anybody over four years old. After eight back-to-back appointments, one of which cost you your lunch break. After your team loses the game; after you lose your job.

Sometimes you don't want to come in from outside and give a detailed account of your day. You don't want to answer the phone calls on the answering machine right away.

You want to sit in a chair and look at the wall. Or take a long, sweet-smelling bath. Or go out into the garden and pull some weeds, bending, stretching, pulling—anything but talking.

You love them. You'd like to cuddle without talking and or the expectation of anything spicier. You'd like to sit, each in his or her own chair, and read the paper, finally. You'd like to hold your child in your lap and rock back and forth in the rocking chair, listening to the cars pass by outside.

They may not let you do any of these things. People don't always understand why we want to be left alone. How depleted we can become in the course of a day. And people don't always understand how sweet and silent love can be.

Oh, that's okay. You can swing into action for another hour or two and give everybody what they need. And then, finally, in the night, nothing stirring but you—or in the morning, after an exhausted sleep, before anyone else is awake—your blessed silence.

SUNDAY, PROPER 17

Pss 148, 149, 150 * 114, 115
Job 11:1–9, 13–20
Revelation 5:1–14
Matthew 5:1–12

When Jesus saw the crowds, he went up the mountain;
and after he sat down, his disciples came to him.
Then he began to speak, and taught them, saying . . .
MATTHEW 5:1–2

Hmmn. Taught whom? It sounds here like it was just the disciples—that he retreated from the press of the crowd and offered this famous teaching to his disciples alone. Not the picture we usually see in our minds of the Sermon on the Mount, in which the crowd, not just the disciples, is Jesus' audience.

What would it mean if it were a private teaching, one just for the disciples? Certainly the oddness of the paired thoughts in the beginning of it, what we now call the Beatitudes, should make sense to the disciples, who had lived with Jesus and knew his way of inverting the world's values. It is the poor who are blessed, the meek, those who mourn, not the ones we think are happy: the rich, the powerful, the successful. The disciples knew Jesus well enough to expect things like this from him. They would get it better than the crowds would.

Or would they? Over and over, we see them *not* getting it, these most intimate friends of Jesus. They continue to jockey for position even after he has told them that position is impermanent, that it carries with it an awesome responsibility they may not have counted on. They are unrealistic in their assessment of what they can and cannot do. They are vain and competitive with each other and with other people. They look down on children, on humble people. They don't understand why the crucifixion has to happen, and they all run away when it does.

So maybe our mental picture of Jesus talking to the crowd, using a mountain as a speaking platform, is something like it really was when he spoke. Maybe it was clear, out there for anyone to hear who had ears to hear, as he put it more than once. And maybe sometimes the very people who ought have understood it best took the longest to catch on to what he meant.

MONDAY IN PROPER 17

Pss 25 * 9, 15
Job 12:1–6, 13–25
Acts 11:19–30
John 8:21–32

*"You will know the truth,
and the truth will make you free."*
JOHN 8:32

There was another thing that was going to make people free—what was it, now?

Ah, yes, over the train gate of the death camp at Auschwitz, a scrolled metalwork sign: *Arbeit Mach Frietag.* Work Will Make You Free. That's what people saw when they got off the train. The next thing they saw might have been Dr. Mengele, quietly pointing his finger to the right and to the left, the first of many sortings of who would live and who would die. It's true that a lot of work went on in that camp. But it didn't make a single prisoner free.

Arbeit Mach Frietag was a cruel lie, dangling hope in front of people who had reached the last stop on the train to despair. Well, does the truth make us free, then? Why does Jesus say that?

Because all human oppression, of any kind, is erected on a foundation of lies. It presupposes the inferiority of the other and derives from that presupposition the fraudulent right to do him/her harm. It assumes freedom for the self and the community in which it resides, and derives rights from that assumption, rights that it denies to others. And the lies turn inward just as readily, in a thousand ways, erecting a self-image other than the image of God that is the true one in every person. We oppress ourselves with our feelings of unworthiness and shame, with fear, with unshakable anger. We convince ourselves that God would not receive us if he really knew who we were, forgetting that it is God alone who really does know, not we ourselves.

There are pacts of silence in love, even in love that's strong and sturdy, love that lasts a lifetime. There are things you just don't say, because you know where the soft spots are and you don't want to pierce them; you know exactly what would go right to the heart, so you keep quiet. And so you don't ask certain things, and don't mention certain things. There are failures and weaknesses that need not be spoken aloud, except in very careful circumstances, and those circumstances are few. He already knew he had those failures and weaknesses.

The truth is powerful, and its use as a weapon is not always a healing thing. Many things are true that ought not to be said, but aggressive truth-tellers plunge their daggers squarely into the heart of their victims and then, wide-eyed and hurt to be rebuked for their cruelty, defend themselves for the hurt they do: *Well, I was only telling the truth!*

That is one of those "true lies," like *Arbeit Mach Frietag.* Yes, what she said was true. But telling the truth wasn't all she was doing.

V TUESDAY IN PROPER 17

Pss 26, 28 * 36, 39
Job 12:1; 13:3–17, 21–27
Acts 12:1–17
John 8:33–47

All of you are worthless physicians.

JOB 13:4

I love all my doctors, even the tall, gaunt neurologist who never smiles. I love their engineers' curiosity about the elegant systems of the human body, their weary patience. One of them moonlights as a standup comic to blow off steam. Another backs out of the room discreetly when he catches me with my shirt off—odd, for someone who has seen me in as many compromising positions as he has. The pacemaker doctor teases me about having fainted in church, not one but *four* times. *Have you ever considered another line of work?*

Well, whether you love them or not is irrelevant, my daughters tell me severely when we talk about an upcoming hospitalization. You have other friends. What matters is how up-to-date they are. You need the very best.

I think mine are pretty good. But I know that I myself am the most important member of my health care team; my health is between me and God, with more than a little help from my friends in white. I am the one who must keep track of what happens and ask the right questions. And I must decide how—or whether—I will accept what they can do.

What a blessing, all this care. Medicine available when I need it. Time to rest when I need to. Hardly anyone in the world has it anywhere near this good.

Job's friends weren't really useless physicians: they weren't even doctors at all. He was just mad because their advice didn't help him much. In the end, he had to learn what everyone who is ill must know: nobody but you can come to terms with your illness. Medical people can help you, but in the end, it *is* what it *is*, and you and God face it together.

WEDNESDAY ON PROPER 17

Pss 38 * 119:25–48
Job 12:1; 14:1–22
Acts 12:18–25
John 8:47–59

Oh, that thou wouldst hide me in the grave ...
JOB 14:13

We look like defeated prizefighters when we've been crying: puffy eyes, swollen, mottled faces. We want to hide until we've had a chance to splash with cold water, find our sunglasses and put them on, but people can tell even then. So we are embarrassed; somebody has seen our weakness. Instinctively, perhaps, we are reluctant to let this happen: you don't want to show your soft underbelly to another animal. You don't know what might happen.

Many people protect themselves from this dangerous vulnerability by converting their sorrow into anger. The advantage of this is that anger is energizing, full of adrenalin, ready to put its fist through the wall. It feels a lot better than sorrow, which drains you of energy and confidence. The disadvantage is that it is one layer away from what's really going on with you: you're really *not* angry, and if you habitually transpose all your sorrow into spleen, you'll lose the ability to tell which is which. You're really brokenhearted, but not too many people will investigate that fact as long as you're still punching the wall.

We are a paradox: we long for people to know us truly, and that someone might do so is also our worst fear. What if someone is close enough to see my fear: mightn't he take advantage of my weakness? Well, he might. But you will choose the person to whom you reveal yourself, and you will choose someone you trust. And, if you trust no one, you will want to pray for the gift of faith in God, and for the grace of trust in the human community.

THURSDAY IN PROPER 17

Pss 37:1–8 * 37:19–42
Job 16:16–22; 17:1, 13–16
Acts 13:1–12
John 9:1–17

Some were saying, "It is he."
Others were saying, "No, but it is someone like him."
JOHN 9:9

The formerly blind man was out of his normal context, and people who had known him for years didn't recognize him. I doubt that anyone had really looked at him in a long time. Maybe nobody *ever* had. He had been "that blind man" for so long that his blindness had become the most important thing about him. Maybe the only important thing.

But no one fact about any of us sums us up. He had always been more than his disability, whether anyone else knew it or not. His healing did not make a new man of him. It just set the old one free.

Surely one of the greatest challenges he faced in his new life as a sighted person was the adjustment the people in his life made—or didn't make—in the way they interacted with him. We meet his parents later in the story, for instance: it would be rare for the family of such a person not to have arranged their lives around his needs. They must have been extremely protective of him from the time he learned to walk. It would be hard to let go of that.

Who are you? Are you your job? Your marriage? Your health? We aren't any one of these things forever—all are passing away. Just children of God, each of us, unique and wonderfully—differently—formed.

FRIDAY IN PROPER 17

Pss 31 * 35
Job 19:1–7, 14–27
Acts 13:13–25
John 9:18–41

"Ask him; he is of age."
JOHN 9:21

The authorities come to the house. They want to talk to our son. *They are not happy. Our son didn't do anything wrong and neither did we, but we are afraid. He has been disabled all his life and maybe he was so excited by his healing that he didn't answer them with the proper respect. They seem angry. We are afraid to talk to them.*

Our children are old enough to speak for themselves. But they don't feel as old to us as they look to the rest of the world. They're not as mature as they might be, we can see that. Their judgment isn't always the best. They need us.

But probably the thing they need most from us is not our help. They probably need our confidence more, our trust that they can manage on their own. We don't help them by doing their lives for them: we just delay their maturation, and that never helps anyone. The best way to help them is to let them do things on their own, asking our advice if they need it. To let them risk falling, and let them fall, as we did when they were learning to walk.

Nothing is harder to do. And nothing is more important.

Christians are often told to bear one another's burdens. But we are never told to inhibit one another's growth. Carry a child everywhere and he won't walk. Carry a young adult everywhere and he won't stand. He won't know for sure that he can.

We won't be here forever. We need to leave behind people who can manage without us. If we do otherwise, we will not have done them a favor—no matter how much we loved them.

SATURDAY IN PROPER 17

Pss 30, 32 * 42, 43
Job 22:1–4, 21–23:7
Acts 13:26–43
John 10:1–18

Would he contend with me in the greatness of his power?
No; but he would give heed to me.

JOB 23:6

One thing that cannot escape even the most inattentive reader of scripture is the freedom many of the writers feel to argue with God. They complain bitterly, shake their fists, haul God into an imaginary court, demand God's attention *right now*. They base all this on the relationship they have with God: *You are you and I am I, so where the heck are you?! We are covenanted! Step up to the plate!* These people don't mind a fight.

And neither does the Almighty, it seems. Nobody is ever struck by lightning for arguing with God.

They appeal to God on the basis of who they know God to be. *Don't act in a way unworthy of yourself*, they shout, and God hears them.

Job will soon understand, if he does not already, that he will not win this argument: he is fighting for life to be fair, and it is not. It is unfair and uneven. The mythic initial setting of the book, the court of heaven with God giving Satan free rein to torture Job, ought not to obscure its more essential truth: we don't know where all our suffering comes from, and we're not going to know. We can be angry about it, and our anger is never held against us. It is heard and, in the hearing, it is honored.

ꜜ SUNDAY, PROPER 18

Pss 63:1–8 (9–11), 98 * 103
Job 25:1–6; 27:1–6
Revelation 14:1–7, 13
Matthew 5:13–20

. . . but if salt has lost its taste . . .
MATTHEW 5:13

B ut salt *doesn't* lose its taste. Salt is a mineral; its saltiness is inte-
gral to it. If it's not salty, it's not salt.

Be who you truly are. Present the truth of you. The basic you-
ness of you, to God. That's all you really have anyway, and it's all
God really wants.

Those who live in the truth, live in Christ. This is true even if
they have never heard of Jesus; they don't have to be in our club to
be beloved of God and live a godly life, and God doesn't check with
us about who should be allowed into his kingdom.

This thought would be troubling to many Christians, who have
been taught that membership in the club *is* necessary in order to
avoid the fires of hell. But it is not membership that makes us holy:
it is our *salt*. Our truth. The sorting of people into in-groups and
out-groups, as beloved a human pastime as it is, is not a holy one. It
is extremely worldly. It's about power and recognition, exclusion
and hierarchy—all things to which Jesus of Nazareth seems to have
been strangely indifferent.

A person can be very busy in the service of the church, running from meeting to meeting, organizing services and projects,
and not notice for a long time that all his salt has run out of a hole
in his pocket. He fights the put-upon feeling that has descended
upon him of late, tells himself he doesn't really feel that way at all,
that he's fine, tells himself he didn't really mean to snap at three
people in one day and that anyway it's okay because everybody
understands.

We are holy first, connected with God from the very bottom of who we are, before we are anything else. The salt of the earth. We won't do anything else for very long if we don't attend to our supply of salt first.

MONDAY IN PROPER 18

Pss 41, 52 * 44
Job 32:1–10, 19–33:1, 19–28
Acts 13:44–52
John 10:19–30

"These are not the words of one who has a demon."
JOHN 10:21

It is a brave thing to be part of a power structure and yet able to see and appreciate something that might replace it. To be right there when the old is changing to the new, at the moment of its transformation, and not to be afraid.

When something new comes along, a conservative spirit in most of us eyes it with suspicion. A body at rest tends to remain at rest; most of us resent change. But some of us manage to maintain open minds. Some of us can question our questions. It takes maturity and guts to wonder aloud if it is possible that things we love might not someday be other than they are.

And yet we know it's true: every human edifice undergoes change, even religious ones. God alone is unchanging; the church is not. This we don't like at all: we hope to secure a piece of the divine immutability and hold onto it, and it seems to us that our thoughts about God deserve to be the place where that piece of immutability might permanently reside. Surely that is only fair, we think. Surely I deserve some protection from the changes of the world.

But there is no protection from the changes of the world, and we do well to be ready for them. So don't dismiss the new thing before you really know what it is. You might throw out something you're going to need later on.

TUESDAY IN PROPER 18

Pss 45 * 47, 48
Job 29:1–20
Acts 14:1–18
John 10:31–42

O that I were as in the months of old!
JOB 29:2

So many changes—none for the better—for poor old Job, the most famous unfortunate in history. But even we feel the passing of the years, and cast a wistful eye on our former powers.

How did we do the things we did in those days? Where on earth did we find all that energy? Did I really fit into those trousers? Where did these crow's-feet come from, this aching back these spider veins?

But still, I wouldn't want to go back there, not for all the tea in China. I wouldn't trade what I know and who I am now for that smooth skin or even for a back that didn't hurt. I look at photographs of my younger self: I am pretty but oddly blank, like a page that has not been written on yet. I wince when I remember things I said and did in those days: how could I have been so arrogant, so shallow, so self-centered? Ugh.

But God loved me then. Not because I was pretty: God thinks we're all beautiful. God must have known what I could be, must always have been willing to mold me, is willing even now to form me, more and more. Willing to do so until I die and step into the goodness of the larger life where all of us are in Christ and Christ is all in all.

St. Paul said that, about Christ being all in all. Job didn't know about it yet—born too soon. But he knew to hope for it: I know that my Redeemer lives, he says in the midst of his sorrows, and that I will see him my very self. He knew that, in the absence of even one tiny sign that things might be turning his way at last; they were getting worse and worse.

So I guess God was molding Job, too, helping him to get through it, as we all are molded in the midst of whatever happens to us. If we live through it, we get stronger because of it.

ⅴ WEDNESDAY IN PROPER 18

Pss 119:49–72 * 49, (53)
Job 29:1; 30:1–2, 16–31
Acts 14:19–28
John 11:1–16

Was not my soul grieved for the poor?
Bu when I looked for good, evil came . . .
JOB 30:25–26

Surely there will be a symmetry of reward and punishment in my life: surely I will derive some material benefit from my good deeds. It will be like a bank: I will deposit my goodness and withdraw prosperity, safety, health.

Well, maybe. Or maybe not. It's hard to shake, the ancient hope for that sensible equation. We can wade through oceans of evidence that life doesn't really work that way, and still we expect it. *What did I do wrong?* we wonder when evil strikes, hoping that we can somehow locate the sin that brought it on, so we can stop doing it and turn things around.

But we must find other reasons for behaving ourselves besides fear of punishment or expectation of reward, because the unfolding of our lives is much less precise and much less predictable than that easy equation.

I suppose that is the important message Job has for us: a counsel to grownups not to expect a child's reward. An introduction to a more adult relationship with a God who inhabits all human experience at once, the good and the bad, who is a stranger to none of them. A sobering sense of human smallness—it would be hard to read Job and still think humankind was the center of anything, let alone of the universe.

So unappealing is this hard lesson that someone went back and changed the book. Scholars believe that the ending, in which Job gets back even more cattle and sons and daughters than he had to begin with, is certainly a later addition. A later scribe just couldn't stand the bleakness and added a happy ending, in which everything came out right.

But it is not bleak to have a realistic view of one's position in the cosmos. We are small, and our lives are short, as full of sorrow as they are of joy. And yet living itself is lovely to us, for all that. In the midst of all his suffering, Job refused to curse God and die.

THURSDAY IN PROPER 18

Pss 50 * (59, 60) or 93, 96
Job 29:1; 31:1–23
Acts 15:1–11
John 11:17–29

*Now therefore why are you putting God to the test
by placing on the neck of the disciples a yoke that
neither our ancestors nor we have been able to bear?
On the contrary, we believe that we will be saved
through the grace of the Lord Jesus, just as they will.*
ACTS 15:10–11

Peter takes an interestingly practical approach to the law: *we haven't been able to obey it yet*, so why require it of people who didn't grow up with it? Most law and order enthusiasts wouldn't say that a law should be shelved because people don't obey it.

Of course, that *is* one way law changes in a society. Widespread disregard of marriage laws, for instance, is a common preamble to official changes in them. Widespread illegal gambling leads to legalization of gambling; widespread illegal drinking led to the repeal of Prohibition. Illegal assemblies have heralded the fall of many repressive governments and are a sure sign that the times are changing.

Always we are thrown back upon the discernment of what law is for. It embodies the moral consensus of a society. It protects the weak from exploitation by the strong. It secures the public safety. The law is never for itself alone. It has a purpose for human beings.

The law of society changes as society does. What about the law of God? It does, too, since it is law for human beings as well. We can watch it change in the pages of scripture: this moment in Acts is such a moment of change. Something will no longer be required that was required. The law will reflect a change in the community. It must, again and again, or it cannot move into the future with us.

⤳FRIDAY IN PROPER 18

Pss 40, 54 * 51
Job 29:1; 31:24–40
Acts 15:12–21
John 11:30–44

Jesus began to weep.
JOHN 11:35

Sometimes the Jesus we meet in the gospel of John seems so much larger than life that we find it hard to get close to him. He is confident, possessed of secret knowledge about many things, secret communications with God. He is given to long convoluted speeches that make hardly any sense to us, whatever they may have meant to those who first heard them. He does not shy away from identifying himself as the Son of God, and it can be hard to see the "fully human" part of "fully human and fully divine" in him.

Except here, in this one verse. This is the only record in any gospel of Jesus weeping. He goes to his friend's grave and is overcome by sorrow.

Notice that the people who see him cry are divided in their opinion of this sight. Some comment on the depth of Jesus' love for Lazarus. But others, accustomed to the larger-than-life Jesus in the rest of John, balk at it: Why is this God-man who can raise the dead stumped by the death of his friend? What's going on here?

We can't reconcile or understand how it is that God comes to us in Jesus. Fully God and fully human makes no sense, and it's not *going* to make sense—that's the scandal of the Incarnation. Sense has little to do with it; sense comes to the end of its usefulness in grasping the coming of Christ. Such knowledge as we possess of it comes to us another way.

One last human moment, then. A moment of sadness that makes sense for a human being who is bereaved. One moment, and then the mystery of who Jesus is continues.

SATURDAY IN PROPER 18

Pss 55 * 138, 139:1–17 (18–23)
Job 38:1–17
Acts 15:22–35
John 11:45–54

. . . when the morning stars sang together,
and all the heavenly beings shouted for joy . . .
JOB 38:7

So when God made the earth, there was shouting and song in heaven. Job 38 is a third creation story, even more poetic than the one in Genesis 1. It is a literature unexcelled in beauty anywhere in scripture.

One thing all three have in common, though, separated though they may be by hundreds of years, is the essential joy and goodness in creation. In Genesis 1, God admires each phase of the creation. In the second, he forms humankind out of his own desire for love, and bestows love upon the human race as well, only out of a desire that life should be "good" for us. It isn't enough that we should be. There should be goodness in life.

In the artistry of the Job account, the grandeur of what God has made sweeps across millennia and lands in front of us, beautiful beyond comprehension. It is a wonder we can even see it, we are so puny in comparison with it. Its beauty and depth answers our sorrows, in a curious way: who are we to weep when everything is such a miracle?

This is cold comfort in the acute moment of pain: we just want it to stop! But pain over time, pain that has become part of life—this pain can find healing resonance with the grandeur of the universe. My pain is part of things; it is not the whole of things. There is glory here, not just my sorrow. I have an end, and still the glory goes on.

It will not be apparent at first that any of this is in the least helpful to the suffering. But the passing of time brings it forward into the heart. Ah—we are one in this majestic creation. We are not alone in it, whatever happens, and we will not miss any of it if we will only see.

SUNDAY, PROPER 19

Pss 24, 29 * 8, 84
Job 38:1, 18–41
Revelation 18:1–18
Matthew 5:21–26

*Come to terms quickly with your accuser while
you are on your way to court with him . . .*
MATTHEW 5:25

Everyone wants to settle on the courthouse steps. Or they should want to: lawyers are expensive. By the time you're finished going to trial, you may well have little to show for the anguish of a trial even if you win. And besides, you may lose.

But sometimes people in a dispute are so angry they just can't stop. They'll risk doing themselves real harm if they think they can do harm to their opponent.

A dispute acquires a life of its own. The more you invest in its continuance, the less willing you become to see its end, and you may be the very last to realize this has happened to you. You still think you want resolution and justice, but you long ago crossed over into a thirst for vengeance. *Who would I be without my enmity?* You lose the desire to find out.

Jesus isn't really saying that being angry is equivalent to murder. He's saying that anger clings, if we let it, that it will get in the way of every good thing we attempt, intruding into things that have nothing to do with it at all. It always changes us for the worse, if we do not intentionally seek to move through it and out, finally free and clear, on the other side.

MONDAY IN PROPER 19

Pss 56, 57, (58) * 64, 65
Job 40:1–24
Acts 15:36–16:5
John 11:55–12:8

Mary took a pound of costly
perfume made of pure nard . . .
JOHN 12:3

Now, wait a minute—is this going to be another St. Francis's tunic thing? Didn't we read about a woman anointing Jesus' feet in another gospel? Wasn't she supposed to be a prostitute? It can't have been Mary of Bethany, the theologically minded sister of Martha and Lazarus, can it?

I don't think so. Everyone gets the story, but they all get the details differently. *Who* was the woman, again? And *where* were they? In drafting Mary of Bethany, John really succumbs to the confusion, but they all partake of it.

The same thing happens to Mary Magdalene in scripture: she is identified with the prostitute with the ointment, too, in a confusion that has lasted for two thousand years. The biblical writers seem to have had a hard time keeping track of the women in Jesus' life. Why? Probably because they were a little suspicious of their presence, and minimized their importance in his life and ministry. They can't have been that many women around him, they must have thought. They must all be the same one.

Blind.

But then I remember that I myself, a priest these twenty-five years, was opposed to women priests when I first heard that such a thing was being discussed. Our voices would be too high-pitched for public reading, I thought. Good Lord.

I was as well-schooled by my culture as the biblical writers were by theirs, it seems. So I am in no position to criticize.

TUESDAY IN PROPER 19

Pss 61, 62 * 68:1–20 (21–23) 24–36
Job 40:1; 41:1–11
Acts 16:6–15
John 12:9–19

*So the chief priests planned to
put Lazarus to death as well . . .*
JOHN 12:10

One by one, the logical objections to the gospel stories are "handled" by the writers.

If Lazarus was raised from the dead, then where is he now?

Well, dead.

Dead? What, again?

Yeah, the chief priests had him killed.

Oh.

If we come upon the biblical writers covering their tracks, it doesn't necessarily follow that the biblical witness is of no use to us. It helps if we take a step back from our twenty-first-century focus on journalistic truth and come closer to the goals of the first-century writers.

None of them were writing while all this was happening. Probably none of them knew anybody who was there, either. They are preserving and arranging material they have received: they are making it into a narrative. They are not covering an event for the newspaper.

But, although they are not like modern reporters, they do want people to believe that their own powerful experience of the risen Christ, decades after Calvary, is real, and connects events in the life and death of Jesus of Nazareth. They anticipate logical objections—*Where is Lazarus now?*—and try to counter them, but only because they cannot deny the grace and power that has been released in their own lives, and they want others to know that grace and power.

WEDNESDAY IN PROPER 19

Pss 72 * 119:73–96
Job 42:1–17
Acts 16:16–24
John 12:20–26

*"Unless a grain of wheat fall into the earth and dies,
it remains just a single grain;
but if it dies, it bears much fruit."*
JOHN 12:24

I, for one, do not wish to live forever. Would not want to, even if I could be assured of remaining young and strong the entire time. I want to be part of the cycle of things, to be intimate with the earth and with people, and I could not be part of it as an equal if I never made my exit. I would never have experienced its pathos as something that applied to me.

And our part of the world cannot come into its own until we leave it. We cannot make our complete contribution while we are still alive, since the most important part of it—the only *lasting* part—is what those we leave behind do with what we gave them. We more or less control our gift as long as we are here. We can set it free only by leaving it behind.

We see that our earthly walk toward death is a process of steady weakening, and physically, it *is*. But it is also the journey of the spirit toward greater and greater strength, until it finally becomes too strong for the weakened body to hold any longer. I want my spirit to progress toward that strength, to shake free, finally, of something I once loved but that has become a burden. And then I want to fly away.

THURSDAY IN PROPER 19

Pss (70), 71 * 74
Job 28:1–28
Acts 16:25–40
John 12:27–36a

"Do not harm yourself, for we are all here."
ACTS 16:28

Two New Orleans police officers are said to have taken their own lives in the days after Hurricane Katrina devastated the city. I only heard this once, and I still do not know if it was really true. News of the disaster traveled fitfully, and it was difficult to know what was so and what was not.

The newscaster didn't say why they killed themselves, but surely it had something to do with their duty. With their execution of it, one thinks. Did they despair of ever getting to the end of the rescue and recovery? Did they encounter members of their own families among the dead? Or was the memory of what they saw in the filthy water just too terrible to endure?

This prison guard began his suicide attempt because he thought the prisoners in his care had escaped: he would surely be executed anyway, if that were so. Events had spiraled out of his control, he thought. *I am trapped. I did nothing to create this situation and I can do nothing to fix it, but it happened on my watch and so I am sure to die for it.* But there was one more thing he could do, before every shred of his autonomy was taken away.

He didn't have to do it, though. The prisoners were free, but they had not run away. What kindness, he must have thought, who *are* these people? And his own conversion process began.

FRIDAY IN PROPER 19

Pss 69:1–23 (24–30) 31–38 * 73
Esther 1:1–4, 10–19 or Judith 4:1–15
Acts 17:1–15
John 12:36b–43

After Jesus had [spoken of his death to the crowd],
he departed and hid from them. Although he had performed
so many signs in their presence, they did not believe in him.
JOHN 12:36b–37

He must have had a bad response from the crowd to what he said about his own death—only that would explain why he hid. Were they indifferent? Hostile? Were some of them already crying, "Crucify him!"? Whatever they gave him back, I have a feeling it was not fear that made him hide. I think his heart was broken, and he didn't want people to see.

Always remember that Jesus was truly human as well as truly God. His heart could be broken as thoroughly as anyone else's. The humiliation of indifferent eyes upon his sorrow was as painful to him as it is to any of us.

To that humiliation must be added his own questioning of his life's work, if we are to be honest and allow our Jesus to be honest. I do not believe it is at all disrespectful to suggest this: it would be a mistake to think he knew every last detail of what would happen to him. He went forward willingly, but that doesn't mean he went forward without any doubts. Was this really the way things were supposed to work out? Was he really supposed to heal people who didn't grow in faith as a result? Had he been faithful in the path he had chosen, or was the fact that people did not believe a sign that he should have done it another way? At the end of it all, had he done the right thing?

Part of faith is the ongoing asking: *Am I on the right track? Show me the way. Turn me around if I am heading backward.* That is the way a human being believes, by following the guidance of God. And the guidance of God is unclear at times.

SATURDAY IN PROPER 19

Pss 75, 76 * 23, 27
Esther 2:5–8, 15–23 or Judith 5:1–21
Acts 17:16–34
John 12:44–50

Jesus cried aloud: "Whoever believes in me believes not in me but in him who sent me."
JOHN 12:44

The relationship between God the Christ and God the Father is intimate, but it is paradoxical. How can they be one but not identical? And isn't this all theoretical jargon anyway: how important is it, really? Of what good is this essential unity to any of us?

The most important gift the Trinity brings us is the perception of the universality of God's love. If Jesus is just God on a one-time visit, only those who know Jesus can claim to know God. But Jesus isn't God in a human suit: he *is* God and human at once, in a mysterious bond we cannot fathom. And so those who did not know the earthly Jesus can know God now through the power of the Spirit, wherever and whenever they live, adopt the Jesus story as their own story, and enter the community from the place in which they first heard and continue to hear it. The Trinity unifies all times and all places, including those still in our future, living now in the eternal present of God.

Hear how yielding Jesus is to God the Father in the Gospel of John. Later, we hear him yield also to the Spirit, the Comforter who will come to animate the church. They hand off one to another in a graceful dance, available in myriad ways to those who wish to take their hand and join in. There is a way into the living presence of God for everyone.

SUNDAY, PROPER 20

Pss 93, 96 * 34
Esther 3:1–4:3 or Judith 5:22–6:4, 10–21
James 1:19–27
Matthew 6:1–6, 16–18

. . . your anger does not produce God's righteousness . . .
JAMES 1:20

A common mistake: we keep thinking we're the instruments of God's instruction in the world, and that God endorses all the likes and dislikes of our culture. We'll go after people who don't fit in, and we'll think we're serving God as we do so.

The current Christian Marriage movement is an example of this. People should arrange their families according to biblical principles, we are told. We think this means one man and one woman who raise their children together, since that's the model of family life we see when we look around us. But then we look at scripture and noticed that some families in the Bible were polygamous, that some practiced child sacrifice, that it was considered especially holy to donate a child to the service of the priests in the temple at a very young age. We see that a man was honor bound to add his brother's widow to his stable of wives, and that any children resulting from that marriage were to be considered the dead man's offspring. The biblical family begins to looking distinctly un-suburban: which biblical family are we supposed to model our own families after?

Well, *ours*, of course! And few issues in the news lately generate as much anger as does the debate about who can and cannot marry. It's not just a difference of opinion for some of us: it's a crusade.

God's righteousness doesn't win on a field of battle. That is where human wars are fought, and the end of such conflict is never pure. Sooner or later, violence always begets violence and ill becomes those who follow the Prince of Peace.

Is God inviting you to injure someone as a means of honoring your faith in him? To harden your heart to all compassion? Listen again. That may be someone else speaking.

MONDAY IN PROPER 20

Pss 80 * 77, (79)
Esther 4:4–17 or Judith 7:1–7, 19–32
Acts 18:1–11
Luke (1:1–4); 3:1–14

"You brood of vipers!"
LUKE 3:7

Well, John the Baptist was not Dale Carnegie. He seems not to have cared at all about what people thought of him or if anyone besides his mother loved him. One comes away for this scene with the impression that he may have been a little, um, difficult.

So what had the crowd done that was so awful that it moved John to refer them as snakes? They'd come all the way out of town to the river to hear him speak and get themselves washed clean of their sins, just in case, and here the first words out of his mouth were enough to make anyone turn around and head back home.

Perhaps it was this: they came out for baptism as insurance against the consequences of their behavior, rather than to find out how to change it. *The holy man can dip you in the river and your sins will all be washed away. We'd better go.* But John was doing something else: inaugurating lives that would be different from the lives that had presented themselves to him for baptism. After his initial scolding, John responds to questions from several individuals in several different walks of life—a tax collector, a soldier, a merchant—about how they should conduct their business henceforth.

Baptism doesn't just get you "in" so you can forget about it and get on with your life. It changes your life and your priorities, or it's not baptism, no matter how holy the officiant.

It's just a warm bath.

❦ TUESDAY IN PROPER 20

Pss 78:1–39 * 78:40–72
Esther 5:1–14 or Judith 8:9–17; 9:1, 7–10
Acts 18:12–28
Luke 3:15–22

"If it were matter of crime or serious villainy,
I would be justified in accepting the complaint of you Jews;
but since it is a matter of questions about words and
names and your own law, see to it yourselves;
I do not wish to be a judge of these matters."
ACTS 18:14–15

Just a few lines, for people who think the separation of church and state is a new-fangled notion. The Romans depended on it for stability in their widespread empire: you could worship anything you wanted to, as long as you didn't try to overthrow *them*. The fact that our Jewish forebears chafed so under Roman rule makes us think it was brutal, but at this stage in its history it was comparatively benign. We notice elsewhere in the book of Acts that Paul capitalizes on his status as a Roman citizen: a citizen was a good thing to be. Most of the people under the authority of the Roman Empire were glad to be part of it.

And so Gallio the proconsul of Achaia declines to make a judgment about a strictly religious dispute. He did not want to navigate those waters. He wanted to keep his jurisdiction safe and quiet for everyone who lived in it, and he wanted to be known to his superiors as an official who could deliver that happy state of affairs.

What is government for? Is it to bring in the kingdom, or does God do that? I think its purpose is to promote justice, not necessarily righteousness; there is a difference. Justice levels the playing field, so that those who wish to strive for righteousness and those who don't give the matter any thought at all can co-exist in peace and safety.

WEDNESDAY IN PROPER 20

Pss 119:97–120 * 81, 82
Esther 6:1–14 or Judith 10:1–23
Acts 19:1–10
Luke 4:1–13

*When the devil had finished every test,
he departed from him until an opportune time.*
LUKE 4:13

Temptation didn't just come to Jesus once. When he encountered evil—as he often did—his vanquishing of it wasn't once for all. He cast out whole groups of demons, but there were always other demons waiting their turn in other places. This time, at the beginning of his ministry, his victory over temptation is temporary: the devil will be back.

Jesus thinks he sees him, now and then—when Peter tries to talk him out of giving up his life, for instance. Perhaps when his resolve weakens in the Garden of Gethsemane, although he does not mention the devil there. He sees the devil in his opponents, sometimes, and they certainly think they see the devil in him. And he sees the devil at work in his betrayal by a close friend.

It is important that we who follow him understand his temptations as real. If they were not, there was no particular victory won in resisting them, not if there was nothing here he wanted or needed anyway. But there was: he loved life, wanted to live, loved his friends and his family, loved children, loved his country, loved his tradition. Loved it all.

So when my temptations are difficult to resist, I am in good company. It is not a sign of infidelity that I long to yield, that it is difficult to hold out against it, that sometimes I fail to do so: that's what temptation *is*. Perhaps the reality of it for Jesus is the most important aspect of temptation for us: he really *does* know what it's like. We go nowhere he has not gone before, including into the dark forest of our longings for things that are not God's will for us.

THURSDAY IN PROPER 20

Pss (83) or 116, 117 * 85, 86
Esther 7:1–10 or Judith 12:1–20
Acts 19:11–20
Luke 4:14–30

They got up, drove him out of the town, and led him to the brow of the hill on which their town was built, so that they might hurl him off the cliff.
LUKE 4:29

Few things hurt more than being the object of public scorn without having earned it. People, even old friends, avoid you, as if your humiliation were contagious. You find yourself tried and convicted in the court of public opinion and you never even got a chance to testify. People who don't even know you think they know what you did.

This is precisely what happened to Jesus, of course. Was it beginning to happen already when he spoke the words that so infuriated his homefolks, or did he just see it coming? Nobody who knew and loved him wanted to hear him talk about what might unfold, but he kept trying to bring it up with his friends. *Get behind me!* he said to Peter, who loved him. But not even Peter was able to withstand the pressure of popular scorn that enveloped Jesus.

As long as they could not find the courage to stand with their murdered Lord, they saved their lives at the expense of having a real life. They were in hiding, afraid to reveal who they really were to anyone outside their small circle. Once they found it within themselves to own up to their identity, the power of Christ filled them. They saw power where before they had seen only humiliation.

Maybe that's how it is. Maybe you get your life back when you become willing to lay it down. Maybe your reputation, dragged through the mud, really becomes your own when you stand up in the midst of humiliation and assert your true self, your actual deeds, your true ideals, regardless of what anyone else thinks and regardless of what happens when you do.

FRIDAY IN PROPER 20

Pss 88 * 91, 92
Esther 8:1–8, 15–17 or Judith 13:1–20
Acts 19:21–41
Luke 4:31–37

Then she struck his neck twice with
all her might, and cut off his head . . .
JUDITH 13:8

Well, here we are again—a much more drawn-out and enticing story than that of Jael has led to another man being killed in a grisly manner by a Hebrew woman. People must have loved these thrilling tales. The beautiful Judith, with a bloody sword in one hand and Holofernes' head in the other, was a popular subject in Renaissance art. It had everything: sex, violence, with just enough salvation thrown in to make it religious.

One thing that these stories of fierce women have in common with many other Bible stories is the killing that goes on. The Ten Commandments seem far away from Judith and Jael, but it is an equal distance from Joshua and Gideon. There appear to be many situations in which it can be put aside for an eventual greater good.

People who describe themselves as "pro-life" need to remember this. The Bible is full of killing. Rarely if ever, in scripture, is life itself the final word in deciding who will live and who will die: it's always something else. In this, the Bible mirrors the rest of life: thou shalt not kill, unless thou art a soldier. Or an executioner or a judge in a state where the death penalty is the law. Or someone is trying to kill you.

Life sometimes impales us on terrible dilemmas, solomonic choices nobody ever wants to make. We choose between two lives often, much more than we think we do, directly or indirectly, and we hate doing so. Hate it when someone points out that our swollen lifestyle involves us indirectly in choosing life or death for someone else. It's not *my* fault, we say indignantly. But then we remember that whatever else the choices we must make may be, they are not simple. And nobody's hands are really clean.

SATURDAY IN PROPER 20

Pss 87, 90 * 136
Hosea 1:1–2:1
Acts 20:1–16
Luke 4:38–44

*A young man named Eutychus, who was sitting
in the window, began to sink off into a deep
sleep while Paul talked still longer.*
ACTS 20:9

Ed Towt used to do that when I preached. I'd look out at the congregation from the pulpit and there he would be, sitting bolt upright with his eyes shut. He always insisted that he wasn't asleep, that he was just resting his eyes, but I was never quite sure. Sometimes he would come in on Monday morning to take issue with something I had said the day before, but I always half thought he just took it all in through his own peculiar form of sleep-learning.

Of course, Ed died a natural death: he didn't succumb during one of my sermons. Young Eutychus wasn't so fortunate. The moral: if you think you're not going to make it through the sermon, play it safe and stay close to the ground.

Sermons are funny things. Sometimes people hear something in a sermon that wasn't there. Or a maybe it *was* there, and the preacher just doesn't know it. Sometimes a sermon seems intended for you and you alone, and you think the preacher must have read your mind; he didn't, but God can, and may have worked a modest miracle that morning. Sometimes a sermon feels just terrible to the preacher, and it's only after the service that she finds out it touched dozens of people very deeply, that it was just what they needed to hear. *Who knew?* she thinks as she goes back to the sacristy to get out of her vestments.

The most important thing about a sermon is not its length, although preachers should remember poor Eutychus and keep it under control, because most of us won't be able to raise anyone who dies from one of our sermons. The important thing is to remember that God is present in its delivery: the preacher has been appointed by God to give the word, and God will see to it that it happens. Just ask for grace, prepare as best you can, ask for grace again, open your mouth, and speak.

Amen!

SUNDAY, PROPER 21

Pss 66, 67 * 19, 46
Hosea 2:2–14
James 3:1–13
Matthew 13:44–52

Not many of you should become teachers,
my brothers and sisters, for you know that we
who teach will be judged with greater strictness.
JAMES 3:1

Q sits in his chair, the golden lamplight on his book. He will sit there for hours the night before a class, preparing his lesson. He prepares for new material, but he also reads over lessons he has taught for fifty years, lessons typed on a manual typewriter that appear limp with age and use. He never teaches anything without preparing.

Sometimes I tell him he over-prepares, but he shakes his head and smiles. Each class is new, each lesson is different in some small way. Time has passed and the world is different since the last time he taught this. Students are different. Somebody has written something new about it. Nothing is ever the same. *I used to think that of the teaching profession as kind of a priestly one*, he has said, and it is clear that he still does. I tell him that he was right, that it is. That the responsibility of it is sacred: it is the care of souls.

He began his teaching career half a century ago in Turkey. The old word for *teacher* in Turkish was roughly translatable as "holy man." Literally, it meant "man who is ready to go to Mecca." The teacher was likely to be the only literate person in a remote village, the one to whom people turned when they needed something read, something that came from the government, an authority even for people who were not his students. But later, the Turks were eager to become a modern secular nation. So they changed the word for *teacher* to something more neutral, a word roughly meaning "giver of discipline."

Are you ready to go to Mecca? I ask him. He says he'd love to go. There's nothing he doesn't love to learn, love to teach. Hours of preparation are worth it to him if he can only teach and see people learn. That seems pretty priestly to me.

MONDAY IN PROPER 21

Pss 89:1–18 * 89:19–52
Hosea 2:14–23
Acts 20:17–38
Luke 5:1–11

"And now I know that none of you,
among whom I have gone about proclaiming
the kingdom, will ever see my face again."
ACTS 20:25

A dragonfly zoomed across the patio, just three feet from Noodle's head. She sprang straight up, one paw raised like a basketball player going for a dunk. Reaching for the insect, she reached too far and did a complete backwards somersault in midair. I let out a little yelp for Q to look, but it was too late: she was neatly on the ground again, daintily washing her face and behind her ear with one paw.

You should've seen that! I told him. *She did a complete flip three feet off the ground from a standing position.* Noodle pretended not to hear me and began to wash the other side of her face with the other paw.

The dragonflies have been plentiful this summer: a good thing, since they eat mosquitoes and flies, and their very presence is a sign that the ecosystem of the garden is in tiptop shape. There have been many different kinds of dragonflies: inky black ones with luminescent blue wings, strange golden biplane ones with double-decker wings, enormous red ones whose wings glint green and gold. It was no wonder Noodle sat and watched for about an hour last night before she made her spectacular jump. They were zooming around in great numbers: I counted twelve different ones in one minute.

How splendid they all are. The cats, the hummingbirds, the dragonflies, the monarchs and viceroys and cabbage butterflies and those black butterflies whose names I don't know. Even the Japanese beetles are beautiful to look at, although beauty is as beauty does.

Now the garden is growing old. Now the insects are adults, numerous, reminding us, as they go about their business, that they were here long before we were and will be here long after we're all gone. Built to last, bugs, taken as a group, and they mostly take themselves as a group. Not like us, cerebral but ephemeral fools that we are, thinking that we can have immortality as individuals when we can't even have it as a species. We will meet again, we say when someone we love dies. And we know it is true. But we also know that it won't be like this life: this life is over when it ends. We are as prepared for eternity as the unreflective ant, clueless as to the next stage of life. But we live as though there were a next stage, as they do. They munch on their leaves in preparation for becoming pupas or laying eggs or turning into butterflies or flying away to somewhere else, and they don't know anything about any of that yet. We are just the same, working and munching and shopping and making love as if we would live forever, and we are right about that. We're wrong about immortality having anything to do with our looks or our personalities, but we're right about never really losing anything we really need.

↘ TUESDAY IN PROPER 21

Pss 97, 99, (100) * 94, (95)
Hosea 4:1–10
Acts 21:1–14
Luke 5:12–26

And it shall be like people, like priest . . .
HOSEA 4:9

The sign in front of the church tells passersby that it's St. Luke's Episcopal Church and what time the services are. At the top of the list of the church leadership, it reads: "Ministers—All the People of God." The clergy's names are listed at the bottom.

That's not just a lovely ideal: it is also true. The life of faith is not a spectator sport. If you're in it, you have a job to do. If you're not a minister yet, what are you waiting for?

Maybe you're waiting for someone to help you discern what your ministry is. The clergy have discerned and been discerned within an inch of their lives, so the ordained minister of your church is probably a good person to help you begin to think about it. But, because he or she administers a parish, the ministries that will leap to mind will probably all be located in the community of the people of God. That's what clergy think of first.

Still, because the priest's ministry is usually in the church doesn't mean yours is. The theatre of operations for the most numerous and most important part of the church, the body of the laity, is wide. Ministry can and does happen anywhere. Because the laity are numerous and carry among them all the talents the human race possesses, its ministry takes many forms.

Consecrate each one. A secular as a service may be, one thing is certain: if it is good, it is of God. Your service in the world is as much an offering to God and as important to the church as the check you put into the collection plate.

WEDNESDAY IN PROPER 21

Pss 101, 109:1–4 (5–19) 20–30 * 119:121–144
Hosea 4:11–19
Acts 21:15–26
Luke5:27–39

Wine and new wine . . .
HOSEA 4:11

Everybody in the choir was in recovery from addiction except one young woman, whose mother was. They all met in rehab. They sing only songs they've written themselves, out of their own experience. This provides more than enough material, since their experience consists of having been raised from the dead.

We made an interesting double bill: I went first, speaking about New York during the recovery effort after the bombing of the World Trade Center and New York now. Then they sang, and in between songs choir members spoke briefly about where they had been when they were drinking and using drugs and how God had led them out of there. More than one of them found the story of what New Yorkers have gained from surviving tragedy a familiar tale. They already knew about learning from something you wish with all your heart had never happened, about losing absolutely everything and then feeling the first stirrings of new life right in the ashes of what can never be regained.

Most of the songs had a heavy bass line: that and the rhythmic swaying of the choir made it impossible not to clap along. "One Day at a Time," went the refrain of one of the songs, and we sang it over and over and over. I woke this morning still hearing it, and I always pay close attention to my first waking thought.

Sufficient unto the day is the evil thereof, Jesus said. One day at a time. I can deprive myself completely of today's blessings by living in anger about yesterday or in dread of tomorrow. Yesterday is over: I can't fix anything in it. Tomorrow may not come for me: none of us get a guaranteed tomorrow. I have only today, the moment I am in right now.

Of course you have to plan for the future, as best you can. *Of course* you have to clean up the messes you made in the past, as best you can. But you can't live in either place. We only live now. If "now" is a place of pain, be present to it and let it be a piercing reminder of that for which you long. Let it burn the extraneous nonsense right out of you, as it certainly will do, leaving only the gold of what is truly important. If "now" is a place of sunshine, be present to it. There will be other moments when you will need the memory.

THURSDAY IN PROPER 21

Pss 105:1–22 * 105:23–45
Hosea 5:8–6:6
Acts 21:27–36
Luke 6:1–11

He will come to us as the showers,
like the spring rains that water the earth.
HOSEA 6:3

Maybe I'll put a few pumpkins out in the scraggly remains of the garden, to please the eyes of those who walk past. Kids may steal them, but that's okay. Winter is coming and they'll be buried in the snow anyway.

It is a garden of skeletons now: the skeletons of black-eyed susans, the dried plumes of the butterfly bushes, minus their leaves. The thick spiky leaves of iris, the thorny canes of the roses on their bamboo tripods. When the snow comes—soon—it will settle thickly on all this architecture, and the garden will be a different place. For now, fat orange pumpkins amid the bones will be a nice touch.

Pumpkins are ready after the soft fruit of the summer are gone. Their hard shells protect their tender flesh from the cold. They will last all winter, if you don't let their bottoms get wet. They are tough, the pumpkins. Winter vegetables.

The giddiness of spring excitement is different from the excitement of the coming winter: I have to work at winter excitement a bit. But it is definitely there: a fairyland of white, the piercing blue of a bright sky against melting snow, heavy clumps of snow bending the tall bamboo all the way to the ground, the delight of a crackling fire, the slow sipping of hot tea.

We will enter our rest, the garden and I, inside, hidden from the worst of the cold. And soon the gentler rains of spring will come, and we will begin it all again.

FRIDAY IN PROPER 21

Pss 102 * 107:1–32
Hosea 10:1–15
Acts 21:37–22:16
Luke 6:12–26

Sow for yourselves righteousness . . .
HOSEA 10:12

L ook, I say to Q, pointing up to the branches of the redbud tree. Oh, no—rows and rows of seed pods, poised to drop to earth and make dozens of little redbuds in the spring.

Just what we need, he says. *More redbuds*. Not that the redbud trees aren't beautiful. They're lovely in the spring, each branch edged with lavender pink flowers, pink arms that reach into the blue sky and out over the new garden. And they're lovely in autumn, with their pale yellow leaves.

Q tried for years to grow one at his old house, but not a redbud would thrive there. Then I moved and married you, he says loyally. And we've had redbuds coming up all over the property ever since. They appear in the driveway, in the tomato patch, in my flower gardens at the feet of the roses, amid the asters. We plant them in friends' gardens: Grace next door, the church across the street, Delphine across town, Mary over on Hazelwood Street. Charlotte and Chuck have a redbud now, and so do Pam and Bob.

To us, the redbud means happiness in the home: hard to grow before, and growing like a weed now. To us, it is the sign of a blessing we each waited a long time to receive. And, apparently, the redbud is a sign that our happiness isn't just for us. We're supposed to spread it around.

And this year's seedpods shake in the wind a little. Want one?

SATURDAY IN PROPER 21

Pss 107:33–43; 108:1–6 (7–13) * 33
Hosea 11:1–9
Acts 22:17–29
Luke 6:27–38

I was to them like those who lift infants to their cheeks.
HOSEA 11:4

So carefully her mother shops with her, thinking long and hard before picking up something and saying, "Hey, how about this?" She doesn't go into the dressing room with her; this young woman whose diaper she used to change six times a day doesn't want even her mother to see her undressed.

It breaks her mother's heart to see her look sidelong at the models in the posters, wearing the very clothes hanging on the rack she is walking past. They are slim as snakes, all of them, and seem so very happy: they laugh uproariously together at something off camera, something we cannot see, something that must be really, really funny. It is obvious that they have been best friends for years, all of them, beautiful thin girls whose progress through their teens has been a seamless triumph of popularity and beauty and success, girls most likely to be most likely forever.

Only one of the seven items she carried into the cubicle fit. "Well, you got some good stuff," her mother says as they walk to the car, and her daughter nods in a way not unfriendly and asks if they might stop somewhere for lunch. Her mother agrees readily and thinks that the shopping trip was certainly not as bad as it could have been. She herself feels her heart in her throat when she enters a store, even all these years after her own girlhood, remembers not being the right shape, the right height, remembers just being all wrong, somehow, everything about her wrong. How thin and beautiful everyone else was, how hulking she always felt looking in the three-way mirror, how she hated having her skinny mother looking in it with her, hated knowing that her mother was choosing her kind words so carefully, searching for encouragement to offer in the face of what was so clearly a lost cause.

They settle on a Thai place, enter, and sit down in the cool darkness. The waitress brings water and they order. Her daughter always has *mee krob*. Her daughter seems okay, talks about her plans for the evening and about Tiger Woods and why people play golf. She tells her daughter that she once knew someone who had played tennis against Arthur Ashe when they were both young, had thought sure he'd beat the socks off the skinny black kid and had learned otherwise by the end of the match. People gain control of more and more as they grow up, create and shape themselves as they come to understand that they can, that they are the primary shapers of themselves, that their impact on themselves will be more lasting than that of their parents or their friends or anyone else.

That the beginning is not the end.

SUNDAY, PROPER 22

Pss 118 * 145
Hosea 13:4–14
1 Corinthians 2:6–16
Matthew 14:1–12

Herod the ruler heard reports about Jesus; and he said to his servants, "This is John the Baptist; he has been raised from the dead, and for this reason these powers are at work in him."
MATTHEW 14:1

Herod is like Lady Macbeth: his guilt is everywhere before his eyes. He can't see anything in his world except through its lens.

We know that he was intrigued by John the Baptist, and often sent for him to discuss things with him. It was during one of these talks that John denounced him, and Herod accepted the criticism with something approaching grace. It was his wife who did not take it well.

But it was Herod who gave the order for John's execution. His own favorable disposition toward John didn't mitigate his guilt in his own eyes: it made it worse. Maybe he didn't really want to have him killed, but he could have prevented it and didn't. Same thing, in the end.

We know about our duty to do no harm—that seems clear enough. But do we have a corresponding duty to prevent the harm others may do, and it is as clear and strong an obligation? What about harm to others that originates far from us. Do we have an obligation to go and stop it? Wasn't that what Vietnam was all about? Iraq?

A pre-emptive strike against evil is a hazardous undertaking: you'd better know the danger is "clear and present," as we say. You'd better be brutally honest with yourself about what other benefits you may reap from your action. Are you really as altruistic as you appear, or do you and yours stand to benefit?

\MONDAY IN PROPER 22

Pss 106:1–18 * 106:19–48
Hosea 14:1–9
Acts 22:30–23:11
Luke 6:39–49

"Can a blind person guide a blind person?"
LUKE 6:39

Well, Helen Keller's teacher was blind, and she led a little girl who could not see, hear, or speak into the world beyond her own darkness, when nobody else had been able to reach her. It took another blind person to meet Helen in her isolation.

The bereaved often help the bereaved with grace and wisdom: they know when not to speak, know what days might be unexpectedly different. They don't expect order or consistency in other people's grief; they remember their own turmoil too well ever to be that naïve.

And someone who is not an addict usually can't help someone who is. She doesn't know exactly where the lies are, and how they function to protect the deadly habit. It takes someone who's been there, too, who continues to struggle against the same demon.

My gym is full of people who have not been in good health and are now doing what they can to become stronger. Not all of us— hardly any of us—are young and strong and shapely. But we are the best encouragers of each other.

So sharing a disability with the victim doesn't rule out a guide; on the contrary, it qualifies him. What *would* rule him out would be not wanting to be healed himself. Because you can't walk to a new place with someone who doesn't want to go there.

TUESDAY IN PROPER 22

Pss (120), 121, 122, 123 * 124, 125, 126, (127)
Micah 1:1–9
Acts 23:12–24
Luke 7:1–17

*"Lord, do not trouble yourself, for I am not worthy
to have you come under my roof. . . . But only speak
the word, and let my servant be healed."*

LUKE 7:6–7

From this passage comes the couplet that prepares the faithful at a Roman Catholic Mass to receive the sacrament. Anything is possible, it says, not because of what I bring here, which may be only my own broken spirit, but because of what Christ brings: the power to transform me.

It excites me every time I hear it: so hopeful and yet so realistic. It is never too late for us to be transformed. This moment of the Mass joins us with everyone else who has ever turned to Jesus for help.

People who are dying receive the sacrament. People who are in prison and will never be released receive it. People condemned to death receive it. The bereaved receive it. People who will never be anything but poor receive it. None of them will be magically cured of whatever ails them by receiving it, but all of them will be healed as they draw near to the body and the blood, for the life of Christ once again to become part of their own lives through this holy encounter.

Here we see that the first person to say these words was someone outside the faith—a Roman centurion. He did not belong to Jesus' inner circle or even to Jesus' religion. He brought with him only a secular power that Jesus didn't need and his own desperation. He does not mention his power: somehow, he knows that his desperation will be enough.

WEDNESDAY IN PROPER 22

Pss 119:145–176 * 128, 129, 130
Micah 2:1–13
Acts 23:23–35
Luke 7:18–35

*"For John the Baptist has come eating no bread
and drinking no wine, and you say, 'He has a demon';
the Son of Man has come eating and drinking, and
you say, 'Look, a glutton and a drunkard . . .'"*
LUKE 7:33–34

Most people don't realize how funny Jesus was. Maybe they think it's disrespectful to think that the Son of God was also a very funny man. But he was a brilliant satirist of the customs and assumptions of his society, and people must have roared with laughter when he came out with this one.

Q. What's wrong with John the Baptist?

A. He doesn't eat or drink.

Q. Well, what's wrong with Jesus, then?

A. He eats and drinks.

Reminds me of the one about the man who complained to the waiter: *The food is terrible and there's not enough of it.*

A funny way of saying that there are those who simply will not listen and learn, no matter what you do. That the message is a new one is itself the problem, and nothing is going to overcome it.

How we will respond to God is up to us. Nobody on earth can make us follow Christ. Even God can't make us. Anybody who wishes to can deny himself joy; nobody will ever make us go to heaven if we insist on going to hell.

THURSDAY IN PROPER 22

Pss 131, 132, (133) * 134, 135
Micah 3:1–8
Acts 24:1–23
Luke 7:36–50

*"If this man were a prophet, he would have known
who and what kind of woman this is . . ."*
LUKE 7:39

The proper thing to do, of course, would be not to permit her touch: not just hers, but any woman not his wife, and certainly not this one, whose reputation as a fallen woman has preceded her into the room. And, since the folks at the dinner party can't imagine Jesus *choosing* to be touched by an unclean person, they conclude that he doesn't realize what she is.

Which he does, of course. And he doesn't seem very worried about being contaminated by her, or by any of the other hundreds of unclean people he has touched and healed.

There are more important things about a person than what bad things he hasn't done. A person could avoid every one of the seven deadly sins and still accomplish no good for anyone else in world, including himself.

⚶ FRIDAY IN PROPER 22

Pss 140, 142 * 141, 143:1–11 (12)
Micah 3:9–4:5
Acts 24:24–25:12
Luke 8:1–15

*They shall beat their swords into ploughshares,
and their spears into pruning hooks . . .*
MICAH 4:3

My current blood lady is the best one I've ever had: she enters my vein quickly, so gently I don't feel a thing. *Now open your fist*, she says quietly, and together we watch in silence as two little tubes fill rapidly with my deep purple blood.

The ancients believed that life lived in the blood itself, having seen what happened when too much blood left the body. And it is true that the history of life lives in the blood: it shows us what victories have been won against what diseases, and what battles are still in progress. It tells what is happening to the muscles right now. It shows us when death has begun in the heart, and when its progress has been interrupted. It tells us about food and water, and signals frantically if kidney or liver or pancreas is overwhelmed.

The first blood transfusion was attempted in 1492 on the Pope, who managed to receive most of the blood but died anyway. Doctors in the sixteenth century hoped to cure illness by transfusing blood from animals to humans, but too many people died. The first human-to-human blood transfusion was successfully performed in Philadelphia by the appropriately named Dr. Philip Syng Physick in 1795. In 1818, a British husband gave blood to his wife to save her from a terrible postpartum hemorrhage. During most of the nineteenth century, doctors in the United States transfused milk from sheep and cows into the veins of people who had lost blood—saline solution was substituted for the milk later on the century with much better results. In 1901, blood was "typed," and the universality of type "O" donors was recognized.

Just in time for World War I, a technique was discovered to arrest the coagulation of blood so that it could be stored and transfusions performed when donor and recipient were not in the same place. Treating patients for shock by injecting albumin into the blood arrived on the scene in time to treat the victims of Pearl Harbor, and the heavy plastic blood bags familiar to us in hospitals and laboratories replaced the older and very fragile glass blood bottles in time for the Korean War. The discovery that blood platelets could be stored at room temperature was made during the Vietnam War.

I suppose the science of hematology always advances during a war; there is so much blood.

SATURDAY IN PROPER 22

Pss 137:1–6 (7–9), 144 * 104
Micah 5:1–4, 10–15
Acts 25:13–27
Luke 8:16–25

*A windstorm swept down on the lake,
and the boat was filling with water . . .*
LUKE 8:23

I'm going down, a friend writes. I leave tomorrow for Houston. Some firefighters and some police officers missed our observance of the fourth anniversary of the World Trade Center tragedy: they're working down on the Gulf Coast. Many widows and other family members are working, too, collecting money and emergency goods for the hurricane victims. It's really helping me get through this week, one of them said.

Everyone from everywhere came and helped us. Everywhere, including Louisiana. A truck full of firefighters arrived to help: they'd driven to New York nonstop, taking turns at the wheel. They had to: time was everything at the site in those first days when there was still hope of bringing people out alive.

And there was another reason they were in a hurry: the back of the truck was full of the best thing the folks back home could think of to send, to fill our stomachs and warm our hearts: tray after tray of wonderful jambalaya. Warm and spicy. Beautiful and red. Made with love you could taste and smell for our rescue workers by some of the best cooks in the world.

Oh, what good people! How generous and funny they were, how charming the way they talked, so different from the way we talked. How kind it was of them to drive all that way and to work so hard. And to bring us jambalaya. I've never had anything so good.

And now they struggle through the long days and don't stop through the nights. Up to their necks in filthy water, as they were up to their necks here in terrible dust. Our folks are there, now, and more are on the way. Now the devastation is a thousand times worse than what they saw when they were here: a whole city, whole towns, everything, everywhere you look.

Nothing is too good for them.

SUNDAY, PROPER 23

Pss 146, 147 * 111, 112, 113
Micah 6:1–8
1 Corinthians 4:9–16
Matthew 15:21–28

Indeed, in Christ Jesus I became
your father through the gospel.
1 CORINTHIANS 4:15

I didn't find out until Monday, I think it was. There was so much going on last weekend, so much running here and there, so many miles of driving, so many things to which it was important to arrive on time. Besides, other news occupied the secular press: Tony Blair's visit, the daily civilian and military death toll in Iraq, theatre in the senate about judicial confirmations. And Brad and Angelina are in love now, not Ben and J.Lo, so that's news. And so it was Monday before I heard that Fr. Basil Pennington had died.

It wasn't easy even this morning to find out more: Googling him yields reviews of his books, old announcements of workshops that have already happened, nothing recent enough to tell me anything about his death. I decided to ask the Trappists. I typed in "Order of the Cistercians of the Strict Observance" and hit pay dirt: a loving announcement of his passing, a brief account of his last days, a photograph of him, ruddy and laughing, looking like a Trappist Santa Claus with his white beard.

What to say? Fr. Pennington's book on centering prayer was the first one I read on this ancient practice that carries me into the still place beneath all the frantic running around I do every day, in my car and on the train and in my mind. He and Thomas Keating and Joan Chittister helped free me from the self-conscious dance of words that had gotten in my way for years when I was trying to pray. I didn't have to find the words. I didn't have to make them elegant. I didn't have to tell God what I thought he wanted to hear. I didn't have to say anything at all. There was a way to go beneath all that.

He had been in a terrible car crash. He was doing well, considering, and was working hard on getting off his respirator, but something went wrong and he died instead. He decided himself to allow death to come naturally when he took a sudden turn for the worse. There had been so many surgeries, so many machines: he was finished with all that. It was time to go home.

Spiritual leaders live on here, even when they enter the larger life. The world barely notices their passing. C. S. Lewis died on the same day that President Kennedy did, and so hardly anybody here noticed. But they continue to teach us: they leave us books and sermons and students and colleagues and strangers into whose lives they came, even if it was only for the exchange of a few sentences. They do what they came here to do, and then they go home. We let them go—we have no choice. Then we are surprised by their peculiar legacy: we are stronger after they leave.

Thank you, Father. Brother. Teacher. Guide. Friend! I never shook your hand, but I will always feel your embrace.

MONDAY IN PROPER 23

Pss 1, 2, 3 * 4, 7
Micah 7:1–7
Acts 26:1–23
Luke 8:26–39

The official and the judge ask for a bribe,
and the powerful dictate what they desire . . .
MICAH 7:3

Another Wall Street scandal broke today, exposing practices that left a few executives unbelievably rich and many stockholders substantially poorer. The accused have issued the traditional outraged denials, and now the conviction and defense machinery will begin to grind to a conclusion it will not reach for years to come. We who watch are always a little surprised when the great are actually convicted of a crime, and even more surprised when they actually do time. They look to us to be too big to fall that far. They must have looked the same way to themselves.

Unfair business practices are old, judging from this passage, which dates from about 500 BCE. Americans who do business in other countries are often shocked at how universal a practice bribery is in some places, and assume that it doesn't offend the indigenous moral sense when it occurs. Oh, everybody's like that over there, they tell their wondering friends. You can't get anything done there unless you play the game. And that is often true.

But even if it is true, it doesn't follow that it doesn't offend, then as now. Listen to indignant Micah: this ancient Middle Eastern prophet scolds his own society about its venality. He, at least, doesn't think it's fair that some people can buy their way out of any problem or into any benefit. Injustice hasn't been absent from any human society since Cain and Abel. But it has been named and denounced in every age, too, by people who knew better. Even there. Even then.

⌄ TUESDAY IN PROPER 23

Pss 5, 6 * 10, 11
Jonah 1:1–17a
Acts 26:24–27:8
Luke 8:40–56

*"Pick me up and throw me into the sea; then the sea
will quiet down for you; for I know it is because of
me that this great storm has come upon you."*
JONAH 1:12

Jonah volunteers to be the scapegoat for the unlucky vessel in the
midst of the storm. He might as well: he knows God is after him.

Usually, though, the scapegoat is not a volunteer. Somebody's
head needs to roll, and roll quickly, in order for those in charge to
demonstrate appropriate firmness, and you know it's not going to
be the boss's head. Once in awhile, law enforcement under pressure
to find a perpetrator—and find one yesterday—has been known to
round up the usual suspects and just choose one of them, defend-
ing the choice right up to conviction and through many appeals, all
on the basis of a profile questionable at best. The community feels
safer with somebody in custody. People have died for crimes they
didn't commit, just to preserve that communal feeling of safety.

It's hard to face our shortcomings. It's much more comfortable
to find a way to think they're someone else's instead, and we can
usually find some evidence for this if we try hard enough. And it's
hard to face the randomness of human suffering, to accept the fact
that sometimes bad things just happen to people: surely somebody
somewhere is to blame. Surely I can make somebody pay the debt
of my sorrow. And surely I will feel better if I do.

The scapegoat gets in between me and the painful details of my
history, unfairly inserted there, delaying my encounter with a truth
I need to face, even if facing it hurts me. My errors are mine: if I can
correct them, I must. My misfortunes are mine, too: while they may

feel profoundly unfair to me, it would be no better to allow someone else to bear the burden of them.

We see that Jonah the scapegoat behaves in a way we now would characterize as Christlike: he offers his life for the lives of his companions. Perhaps all scapegoats, including the unwilling ones, participate in Christ's self-giving. Perhaps this helps us find meaning in meaningless suffering. It doesn't make bad things good; they're still bad. But it honors the nobility of the innocent victim, and that's a communal value far above a fraudulent feeling of safety.

WEDNESDAY IN PROPER 23

Pss 119:1–24 * 12, 13, 14
Jonah 1:17–2:10
Acts 27:9–26
Luke 9:1–17

*"Wherever they do not welcome you, as you are
leaving that town shake the dust off your feet . . ."*
LUKE 9:4

Nobody has to accept love. Human love or the love of God—we are always free to turn it down. We can offer ourselves, but nobody has to accept us. And sometimes people don't.

What we can't offer anybody is someone else. Certainly we can change our behavior, begin doing something desirable or stop doing something unworthy of us. But we are still ourselves. We can only be ourselves. In the end, take us or leave us. And nobody has to take us.

That we offer love doesn't mean we are perfect people. The self I offer is a flawed self, definitely a work in progress. But the love I offer, insofar as it is love and not some manipulative dance of my unconscious devising, is pure. It is the best I have right now. Perhaps in the future I will be a better person, but right now, this is what I have.

Accept the gift of love, even if it arrives in a flawed vessel. Even if there are loose ends. Even if there are places you cannot go together, things upon which you do not agree. Insofar as it is love, it is always of God.

And, insofar as it is love, it will always be generative. Everyone knows that love between men and women often makes babies, but all love is generative in some way: it brings forth more life, seeds the possibility of a common future. All love does this, from the patience of a teacher with a struggling student to the stormy give-and-take between parent and teenager to the careful hand-in-hand walk of ecclesiastical cultures that simply do not understand each other's ways. It will not always be like this, because both sides will change as history unfolds, and avenues of intimacy will open that were not there before. Life never stands still; it develops. The relationship you cannot have today may be possible tomorrow, and you have to stay connected in order to be there when that possibility first appears.

THURSDAY IN PROPER 23

Pss 18:1–20 * 18:21–50
Jonah 3:1–4:11
Acts 27:27–44
Luke 9:18–27

*"For those who want to save their life will lose it,
and those who lose their life for my sake will save it."*
LUKE 9:24

What does this mean? Jesus says it all the time, but it doesn't seem to make much sense, taken literally. So how are we supposed to take it?

It must have to do with refusing to accept the risk that goes along with living. With refusing to spend any of the life you've been given. Holding yourself back from everything, for fear of injury or loss.

Refusing to enter into a game you might not win. For it is certain that we're not going to win, not every time. But we never win if we refuse to play.

Love gives people the courage they need to risk living. It makes us willing to take a chance on running short ourselves in order to bless the one we love. Willing to be foolish in order to come closer. Love helps us overcome our terrible self-consciousness, to forget ourselves and our fuming about how we must look to others. In love, we don't care about that any more. We have more important things on our minds.

Actually, we are under no illusions about human love, anyway, if we give the matter even a minute's thought: we know in advance we're going to lose it. You will die or he will—one or the other. None of us live forever. Nothing here on earth is eternal. Put all your love into anything here, and you will certainly know the pain of loss. Guaranteed.

After all these losses, there is still a love we can never lose, nor can we be lost to it. Christ is alive in a way unlike our life now, a way that knows no beginning and no ending. We first learn to love from each other, learn the love that always lives in fear of losing its object. And then we complete our learning under the further instruction of Christ.

FRIDAY IN PROPER 23

Pss 16, 17 * 22
Ecclesiasticus 1:1–10, 18–27
Acts 28:1–16
Luke 9:28–36

*And they kept silent and in those days told
no one any of the things they had seen.*
LUKE 9:36

I didn't know who to tell first. So, for over an hour, I told no one that I had finally seen a hummingbird in our garden. I had been longing for one to appear for a good three years, and suddenly there she was, a tiny flicker of dun-colored feathers, borne aloft by a whirr of gossamer wings. So much of me was invested in my longing for a hummingbird, in fact, that I scarcely knew myself now that I actually had seen one. Now I am not the woman who wants a hummer. Not any more. I am the woman who has one.

When you have news that you know will change your world, you're not sure you want to inaugurate that process. You are a body at rest, and that is about to change. An old longing, an old status, an old address in your heart—familiar and comfortable, and we don't leave the familiar willingly. You need to ponder what the world will be like after the cat is out of the bag. What you will be like.

What odd beings we are, reluctant to embrace even a happy change. Too comfortable with the familiarity of our discouragement to trade it in for something more hopeful. That must be why so many people of the time were capable of seeing and hearing Jesus but did not reach for the hope he offered. It was too new. Perhaps it would be taken away. Perhaps they would look foolish. Better just to remain as they were. Almost everyone who heard him in the flesh came to that conclusion.

And why the disciples told no one outside their circle, why they had a hard time believing in the resurrection themselves. Everything would change if they were right about what they'd seen. And they may not have been sure they wanted everything to change all that quickly. Don't tell anyone and it won't really be true. Don't think about it and it'll go away, and you can go on as before.

But you didn't *like* before. You longed for this. Here it is. Go!

ⅤSATURDAY IN PROPER 23

Pss 20, 21:1–7 (8–14) * 110:1–5 (6–7), 116, 117
Ecclesiasticus 3:17–31
Acts 28:17–31
Luke 9:37–50

*[John said,] "Master, we saw someone casting out
demons in your name, and we tried to stop him,
because he does not follow with us." But Jesus said to him,
"Do not stop him; for whoever is not against you is for you."*
LUKE 9:49–50

Some people think the institutional division of Christianity into different denominations is a tragedy. I disagree: why is it so terrible for people to have different ideas about God? Differing ways of worshipping? And what's so holy about uniformity? Let it become too central a value, and it will become possible—no, preferable—to ignore or even attack anything new God chooses to present us, without even exploring the possibilities it offers.

If it sounds good, it *is* good, Duke Ellington said about music. There are lots of sacred cows in music, things a composer absolutely must or must not do. But they change from age to age and from place to place, and the geniuses of composition are never the ones who always obey the rules. The geniuses break them—here and there, never without a reason. And in the breaking of the rules, beauty emerges, right in the crack of the old absolute.

It would be a paltry Jesus who could only work with people who knew him personally—him or one of his disciples. A poor Christ who could only move in history if he were acknowledged: when the world was created through him, as we say it was in the creeds, *nobody* acknowledged him but the Father and the Holy Spirit. There was, as yet, no one to acknowledge him. It would be a weak Lord indeed who could speak to no one but those to whom he had already spoken, and that in only one language: theirs.

That is not our Lord. As elastic as the creation, able to encompass it all. Not bound by the things that bind us, able to leap over our walls with no trouble at all.

SUNDAY, PROPER 24

Pss 148, 149, 150 * 114, 115
Ecclesiasticus 4:1–10
1 Corinthians 10:1–13
Matthew 16:13–20

No testing has overtaken you that
is not common to everyone.
1 CORINTHIANS 10:13

This approach doesn't always help much: knowing that others also feel terrible doesn't make your pain go away. And yet, there *is* something to be said for listening to the experience and seeing the example of people who have gone through what you now face.

A woman loses her husband of many years. She is lost, no longer herself, feels like someone in an awful dream. But then she remembers that she knows other women who have gone through this loss, and that they have made it, somehow. So maybe she will not always be so lost. Maybe life will be good again. It will never be the same. But maybe there can be a goodness in life, a goodness of a different kind.

And they remember the early days of their own widowhood, too, and how they stumbled through them. And how they clung to a friend who was also a widow, who also knew the bizarre aloneness of those first days. And so they seek her out: *Maybe she needs now what I needed then,* they think, and she certainly does.

Coffee or tea and a chat, a quiet moment polishing the silver in the sacristy, the quick pressure of a hand on her hand, a quick hug. The mention of his name without the silly fear of bringing it up that other people feel who haven't been through this: music to her ears, that name, even if it is also an ache in her heart.

MONDAY IN PROPER 24

Pss 25 * 9, 15
Ecclesiasticus 4:20–5:7
Revelation 7:1–8
Luke 9:51–62

"Let the dead bury their own dead . . ."
LUKE 9:60

But they can't, of course. They have done all they will do in this world. It is a holy thing to see the life pass from a person. Surprisingly gentle, for all our fear of it. Perhaps the journey toward death is hard, but the moment itself is gentle.

That moment feels summative to us, more important than the other moments of the life we mourn. We wanted to be there. If somehow we were not, we are jealous of those who were, ridiculously afraid that the person didn't know that we loved him as much as they loved him. The last moment must be the moment of completeness, we think, and surely our absence from it is a sign of spiritual absence from the family, lonely confirmation of all our secret half-fears that we don't really matter.

Actually, the person dying is focused on other things. He is more in the next world than in this one, and as his body weakens he is less concerned about what happens here. It was his life that summed him up, not his death. He was who he was throughout his days, and the last day doesn't sum him up more than any one of his other days did. Your life with him was a whole, for good or ill, a mixed bag of love and trouble, the love well worth the trouble.

TUESDAY IN PROPER 24

Pss 26, 28 * 36, 39
Ecclesiasticus 6:5–17
Revelation 7:9–17
Luke 10:1–16

And God will wipe away every tear from their eyes.
REVELATION 7:17

After the unbelievable news, patently false, some mistake. After hanging up the phone, staring straight ahead, your cup of coffee forgotten in your hand, and you absorb the ridiculous notion that you might have to live without him. Impossible. There is some mistake.

After the circumstances of his sudden death have begun to sound like a poem as you tell them for the fifth time, and the sixth. A stupid poem, an inadequate poem, a vile, mocking poem. You hate the poem and think you may never read a poem again.

After you wake up in the morning, that first morning without him, surprised that you slept. Not sure you really did. You wore his undershirt to bed, and it still smells like him. You won't wash it. But after a while, you will find that it no longer smells like him, and now something else has been taken from you, and it is so unfair that smell doesn't last, that it takes its place in the must of the past along with everything else. After a while, they don't smell like anything. Just old clothes. And you are so angry.

His razor. His toothbrush. His comb. His socks. His library books. *How is your husband?* the nice man at the dry cleaners will ask one day, and you will not have been expecting an ambush and your throat will go dry and you will say that he's fine and then you will change dry cleaners.

Such dry confusion. Such a pile of debris. So much dust. What's my life expectancy again? Can we negotiate that? Because I'm really ready now.

You sit in a chair and look at the wall. Then you go to bed. You go back to work, but you're in the chair again in the evening. And then to bed.

Someone watches you, though. There is someone who sees. There is life for the bones of your life, even if you think you don't want life, don't want it ever again. There will be a rustle of movement, a clicking and popping, legs and arms will re-form and there will be new muscle, strong and fresh, and new blood, fast in its course and red as wine. You need not do this. It will come to you. Open one eye, move one finger just a little, answer one question, talk to one person, and your re-living will begin, in the place where the Watcher sees an opening.

⋁ WEDNESDAY IN PROPER 24

Pss 38 * 119:25–48
Ecclesiasticus 7:4–14
Revelation 8:1–13
Luke 10:17–24

*Do not babble in the assembly of the elders,
and do not repeat yourself when you pray.*
ECCLESIASTICUS 7:14

Could you just repeat what you said a few minutes ago? someone *asked. You said that feelings aren't the barometer of spiritual experience, and then I think you said that the spiritual life doesn't need a barometer.*

No, it doesn't. Nothing in the spiritual life needs to be measured. You don't need to worry about whether you're praying as well as somebody else is, even somebody whose spiritual life you admire. We are not called to grow into someone else's spiritual clothing, only into our own.

Measuring and evaluating your prayer is too much like what happens in school to be spiritually healthy. In school, you get a grade. You try to get a better grade. You hope you get a better grade than your seatmate, because you are competing with him. Your focus is on yourself, and it is a competitive focus.

But in prayer, the focus needs to be wider: it is on you, but it is also on those you love, on the world, on the mystery of God. I can't think of a single way to measure that, or a single good reason for doing so.

And you don't need to fuss yourself about whether you are as devout as you used to be. Human beings are changeable creatures, and the spiritual life is a human enterprise: it has eras, and it will change from era to era. Something that has fed you for years may cease to do so, and that need not mean you're wandering away from God. It probably just means you're changing eras. Don't be surprised or alarmed; it will probably be back. Just do something else for a while: evening prayer instead of morning, journaling instead of either, centering prayer upon awakening. Something new to you. It may be that the new practice will be even better than the old. It may have been time to let the old one go.

Just ask God for the gift of prayer that God wants you to have. Do this especially if you're a smart, liberal person who feels a little embarrassed anthropomorphizing God and asking him for things. Don't be embarrassed: you don't create God in your own image by imagining God; you're just using the tools that human beings have for coming closer to God. You are speaking the language of prayer, of image, of poetry, not the language of journalistic fact. You are right to assert that God is beyond image, beyond body, beyond all that is here. But we're here. The threshold of prayer is low enough so that all of us can take the first step.

THURSDAY IN PROPER 24

Pss 37:1–18 * 37:19–42
Ecclesiasticus 10:1–18
Revelation 9:1–12
Luke 10:25–37

Do not get angry with your neighbor for every injury . . .
ECCLESIASTICUS 10:6

We have choices about how much anger to expend on which annoyances in our lives: we cannot die in every ditch. Perhaps we cannot help the wave of anger that burns through us at the moment, but we are the ones who will decide what to do with it.

But I get mad! someone says in defense of her short fuse. And other people don't? The world is not divided into people who get angry and people who don't. We are all people who do.

Count to ten. Imagine the object of your wrath as a four-year-old; imagine yourself as one too, while you're at it. Give yourself enough time, before you speak, to ask yourself what you really hope will happen now.

Most habitually angry people think that a scolding changes behavior. It doesn't, though. It may motivate a momentary compliance, but that evaporates as soon as the threat does. Something quieter but much more onerous is required: repeated correction issued in a calm manner, again and again. Perhaps concrete consequences to an inappropriate action will be needed—a valuable learning tool. But rage won't do it. It will only plant dread of you in the heart of the offender—dread and a certain rebellious desire to commit the unacceptable act again.

⟍ FRIDAY IN PROPER 24

Pss 31 * 35
Ecclesiasticus 11:2–20
Revelation 9:13–21
Luke 10:38–42

My child, do not busy yourself with many matters . . .
ECCLESIASTICUS 11:10

Ever since church, I have been exhausted, sprawled across the bed without so much as a sheet over me. The services on Sunday morning tire me out much more than they used to, and that that's just fine; I don't have any obligations until evening.

And so I can travel back in time as I doze, back to a country childhood in the fall by means of country sounds outside the window I still have open because the afternoon is warm and because I can't bear to shut myself away from the bird sounds for another winter. I smell the sharp smell of leaves in piles, the smell of apples. It seems that my parents are still alive, that we are still in our old house. A sleepy Sunday afternoon in a time out of time.

Of course, I railed against the quiet of such Sunday afternoons when I really was little, begrudging my poor parents their hard-earned naps. Couldn't we *do* something? Weren't they *ever* going to get up?

Time seems to children to take so *long*: a Sunday afternoon was eternal. It speeds up as we age, though, hurtles along at a pace we never expected. Life is short, we realize. I suppose that means we should work hard and get it all done while we can.

But surely it also means that we must rest when we're tired, in the moment of it, that each fleeting moment should be fully savored.

SATURDAY IN PROPER 24

Pss 30, 32 * 42, 43
Ecclesiasticus 15:9–20
Revelation 10:1–11
Luke 11:1–13

"Search, and you will find . . ."
LUKE 11:9

Rain today?* I Instant Message my daughter. *A ton,* she types back. Good. The ground will probably stay soft from the rain until I get home, even if it doesn't rain again this week. I want it to be soft enough that putting a hundred bulbs in will be easy, and it is much easier when God does the watering.

I think of the garden a lot when I'm away, no matter what the season. Next year, I'm going to fix things so I don't have to leave home in the summer, just stay there and take care of it. I think I said that last year, too.

I get up early most days and go outside for a visit, even now, when hardly a bloom remains. Even in the snow. There is always something beautiful to see, always birds and squirrels and cats to be fed. There is always a flower or two to cut, a branch to bring in for the sake of its remarkable architecture, always a plant to study, green and bursting with life or dormant, seemingly dead.

Oh, but nothing is really dead. Everything is alive, smack in the middle of its current chapter or poised to begin its next one. This is true every single day, no matter what happens outside. Or inside. I make my tea and say Morning Prayer. By the time I get to my computer, the day has begun.

⟍ SUNDAY, PROPER 25

Pss 63:1–8 (9–11), 98 * 103
Ecclesiasticus 18:19–33
1 Corinthians 10:15–24
Matthew 18:15–20

*Do not become a beggar by feasting with borrowed
money, when you have nothing in your purse.*
ECCLESIASTICUS 18:33

Did you have a wonderful time in India? I asked a young friend who had just returned from there.

It was amazing, she said, and we began to talk about southern India where she had been, about its deep spirituality, about the crowds of people everywhere, about the beautiful children.

So you want to go back? I asked.

In a heartbeat. But I cashed in my 401k plan to get there this time, so I don't know when I'm going to be able to go again.

Ah. I had not wanted to ask how she had managed such an expensive trip, but now I knew: she had cashed in her retirement money. Clearly it was worth it in her mind: a once-in-a-lifetime personal and spiritual experience. Of course, she isn't yet thirty years old. Retirement is decades away. It isn't real to her.

Young people really don't think they'll get old. It just doesn't feel real to them, and most of them wouldn't save for that eventuality if they had a choice. Most of them are just starting out and don't have much cash; they need every penny. If they can get at their retirement money, they'll use it: not necessarily foolishly, maybe for a house or for education, good things. But when it's gone, it will be gone.

Lots of young people are fine with that. They don't mind the risk. But then, they don't really believe they will ever get old.

MONDAY IN PROPER 25

Pss 41, 52 * 44
Ecclesiasticus 19:4–17
Revelation 11:1–14
Luke 11:14–26

Have you heard something? Let it die with you!
ECCLESIASTICUS 19:10

I don't remember most of the confessions I hear. I make a point of allowing them to pass through me. They are not *for* me, after all, but for God. I am merely the human being who assists in their prayerful speaking and then assures the one confessing of what we both already know: God is loving and forgives us, is more forgiving of us than we are of ourselves.

I thought this would be hard when I was first ordained: I have a hard time keeping Christmas gifts a secret! But there is a grace to confession and absolution that is greater than the two people involved. It cleanses the one who speaks—whether she expects it or not, whether she feels it or not—and silencing the one who listens, no matter what is said. It is not hard to keep the seal. It comes with the rite.

Death doesn't break the seal. I used to think that would make a difference, too, but it does not, even though I know that the person who has died is free of all care about our sins and sorrows, including the ones he committed while he was here. The matrix of his life remains here, and our sacred time together in the confessional was part of it. It is not mine to change. It was and remains his.

If we understood the depth of the love that awaits us and even now envelops us, we probably would not need the confessional seal. We would promptly admit our fault and ask forgiveness, always, and would never feel the need to conceal anything. But we do not understand. All our shame arises from not understanding the depth of that love.

TUESDAY IN PROPER 25

Pss 45 * 47, 48
Ecclesiasticus 24:1–12
Revelation 11:14–19
Luke 11:27–36

*A woman in the crowd raised her voice and said to him,
"Blessed is the womb that bore you and the breasts
that nursed you!" But he said, "Blessed rather are those
who hear the word of God and obey it!"*
LUKE 11:27–28

Of course people send me animal pictures over the Internet. I write about animals a lot. And I open each one, in case it's one I haven't seen. I forward the best ones to my younger daughter, who shares them with her class of mentally disabled eight-year-olds, and to my older daughter who just loves animals, and to my grandchildren, and to Q.

This one was about a baby hippopotamus, swept away from its mother in the raging waters of the tsunami. It landed smack on top of a giant tortoise, a male estimated to be a hundred years old. The tortoise took it well—considering that his sudden visitor weighed 300 pounds—and the orphaned hippo, who ordinarily would have remained with his mother for the first four years of his life, decided that the tortoise would be a good substitute, and began to follow him around as he would have followed his mommy. The photos show them walking together, sleeping together. They swim together, and the hippo gets aggressive with anyone who seems to him to be threatening the tortoise. They look to me to be happy together, insofar as a human can read the features of species so different from her own.

And it seems not to matter to the hippo that his new mom is a turtle. Or that he's a boy. However hippos love, he loved his dead mother and he loves his new one. He needed love in order to grow up, and he made it his business to find it.

He didn't sit in a corner and die because there were no other hippos. He didn't hold out for something more suitable, or more like his mother, or more like his dream of the perfect hippo. He needed love more than he needed his ideal. Probably we all do.

Might this new friend be the perfect friend, become your perfect partner? Probably not—perfect doesn't live around here. But can you find joy again after you have been cruelly used by life?

Yup. If you're willing to think outside the box a little.

WEDNESDAY IN PROPER 25

Pss 119:49–72 * 49, (53)
Ecclesiasticus 28:14–26
Revelation 12:1–6
Luke 11:37–52

"For you tithe mint and rue and herbs of all kinds,
and neglect justice and the love of God . . ."
LUKE 11:42

Small observances—tiny customs that don't require much in the way of commitment or cost. Something on the order of a tip: just a tiny thing, nothing big. Let me do something small—but *visible*—something I can do that will show the proper respect but won't really affect my life or slow me down much.

Sometimes people who can't—or won't—do the big thing they really need to do will focus instead on minutiae. The person whose house is a mess, but who has a fit if something is out of place in his car. The secret cocaine user who won't allow her children anything but organic foods because she thinks food additives are unhealthy. The unfaithful husband who keeps his expense account scrupulously because he thinks it's important to be honest. *I can't do what I know I must do. So let me do this instead. Let me tithe my mint and my rue religiously.*

But the math doesn't work that way. In fact, there is no math, no equation we can structure that will balance out our righteousness and our sin. This vain enterprise avails no one of anything but self-delusion. It delays the inevitable day of reckoning and guarantees that it will be much worse when it finally arrives.

And it completely ignores the fact that we have a savior. Jesus has done the math. Thenceforth, we need waste no more time trying to prove ourselves free of sin. We're not. And we never have to carry the burden of our sins alone.

THURSDAY IN PROPER 25

Pss 50 * (59, 60) or 103
Ecclesiasticus 31:12–18, 25–32:2
Revelation 12:7–17
Luke 11:53–12:12

"Yet not one of them is forgotten in God's sight."
LUKE 12:6

This was a car trip, just Q and me, through beautiful country, down into lush Virginia and up into the mountains. We drove in and out of cloudbursts. We ate an entire gorgeous dark chocolate bar with real espresso in it. We drove past Civil War battlefields and imagined the houses we passed as they were then, past sad little graveyards filled with dead soldiers and those who loved them.

There were 23,000 casualties in one day's fighting at Antietam. There was no graveyard large enough for all the dead. They were interred in shallow troughs near where they fell, Confederate separate from Union, few identified. Later on, the Union soldiers were interred in a section of the battlefield purchased and set aside for that purpose. Separate even in death, the last of the Confederate fallen did not receive a proper burial until 1877.

Life and death both come close to me when I am away from home. I notice babies more, and small children, but also graveyards, old houses telling silent tales about the lives they once held. A sweet melancholy creeps over me, a wistful tenderness toward our fragile race and all its ephemeral arrangements, all our attempts to be remembered. Their lives were short, as mine will be. Fleeting. They longed to stay but had to go. There was only one of each of them.

FRIDAY IN PROPER 25

Pss 40, 54 * 51
Ecclesiasticus 34:1–8, 18–22
Revelation 13:1–10
Luke 12:13–31

*"And can any of you by worrying add
a single hour to your span of life?"*
LUKE 12:25

I miss writing the eMo when I don't write one, and feel a vague anxiety: *You are inconsistent.* But people aren't as regular as clocks, and it's a mistake to expect mechanistic perfection of oneself or anybody else. We should build a certain amount of failure into every plan we make, in fact, some slack somewhere in it that will enable us to regroup quickly when something goes wrong. For it is just those times in which we get to show just how nimble we can be.

Or how patient. There are *snafus* from which no recovery is possible, mistakes that really do scuttle a whole project and force a return to the very beginning of a major effort. To have been responsible for one of those, squandering the work of people you care about, dashing your own hopes for it as well, is a terrible thing. A close second in awfulness is to be the manager of the guilty party, having to watch him writhe, walking the uncomfortably fine line between consoling him and requiring his accountability.

I am my own boss. This certainly ought to streamline supervision, but for a certain personality, the reverse is true. The self-employed never go off duty. We can never go home: we *are* home.

There is always more that could be done, and what is done could always be better. You can't call yourself in sick.

For those blessed with the gift of moderation, this is an ideal situation. For those of us who range somewhat further afield, it is what my friend Brooke calls *a spiritual discipline*, which is church-ese for *a pain in the butt*.

Oh, do the best you can and then get over it. Try again tomorrow if it's not good enough. Get enough sleep and enough prayer. Get enough exercise and do one beautiful thing each day. Accept the fact that nothing is ever perfect and your work won't be, either.

SATURDAY IN PROPER 25

Pss 55 * 138,139:1–17(18–23)
Ecclesiasticus 35:1–17
Revelation 13:11–18
Luke 12:32–48

And I saw another beast coming up out of the earth . . .
REVELATION 13:11

I've had just about enough Revelation for the year, Harry says. *Me, too*, I say. *But we'll be finished with it soon.*

Devotees of the Daily Office don't choose what scripture passages we'll read every day. They're chosen for us, in a two-year recurring cycle of lessons that you find listed in the back of the prayer book. We just show up and read what's set before us. Often this is fine—you spend weeks in something exciting, like the story of Joseph or the Exodus. But sometimes, like today, it's something very strange indeed: you read it twice, and you're *still* at a complete loss as to how you might be edified by what you just read.

Harry and I sound like a pair of teenagers complaining about their homework. I think it must seem odd to people who don't do this, that modern adult people should sit down and read something we don't necessarily find interesting, just because it's assigned. *Surely I should read things I want to read,* they think. *It's hard enough to make myself to read and pray as it is. How am I ever going to become faithful if what I'm reading isn't interesting?*

It's not hard, though. Your habit carries you through the boring bits, much the same as your marriage carries you through those moments when your spouse isn't quite what you would call *thrilling.* As your friendship helps you sit patiently on the phone and listen to your friend prattle on about something you don't care much about. Maybe this moment isn't our ecstatic union. But I still love her. He is still my friend.

The relationship matters more than the unrealistic expectation that every moment in it will be thrill-packed. We show up every day, because we don't know which it will be: it may be that the passage you expect to be dry as a bone will yield something you never noticed was there, something you absolutely needed to hear today. It may be that a prayer you've said a thousand times, five thousand times, suddenly clicks into place in a new way. You just never know.

In the meantime, the familiar sameness carries you. You and God are both here, right where you always are, you and God and everybody else who prays, throughout the whole world—we are mystically joined to one another in prayer, all of us, whether prayer on a given day turns out to be a mountain-top experience or something considerably less than that. You sit quietly for a time, after the prayers are finished and before you close with "Let Us Bless the Lord." Your mind settles down, turning all its concerns and worries over to God for the day or for the night, commending all that occupies you to the loving care of the one who made you.

The weird reading from Revelation was part what took you to the place from which you could turn all of it over to God. It's not always what you read that counts. Sometimes it's just *that* you read.

↘ SUNDAY, PROPER 26

Pss 24, 29 * 8, 84
Ecclesiasticus 36:1–17
1 Corinthians 12:27–13:13
Matthew 18:21–35

*For now we see in a mirror, dimly, but then we will
see face to face. Now I know only in part; then I will know
fully, even as I have been fully known.*
1 CORINTHIANS 13:12

You come to know Christ by living a life that expects him. Not a life that understands everything about him or a life that never knows a day's uncertainty—just a life that wants him. Knowing Christ begins with the desire to know him, not with a convincing body of evidence. In matters of faith, evidence does not convince.

Longing and following are what convince us. We are convinced about those things in which we have invested ourselves. We are simply bored by the things into which we have poured little or nothing: they may be someone else's passions, but they are not ours.

Ordinarily we do not know at first that it is Christ for whom we long. We think it is something else. A girlfriend, please, the perfect woman for me. Dream children, a dream house. The perfect job. The respect we are due. But we may gain some or all of these gifts, and still there is something for which we long.

Gifts don't last. They end when we end. As we proceed, it is something lasting for which we long, and we come to know that there has never been anything lasting except for one thing. And we see that it is Christ, and we see something else, something surprising. At the very moment when we first behold him, we see that we have known him all along. It was Christ we wanted, through all those years of chasing after our dreams. He stood before us with each of them in his generous hand, and we were so entranced with the gifts that we hardly ever noticed him as he handed them to us.

The sooner we can approach our own longing for Christ the more serene our lives will be. The gifts will come and go into all our lives, and we will greet them with delight and relinquish them with a pang each time we must relinquish them. We lose all, all of them. Only Christ remains with us to the end.

And all will be well because he remains. He is no stranger to us. We have known him all the time.

MONDAY IN PROPER 26

Pss 56, 57, (58) * 64, 65
Ecclesiasticus 38:24–34
Revelation 14:1–13
Luke 12:49–59

*"Do you think that I have come
to bring peace to the earth?"*
LUKE 12:51

Sometime this week or last week: the real Veterans Day. We didn't use to make a long weekend out of whatever Monday was nearest it; we just observed the day, November 11, wherever it fell in the course of the week.

It was a day primarily about memorial wreaths and parades. There were many veterans of the Great War alive when I was a child, and they would march down Fifth Avenue in their old uniforms, if they had remained trim enough to fit into them. Only thirty of them remain now: one, 103 years old, will lay a wreath with President Bush at the Tomb of the Unknowns. He was sixteen when he enlisted. The Tomb was dedicated on November 11, 1921, after his terrible war, and they called it the Tomb of the Unknown Soldier, and it contained the remains of an unidentified soldier of the Great War. I forget why they changed the name, but it wasn't long ago that they did. Younger men from the Second World War and from Korea marched in Veterans Day parades. Vietnam was still in French hands when I was a child. I'm not sure I had even heard of it.

And the soldiers dying now hadn't even been born. Not even imagined. I suppose there will be no end to this parade, not ever.

Sweet Jesus.

TUESDAY IN PROPER 26

Pss 61, 62 * 68:1–20 (21–23) 24–36
Ecclesiasticus 43:1–22
Revelation 14:14–15:8
Luke 13:1–9

*"Or those eighteen who were killed when
the tower of Siloam fell on them . . ."*
LUKE 13:4

An ancient news story, now forgotten. A terrible accident: workers, perhaps, killed while repairing one of the towers associated with the waterworks of Siloam in the city. Or maybe passersby. Or children, maybe, who had wanted to climb to the top of the tower and look out across the city. Who was killed, we do not know. We know of the event only from Jesus, and Jesus doesn't say. He mentions the tragedy only in passing, to make a point about bad things happening to good people. But everyone in the audience knew about it. It must have been relatively recent. Oh, yeah, they thought to themselves. I remember that. That was a terrible thing.

News of the disaster must have spread quickly in the city. Not as quickly as it did when our towers fell, of course, when people all over the world stood in front of their televisions and watched in disbelief as the buildings burned and as they fell. But there must have been the same frenzy of fear and confusion: Was she in that part of town? Did the tower fall on him? Was he working that day? Did she get out? Why hasn't he come home? People must have run there, from all over Jerusalem, to see for themselves. People must immediately have begun pawing through the rubble, must immediately have begun the frantic search for anyone who was still alive. How many they saved, we do not know. Jesus doesn't say how many got out of the tower alive. Or how many were pulled from the wreckage. I guess he didn't have to; everyone listening to him already knew all about it.

There will come a time when the bombing of the World Trade Center will be like that: a moment in history that not everybody knows about. Most New Yorkers know about the General Slocum tragedy now, when more than a thousand people died in flames on an East River pleasure cruise, and about the Triangle Shirtwaist fire, when more than a hundred young women burned to death in a locked sweatshop, but the general memory of those sorrows has only resurfaced since 9/11. Before 9/11, labor or maritime or New York historians knew about the General Slocum or Triangle. Some people recollected, vaguely, learning about them in their school days. Nobody remembered them.

The World Trade Center a minor event in the memory of the world? That can never be, we think, but it will. History closes up quickly around the place where we were. Life moves forward, whether we follow it readily or stumble blindly after it. There will come a time when nobody remembers. If the earth lasts long enough, there will come a time when nobody even knows. When they'll have to look it up.

WEDNESDAY IN PROPER 26

Pss 72 * 119:73–96
Ecclesiasticus 43:23–33
Revelation 16:1–11
Luke 13:10–17

*And just then there appeared a woman with a spirit
that had crippled her for eighteen years. She was bent
over and was quite unable to stand up straight.*

LUKE 13:11

Ah, me. It wasn't a spirit. It was osteoporosis. She was like many older women and some men as well, bowed at first and then bent double because their bones can no longer keep them erect. Scans of the bones reveal a honeycomb structure within them, instead of a solid one. You can break a rib coughing.

There are medicines that help delay its progress. Weight-bearing exercise stimulates the bones to grow, in the miraculous communication of nerve and marrow cell that goes on every minute of every day. Intake of calcium is important, too, and other nutrients play a role.

The person who is bent double is the same person who used to stand erect. The person she was is still inside the body that feels and acts so differently from the way it used to perform. It hurts to walk around bent double, to crane one's neck in order to have a conversation with someone who is standing, but it hurts even more to see other people assuming you're mute or stupid because you can't stand up straight.

Which one was the thing that drove the woman to seek healing from Jesus: was it the physical condition or the social isolation? Both, I suppose. He healed the physical part. It would be up to the people around her to see to the rest.

THURSDAY IN PROPER 26

Pss (70), 71 * 74
Ecclesiasticus 44:1–15
Revelation 16:12–21
Luke 13:18–30

"Lord, will only a few be saved?"
LUKE 13:23

This is never a disinterested question. It is really a way of asking without coming right out and asking, *will I be among them?*

The truth about salvation is so simple it's offensive to most people who care about it: all you have to do to be saved is to want to be saved. Nobody is shut out who wants to come in.

Well, what about all these people in chapter 13, then, who ate and drank with Jesus and now can't come into heaven? Well, they can, as soon as they understand that this is what they want: not just to be away from the storm, not just to be safe, not just to live forever—just to be with Christ. That it is the relationship with Christ they want first, and that they are willing to be anywhere and do anything if they can just be in that relationship. If all else flows from that.

This is actually all we can do. We're going to "be anywhere and do anything" anyway. Life will swirl around us as it swirls around everyone else, and our being centered in Christ won't change that as long as we're living on the earth. But as soon as we can, it will be well with our souls if we put the primary relationship first: all others will be taken from us, every last one of them. Go first to the one you will not lose, and you will be able to endure the loss of everything else, when it comes.

ⅴ FRIDAY IN PROPER 26

Pss 69:1–23 (24–30) 31–38 * 73
Ecclesiasticus 50:1, 11–24
Revelation 17:1–18
Luke 13:31–35

*How often I have desired to gather your children
together as a hen gathers her brood under
her wings, and you were not willing!*
LUKE 13:34

Jesus doesn't seem to mind a feminine image for himself half as much as we mind it for him. In recent years, a blessing has been proposed in my church that makes use of this phrase, blessing the people in the name of Jesus who gathers everyone like a mother hen. Most priests I know use something else. I don't use it myself. Jesus as a chicken is too much, they say. But he's the one who said it first, not any of us.

But I wonder if it is not the kind of bravery the mother hen image shows us. Maybe it's not the kind of bravery we want in a savior. We are used to Jesus as a king, as a mighty ruler, kind Lord, wondrous healer, riveting teacher and preacher—not as a nurturer. Not in so womanly a role. It makes Jesus seem so *domestic.*

But then, the Bible was written by men, who may not have known just what kind of toughness is required to raise children. It is not for sissies. Both women and men undervalue this work. How many times have you heard a mother say she "doesn't work," meaning she doesn't work for money outside the home? *I work like hell,* my friend Linda always used to answer that loaded question about how she spent her time.

If mothering seems to us not to be brave enough to apply to Jesus, maybe we've forgotten just what it's like. Endless, scary, physically demanding, no time off—and full of love that would sacrifice itself without thinking twice if it would save the beloved child. That *does* sound like a savior.

SATURDAY IN PROPER 26

Pss 75, 76 * 23, 27
Ecclesiasticus 51:1–12
Revelation 18:1–14
Luke 14:1–11

Fallen, fallen is Babylon the great!
REVELATION 18:2

*W*e need to put Old Glory up in the morning, Q said last night.
I forgot.

Yeah. I forgot, too. In the morning, I mix up some muffins and, while they are baking, go out front and hang the flag. Our bracket is broken, and so I have to hang it flat. I can never remember which way it goes when you hang it flat, where the field of stars should be, so I must trot back and forth looking at it, changing my mind a few times before I'm satisfied I've got it right.

It's almost time for school to begin for the day, and a few stragglers hurry along the sidewalk. I watch them and find myself thinking of that terrible day when a Russian school that was taken over by terrorists as the festive first day began. The story got worse and worse as the details unfolded; no food, no water, hundreds of terrified children and frantic parents and teachers. I suppose one could imagine a worse conclusion to the ordeal, but the one that actually ensued was dreadful enough: 350 dead, many more injured. A sizable cohort of the terrorist team escaped to kill another day.

Love of country. Love of family and of clan. Longing for freedom, and always the spiritual vulnerability to the siren call of violence in obtaining or protecting it. Willingness to die morphs malignantly into willingness to kill, and a misplaced admiration approves of it all, forgetting that choosing martyrdom for oneself is one thing and choosing it for someone else, quite another.

Both parties' nominating conventions are over now. The gloves will come off now, pundits say, although some political speakers have been bare-knuckled from the beginning. They admire their own pugilism, dismiss those who counsel political civility as morally weak and even traitorous.

I say be careful. Even here, where we say quickly that such things as happened in that Russian school could never happen here, forgetting how many times such things have happened here among even us. Strong opinions and passionate convictions move history, but they never absolve us from teaching the duties of compassion and the obligations that go with membership in the human family. We cannot forget them; no nation can, not ever, or it will live to see its own fatal fall.

SUNDAY, PROPER 27

Pss 93, 96 * 34
Ecclesiasticus 51:13–22
1 Corinthians 14:1–12
Matthew 20:1–16

When I was still young, before I went to my travels,
I sought wisdom openly in my prayer.
ECCLESIASTICUS 51:13

A hint of something even more ancient than this ancient book peeks from behind its pages: the ancient figure of a passionate young seeker of wisdom, who leaves his home and goes on a journey. A story of learning and the transmission of wisdom, as the highest good to which a human being may aspire. The Buddha was such a young man: a story of wisdom from the East that made its way long ago into the crucible of western culture. Ecclesiasticus is part of the "wisdom literature": hymns to wisdom abound in it, but so do maxims for right behavior and common sense advice for living one's life.

Not much here about salvation. No Bible stories here. No history—this could have been written at any time, could have been written even now, perhaps. Certainly no Jesus. Not even a whole lot about God. It is the allegorical figure of Wisdom—a feminine figure—who takes center stage.

She is the overwhelmingly attractive object of ardent desire and hot pursuit. The urgent sexual imagery surrounding her informs us of how essential it is to possess her. The soul in search of wisdom is active, journeying, different from the contemplative soul that waits to be filled by the God who leads it gently beside still waters.

So many books in scripture. So many ways of faith. And so many of us, each to read and—in so many ways—come to understand.

MONDAY IN PROPER 27

Pss 80* 77, (79)
Joel 1:1–13
Revelation 18:15–24
Luke 14:12–24

"But when you give a banquet, invite the poor, the crippled, the lame, and the blind. And you will be blessed . . ."
LUKE 14:13

And why does Jesus say this? Because your friends will have you to dine in exchange, but these people can't. They can't pay you back. So this dinner is not a tit-for-tat social obligation. It is a graceful giving for the pure joy of it.

Sometimes I think that the thing I miss most from parish ministry is the Thanksgiving dinners we used to put on for the neighborhood. Oh, the turkeys! Eight or nine of them, and my husband and Joe Rider—may he rest in peace—used to set themselves up with a door on two sawhorses: the carving station. And the salad makers were stationed on the back stairway, somehow producing 150 individual salads, handing the bowls from person to person down the stairs to gather tomatoes, the carrots, the onions, the lettuce on their way. The dessert station was near the window, and the long table with all the entrée dishes was along that wall, too, aproned and gloved volunteers, serving spoons at the ready, arrayed along one side. Coffee and tea were on the bookcase, and cups of cider on the little tables the children in the after-school program used during the week.

The kids would help set up the tables, which they loved to do: they would fly around the room with plastic cutlery, with napkins, with cups: a big party, and they were helping. And then their parents would come, to be among the first served. People from all over the city came to help us with the meal, and donations flowed in the door all day every day for a week before the dinner.

It was like heaven will be. When all was ready, the doors were opened and the crowd came in: many elderly, many single parents with children, many with canes, many homeless, many not quite all there. Is there something happier than this, I would think as I looked on at all the guests, all the helpers, all the food, all the laughter and talk. No. I don't think there is. I don't think there needs to be.

TUESDAY IN PROPER 27

Pss 78:1–39 * 78:40–72
Joel 1:15–2:2 (3–11)
Revelation 19:1–10
Luke 14:25–35

(Fine linen is the righteous deeds of the saints.)
REVELATION 19:8

Well, maybe it is. This parenthesized guess is clearly an attempt by a copyist to make some sense of the wild goings-on in chapter 19, which depicts the joining of Christ and the church as husband and wife in a wedding quite unlike any you are likely to attend this year.

No modern person can be blamed for being puzzled as to the inclusion of this strange book in the Bible. Many other books didn't make the cut—books that, shall we say, *held together* a lot better—but this one did, which means there was a consensus about it among the leaders who chose which books would be in and which ones out of the Christian canon. Enough of them thought the Revelation to John was necessary that we're reading it in church today, when hardly anyone has a clue what it means.

Because its details and images are so lurid, it's tempting to become fascinated and then utterly bogged down in them. If we do, we miss some of scripture's most comforting words, words that give us a clue about Revelation's lasting importance. It is from this book that we hear that "God will wipe away every tear from their eyes," something we need to hear when our hearts are breaking. It is here that we hear of Christ as the Alpha and the Omega, and begin to understand that time is an earthly reality but not a heavenly one, also an idea that brings us great comfort. Since most of our pain comes from the passage of time—the march toward our own deaths, the decades of separation we must endure, bereft of those we have loved and lost—the idea that God doesn't live in time, and that we also will not, is very good news.

So read. Don't worry if you can't keep track of every monster in Revelation: there are an awful lot of them. But step back and glean from this strange book the gems it has for us today. There are a lot of them, too.

WEDNESDAY IN PROPER 27

Pss 119:97–120 * 81, 82
Joel 2:12–19
Revelation 19:11–21
Luke 15:1–10

*"There is joy in the presence of the angels
of God over one sinner who repents."*
LUKE 15:10

He used to call collect, but now he has his own cell phone. He used to call collect from Rikers Island quite a bit. He went there so many times he must have had his own mailbox. He kept getting in trouble with the police, who knew him and picked him up all the time.

I messed up, he would explain to me when he called me to tell me he was in jail again. It was never much of a surprise. He couldn't handle his anger or his impulses very well: too many drugs, especially crack cocaine. He was out of control. He will never get better, I would think when I hung up the phone.

His mother felt the same way, I could tell. He had abused her welcome so many times that she couldn't afford to let him know where in the city she lived. He would come to my office and I would call her, using a number unknown to him, and then would let them talk. *If he could just get some kind of job*, she would say, and I remember thinking, *If pigs could just fly.*

But somehow he did. A judge gave him rehab or jail, and he chose rehab. Two years he stayed there, and afterward drifted in and out of disastrous living arrangements. But he didn't use drugs and he didn't go to jail—no mean feat.

He's been out for more than four years now. He has a job in a gas station and he has a room in a rooming house in Queens. He'd like to go to school and learn a trade. I'm not sure about that, as he is mostly illiterate.

But then, I'm the one who thought he'd never get out of jail.

THURSDAY IN PROPER 27

Pss (83) or 23, 27 * 85, 86
Joel 2:21–27
James 1:1–15
Luke 15:1–2, 11–32

"I have sinned against heaven and before you;
I am no longer worthy to be called your son . . ."
LUKE 15:18–19

But of course, worthiness isn't really what makes a son. Or a daughter. Love does that.

His father never disowned him, never even came close. He felt that surely he had permanently exiled himself by his disgraceful behavior, but no.

His dad must have been looking for him out the front door: it says in the story that he saw his son while he was still a long way off. Maybe he went out every morning to look and see if he was coming home.

There needs to be a way to come home. You may need to come down hard on behavior that is unacceptable. Notice that, as glad as the father is to see his son, the prodigal isn't going to get any more inheritance: he's spent his. "All I have is yours," his father says to the older brother, so I guess that was that about the money. You may even have to ask a beloved young adult to leave your house. But there needs always to be a way back, whether the young person chooses it or not. You can't help looking out your front door every day to see if your prodigal is coming home, and miracles do happen. People can change if they want to.

It may be that there were some things you couldn't teach him. She just couldn't—or wouldn't—learn them from you. But maybe life will do what you could not. So keep looking, because there has to be a way to welcome repentance if it occurs. The relationship doesn't end.

FRIDAY IN PROPER 27

Pss 88 * 91, 92
Joel 2:28–3:8
James 1:16–27
Luke 16:1–9

*"I am not strong enough to dig,
and I am ashamed to beg."*
LUKE 16:3

But you can always cheat. I can imagine the ripple that must have gone through the audience when Jesus told this story. *Is that any way to behave? What kind of a rabbi is this? Where is the condemnation of the dishonest man?*

The writer tries to help us with an explanation at the end, one that really doesn't explain much: *I tell you, use worldly wealth to gain friends for yourselves, so that when it is gone, you will be welcomed into eternal dwellings.*

No, I can't say I quite got that, either.

But what Jesus said at what was probably the original end of the story is the point: the children of darkness are often smarter than the children of light. Don't be passive and naïve: be as sharp for the good as the evil are for their fell purposes. Put the energy into holiness other people put into sin. Be as zealous for the things of God as you are for all the other things you care about: your job, your house, your investments. Don't just wage war: wage peace, wage justice, wage righteousness.

And don't imagine that the way to do this will always be decorous. Be prepared to use your street smarts.

SATURDAY IN PROPER 27

Pss 87, 90 * 136
Joel 3:9–17
James 2:1–13
Luke 16:10–17 (18)

*"Whoever is faithful in a very little
is faithful also in much . . ."*
LUKE 16:10

We don't arrive prepared to do great things. We have to grow into them. And the earlier we start, the better.

The young man grew up in a tough neighborhood in East Harlem. He lived with his grandmother, who was raising eight children in an apartment too small for all those people. His dream was to get her an apartment that was safe, clean, comfortable, and large enough. It wasn't at all clear how he was going to do this: he was sixteen years old.

But from his pastor, he heard about a sweat equity program the city of New York was offering: you could buy a wreck of a building for next to nothing and bring it back to life yourself—urban homesteading. You had to show the authorities that you had people in your organization with the skills necessary to do the work. *Hmmmn*—all he had was his grandmother, his aunts, uncles, cousins. *Don't worry about that now,* an architect colleague of the pastor told him. *Just get the building, then figure out the rest. He got to work on the proposal.*

Okay. His grandmother worked in a store, but sometimes she had to hammer a nail or replace a missing screw—that made her a carpenter, right? And his uncle was a janitor—didn't that make him a facilities engineer? His other uncle worked in a factory, inserting wires into ladies foundations garments; people who do wiring are electricians, right?

He got the building. It took his motley "construction crew" six years—and everyone learned a lot about the building trade—but the building was renovated and they live in it today.

In one sense, of course, he was *not* trustworthy, insofar as the housing bureaucracy was concerned. In another, though, he was fiercely faithful and tenacious, and his stubborn single-mindedness carried him to a very big thing: a big dream of a home for his family had come gloriously true.

SUNDAY, PROPER 28

Pss 66, 67 * 19, 46
Habukkuk 1:1–4 (5–11) 12–2:1
Philippians 3:13–4:1
Matthew 23:13–24

I press on toward the goal . . .
PHILIPPIANS 3:14

So what do you get if you're a bronze winner? Q wants to know. I get my name on the bronze winner board.

That's it?

Well, and I have the satisfaction of having done 150 workouts. Silver is next—that's 250 workouts.

Then I guess you'll go for the gold.

Oh, yeah. 350. I happen to be wearing my new Elite Member tee shirt, which I got for working out at this gym for two years. They're big on positive reinforcement.

I am like Paul: we both need to run for a prize. Motivation. We know he was competitive: we hear him comparing himself to other people all the time in his letters. The image of a race was a comfortable one for Paul.

But what if you're just not competitive? If you've never cared about winning, just about playing? What if your personality is more peaceful and self-contained than that, and you don't need a prize to keep you in the race. What if it's *not* a race for you?

Christ walks with each of us in the way we walk. Runs, if we are natural runners. But he is just as content to go for a stroll and take some time to smell the flowers.

MONDAY IN PROPER 28

Pss 89:1–18 * 89:19–52
Habukkuk 2:1–4, 9–20
James 2:14–26
Luke 16:19–31

*"... but if someone goes to them from
the dead, they will repent."*
LUKE 16:30

I am far away in an Oklahoma City hotel room, just me and the radio so far, having a leisurely breakfast before my day here begins. In and out, these trips, just time enough to meet the people and begin to enjoy them and then it's time to go. I'll be back in the air by evening, not thirty hours after I arrived here.

There was one thing here I had to see, though, and the bishop and his wife took me over there last night after we were finished for the evening. He showed me just where he was standing that day, where the road was upon which the truck was parked and left there to kill while the murderer sauntered off into the crowd. It is now a reflecting pool, calm and still, showing us the moon and the stars of the night sky. Where the building was, there are chairs now, one for each victim. The large chairs are the adults; the little ones are the children. They are all lit from within.

The chairs are beautiful, I told the bishop. I told him they reminded me of the final scene in *Our Town*, in which the beloved dead sit in chairs and talk, less and less about earthly sorrows and more and more about the stars. I told him about how comforting New Yorkers found the two beams of light that reached from the WTC site into the night sky and dissipated into it, about how many of us wished they could have stayed there forever, reaching into heaven every night, for as long as there is anyone to remember.

We walked on a bit, past the battered partial wall of the building, the informal memorials hung on the chain link fence. Life goes on, of course. New things come into being. The chairs remain, empty, marking the spot of great loss.

They're *missing* it all. Missing their cats and their dogs, their kitchens, their children's graduations, their sons' weddings. They died before they met the person they would have married, before ever having a grandchild, before getting out of the service. They're missing the rest of ordinary life, and we can't abide that. None of us want to leave here.

But they have a different view now. We don't like that, either: we want them as they were, not as they are, and that is not on the table.

I must pack and check out of my room. Get to the airport this afternoon and head home. Walk through the garden in the dark and into the house, climb the stairs and see Noodle curled up on the bed, fast asleep, Q in the office on the computer. Ordinary life: I am not yet finished with mine.

TUESDAY IN PROPER 28

Pss 97, 99, (100) * 94, (95)
Habukkuk 3:1–10 (11–15) 16–18
James 3:1–12
Luke 17:1–10

The brightness was like the sun . . .
HABUKKUK 3:4

Today was a splendid fall day—gorgeous, a bright sun in a blue sky. September 11, 2001, was just such a day. So was the morning of the Oklahoma City bombing.

The day of the Indian Ocean tsunami was like that, too. Sun and sky. Not a cloud.

We remember the weather on days that changed our lives, as if it held a secret key to understanding them better. There ought to have been something ominous, some portent, oughtn't there? Something about the way we should have noticed, so that we might have seen it coming? Surely the whole universe knew how the day would resound, didn't it?

No. The universe never knows our business, nor does it care. We try to wrap some importance around ourselves by reading the stars, as if they convened to decide our fate, but they do not. They are occupied with other things.

Now, you could tell Hurricane Katrina was coming. She had portents: thick, hot air, a gathering wind, building and building to a howl of mythic proportions. You could tell the rain was coming. The meteorologist announced it before it happened.

But the real horror of the hurricane began the next day, after the rains and the wind ceased. When everyone figured the worst was over, and it wasn't so bad. Under a sunny sky.

We knew and did not know.

WEDNESDAY IN PROPER 28

Pss 101, 109:1–4 (5–19) 20–30 * 119:121–144
Malachi 1:1, 6–14
James 3:13–4:12
Luke 17:11–19

"Were not ten made clean?
But the other nine, where are they?"
LUKE 17:17

I guess they were just too excited to remember their manners. Overjoyed, but in shock. Or maybe they were so eager to get back home to their families after years of being separated from them—to

hold their children, their wives, to sleep in their own beds at last—
that they just couldn't wait. One came back to say thanks, though: a
Samaritan, one of several Samaritans with whom Jesus interacts or
whom he imagines in a parable. They all contrast favorably with his
own co-religionists, something one might not expect.

The writer makes sure we know that this healing took place on
the border between Samaria and Galilee. Why does he tell us this?
Why does it matter where it happened?

An in-between location—not Israel and not Samaria. Not in and
not out. A place where nobody is at home—or maybe it's a place
where *anybody* can be at home. A "no-man's land?" It could just as
well be described as an "everyone's land."

The healing of the ten lepers is a break with a tragic past. In
scripture, few are more wretched than a leper, and now these ten
will leave that terrible isolation behind forever. And it happens in a
place that is neither one or the other, a place that is like the ten: no
longer bound by the bitter divisions of the past.

THURSDAY IN PROPER 28

Pss 105:1–22 * 105:23–45
Malachi 2:1–16
James 4:13–5:6
Luke 17:20–37

Remember Lot's wife.
LUKE 17:32

I have never forgotten her, not since I first read this ancient story
as a child. It was on her behalf that I had my first argument with
God. What was so terrible about her looking back to see the home
she loved one last time? Why on earth should a person who does
that be turned into a pillar of salt? It was the meanest thing I had
ever heard of, and it still is.

In those days, I had nothing else to think but that everything the Bible *said* God did or thought *was* something God did or thought. I didn't know then yet that people wrote these things down, that they wrote in different languages and in different centuries and for different reasons. I didn't know that the people who wrote the Bible came after the people who spoke it, that it was oral for decades and more before it was ever recorded in writing. I didn't know that there were stories from cultures beside the Jewish and Christian ones in it. I didn't know it borrowed stories sometimes. I would have been shaken to hear any of these things. *Does that mean it's just made up then? That it's not true?*

I only knew about journalistic truth then: something either did or did not happen, and it happened here and at this time and in this way. I didn't know about poetic truth or spiritual truth or moral truth or psychological truth. I thought there was just one kind of truth. Many people still think that.

But I don't. Knowing as much as we can know about who wrote and why, what life was like for them then, what they wanted people to think and do, makes reading the Bible just about the richest thing a person can do. There is no end to its riches, and you miss way more than half of them if all you can see in it is a record of "what happened."

Or what *didn't*. Remember Lot's wife.

FRIDAY IN PROPER 28

Pss 102 * 107:1–32
Malachi 3:1–12
James 5:7–12
Luke 18:1–18

*The farmer waits for the precious crop
from the earth, being patient with it
until it receives the early and the late rains.*

JAMES 5:7

Now, of course, the crops are in, and the yield was as good as it's going to be for another year. No more fresh tomatoes, sweet corn. Maybe you put in some beets or some Swiss chard or broccoli, and they're yielding, but mostly you're back in the produce department, picking through whatever looks decent.

Here, it is the cold rains of late fall into which we venture. Those hopeful tender showers in the softening air of spring are months away. Not even a seed catalogue arrives to dispel the grayness of the season. They will come, with our income tax forms, the week after Christmas.

What does the garden require of you most often, more often than anything else? More than hard work and long trips with the watering can? More than mulching or fertilizing? It is the ability to wait. Patience.

I am not the first person to observe that the life of faith is like a garden. It is all about waiting and growing, growing and waiting, trial and error, delight and disappointment, life and death. The Advent season of waiting approaches, and we are ready: the long green weeks of Pentecost have grown old, and it is time for a new year.

SATURDAY IN PROPER 28

Pss 107:33–43; 108:1–6 (7–13) * 13
Malachi 3:13–4:6
James 5:13–20
Luke 18:9–14

"I thank you that I am not like other people . . ."
LUKE 18:11

I'm the kind of person who_____. Fill in the blank. But
you never hear anyone begin a sentence that way and continue in
a manner unflattering to himself. It's always *I'm the kind of person
who says what he thinks* or *I'm the kind of person who believes in a
hard day's work* or *I'm the kind of person who puts his family first.*

It's never *I'm the kind of person who just can't be trusted.* Or *I'm
the kind of person who just won't accept responsibility.*

A friend refers to this tendency to confine our self-knowledge to
what is complimentary to us "the limitation of self-report." We do
not allow ourselves to know the whole of ourselves; only the good
parts, and we certainly don't want anyone else to know about the
whole of us, either: we are similarly selective about the public face
we wear. The whole truth does not come naturally or comfortably
to us. We must *learn* to see the truth about ourselves, and it is no
easy task. Many never master it.

So the self-confident man publicly praising God for his unique-
ness was mistaken. He *was* like other men. *Just* like other men. It
was the tax collector who was unusual.

SUNDAY, PROPER 29

Pss 118 * 145
Zechariah 9:9–16
1 Peter 3:13–22
Matthew 21:1–13

Rejoice greatly, O daughter Zion!
ZECHARIAH 9:9

By now, Handel's *Messiah* is in the DNA of western Christians: there are passages in scripture we simply cannot read anymore without hearing them sung in our minds. This is sure one of them: the soprano's tour de force, her sugar plum fairy moment in the entire oratorio, the aria that makes everyone wish, for a moment, that she could sing like that.

In the eighteenth century, music like this was performed in somewhat the same way as jazz is performed today: a singer was expected to add her own cadenzas and glissandos, to insert trills and turns. So no two performances of this beautiful aria were the same; each singer's was different. Probably the same singer's performance was different each time she sang it.

And, of course, there were no recordings. So the aria was truly over when it was over. It would never be heard again, not like that. Not exactly. Some other way, but not that way, not ever again.

Every moment we live is like that: one of a kind. It will never come again.

There is something in this particular aria that captures that very once-in-a-lifetime joy. Don't just rejoice—SHOUT!! What you have longed for generations is happening RIGHT NOW! There has never been another day like it.

MONDAY IN PROPER 29

Pss 106:1–18 * 106:19–48
Zechariah 10:1–12
Galatians 6:1–10
Luke 18:15–30

*If anyone is detected in a transgression,
you who have received the Spirit should restore
such a one in a spirit of gentleness.*
GALATIANS 6:1

It sounds so sweet here, but few things are more painful and awkward than confronting someone in gentleness. You lie awake all the night before you have to do this, planning what you will say, afraid you will be too heavy, or too light. Is there a way to avoid it? Can't somebody else do it?

Maybe sometimes somebody else can. But sometimes you are *it*.

Remembering that no one is well served by a lie can help you wade into a scary situation. What you are about to do is not a necessary evil; it is an active good. The pain you are causing in correcting the behavior is not the first pain that happened in this situation: the person you must confront has caused others pain, too, or you wouldn't be having this conversation. However long this wrong has been going on, today is the day you and its author will bring it to an end.

You hope.

After today, time will tell. Perhaps one remonstrance will be enough. Perhaps it will not, and you must do it again and again. Perhaps the relationship can continue in a new form, but it is also possible that it will end. That would be too bad.

But not as bad as doing nothing.

TUESDAY IN PROPER 29

Pss (120), 121, 122, 123 * 124, 125, 126, (127)
Zechariah 11:4–17
1 Corinthians 3:10–23
Luke 18:31–43

*. . . like a skilled master builder I laid a foundation,
and someone else is building on it.*
1 CORINTHIANS 3:10

Don't you dare ever take a vacation again. This place fell apart without you.

I don't know what we'd do if you weren't here.

When you leave, I'm leaving.

You protest prettily that this is not so, that you are just another member of the team. But in your heart, you also suspect that it is true. They really *can't* get along without me.

Then you leave. And they get along just fine. They do some things differently from the way you did them, and they do some things you counseled against. They seem pleased with the results. *Humph.*

Most great human projects are started by one person and completed by others. The great cathedrals of Europe—none of their architects lived to see the completion of them. Sometimes they would try to ensure that their choices were honored: filling in only half of a frieze, for instance, so that whoever finished it would have to use the same motif on his half. This is known in architecture as "lifting his leg," an indelicate reference to a dog who makes sure he leaves his scent everywhere, claiming the territory as his.

Loving the work of the community more than you love your own work takes practice. It forces us to face ourselves: do I do what I do only for the sake of the applause I get, or am I so committed to the mission that I can take it or leave it? Everyone has an ego that needs stroking, but everyone can learn to keep it in its place. And what we can do together is so much greater than anything I could do on my own that it's well worth the lesson.

WEDNESDAY IN PROPER 29

Pss 119:145–176 * 128, 129, 130
Zechariah 12:1–10
Ephesians 1:3–14
Luke 19:1–10

He was trying to see who Jesus was, but on account of the
crowd he could not, because he was short in stature.
LUKE 19:3

The stairs up from the railway tacks to the concourse above me, three long flights up. I am almost six feet tall, but I felt short and vulnerable as the crowd rushed around me. I stood looking up the stairs, trying to decide how I would climb them with a heavy suitcase and doctor's instructions not to lift anything. Well, all right, I thought, I can probably manage. I would just take it slowly.

And I did, ridiculously slowly, one step at a time, not exactly lifting the suitcase but not quite *not* lifting it, either. Then Sir Lancelot came along, took the suitcase, waiting kindly for me at each landing. *I'm sorry to be so slow,* I said, and he just smiled and waited, Goodbye, thanks, and then Sir Lancelot was gone.

I am not really disabled; this was a temporary condition. But I have been, have known the frustration of always being last, of having everything take so *long*, of having to plan ahead so carefully for the smallest of endeavors.

And of course, we'll all know disability eventually. Mostly we don't get more hale and hearty as we age—we get less so. If you stay here long enough, you'll eventually know weakness.

THURSDAY IN PROPER 29

Pss 131, 132, (133) * 134, 135
Zechariah 13:1–9
Ephesians 1:15–23
Luke 19:11–27

*"But as for these enemies of mine who did not
want me to be king over them—bring them here
and slaughter them in my presence."*

LUKE 19:27

When this passage is read on Sunday, it concludes with verse 26, not verse 27, in which the king in the parable wants to watch his detractors' executions, since the king is a figure for Christ himself. It appears that bad things will happen to people who don't get on board.

However squeamish we have become in modern times about summary executions, they abound in scripture. These writers don't seemed at all shocked when a ruler has someone bound, tortured, and even killed for some trivial offense. How barbaric, we think when we read such things. If we're planning a lectionary, we skip over a verse like that.

Barbaric? Violent? It is easy to see the barbarism of another age, harder to see our own violence. Ours is at a distance; we need not behold it ourselves, and it is a leisurely violence: child labor in faraway places, world hunger coexisting scandalously with an American obesity epidemic, the future of who will live and who will die of AIDS resting entirely upon geographical accident of birth, when the capability exists to level that playing field.

We don't demand to watch our victims suffer. We don't even think we *have* victims. But we're wrong about that. We just don't see them.

◦ FRIDAY IN PROPER 29

Pss 140, 142 * 141, 143:1–11 (12)
Zechariah 14:1–11
Romans 15:7–13
Luke 19:28–40

*"Go into the village ahead of you, and as you enter it you
will find tied there a colt that has never ridden."*

LUKE 19:30

There's that colt again—at least there's only one of them this time. Luke does not succumb to the confusion about the two animals by misunderstanding the parallelism of Hebrew poetry. So the passage makes a little more sense.

Of course, there is still the issue of horse stealing—well, *donkey* stealing. Notice that the disciples aren't supposed to *ask* anybody for the animal first: just untie it and go, unless anybody stops you, and then explain. If the owner hadn't happened to step out of his house right then, I guess he would have just discovered his donkey missing later on and never known what happened to it.

The Lord has need of it was the phrase that was supposed to make everything all right, and sure enough, the owner was satisfied with that. We're the only ones to who it seems odd. *Which* Lord? Was the owner of the donkey a follower of Jesus, and everything about the donkey ride into town pre-arranged? Or is this transaction supposed to be more magical than that? The latter, I imagine: we wouldn't have thought to ask where he got the donkey. It seems an unnecessary detail, unless it is given us in order to make the moment more miraculous than we might otherwise expect it to be.

I guess it was miraculous. An unknown preacher from out of town hailed on the Jerusalem street as the one who comes in the name of the Lord, right under the noses of the people most likely to be alarmed by such a claim. Demonstrating the power of humility in this way first, in many other ways as the terrible week unfolded.

SATURDAY IN PROPER 29

Pss 137:1–6 (7–9), 144 * 104
Zechariah 14:12–21
Philippians 2:1–11
Luke 19:41–48

Let each of you look not to your own interests,
but to the interests of others.
PHILIPPIANS 2:4

Y ou get some retreat time yourself, you hear? An eMo reader chides me in an instant message. I type back that I will try. The retreat involves giving four talks over twenty-four hours and speaking with individuals in between, so it's not a vacation. There have been times when I have returned from one and had to go straight to bed.

But lately my retreats have been easier on me than they used to be. I seem finally to have learned to make more sensible use of the long period of silence in between talks, resting instead of talking to people during some of them. My inner introvert is coming into her own. Perhaps someday I will make a good hermit.

I keep all my old date books, just in case. I look back at my schedules of only a few years ago. How on earth did I do it, I wonder. And why?

I really don't know *how*. But the *why* is easy: it was because I couldn't say no. Couldn't turn anybody down. I also couldn't say no to myself: all the things I was doing were things I loved. That wasn't the problem. There were just too many of them. I guess I was afraid I might miss something.

And I do miss things. Things I would have loved doing but did not do are now being done by someone else. Somebody else got to do them instead. Some are things I won't have another shot at, ever again. This won't kill me; on the contrary, it will help me live longer. We won't get to do everything, for ourselves or for others: We have to choose. All of us.